MW00533501

PRACTICING MEMORY IN CENTRAL AMERICAN LITERATURE

PRACTICING MEMORY IN CENTRAL AMERICAN LITERATURE

Nicole Caso

PRACTICING MEMORY IN CENTRAL AMERICAN LITERATURE
Copyright © Nicole Caso, 2010

First published in 2010 by
PALGRAVE MACMILLAN® in the United States – a division of
St. Martin's Press LLC, 175 Fifth Avenue, New York, NY 10010.

Where this book is distributed in the UK, Europe and the rest of the
world, this is by Palgrave Macmillan, a division of Macmillan Publishers
Limited, registered in England, company number 785998, of
Houndmills, Basingstoke, Hampshire RG21 6XS.

Palgrave Macmillan is the global academic imprint of the above
companies and has companies and representatives throughout the
world.

Palgrave® and Macmillan® are registered trademarks in the
United States, the United Kingdom, Europe and other countries.

ISBN: 978-0-230-62036-0

Library of Congress Cataloging-in-Publication Data

Caso, Nicole, 1970–
    Practicing memory in Central American literature / Nicole Caso.
        p. cm.
    Includes bibliographical references.
    ISBN 978-0-230-62036-0 (alk. paper)
    1. Central American fiction—20th century—History and criticism.
    2. Literature and history—Central America.   3. History in literature.
    I. Title.

PQ7472.N7C37 2010
863'.6099287'09728—dc22
                                                        2009031180

A catalogue record of the book is available from the British Library.

Design by MPS Limited, A Macmillan Company

First edition: March 2010

10 9 8 7 6 5 4 3 2 1

Printed in the United States of America.

To my family:

Juan José, Jo Mary,
and Margot Caso

CONTENTS

ACKNOWLEDGMENTS

This book has benefited immeasurably from the generous support and encouragement of many people. Thank you to José Rabasa, my dissertation advisor at the University of California, Berkeley, for continually challenging me to think against the grain. His keen ability to listen and to understand where my thoughts were headed repeatedly steered me through complex theoretical waters that greatly enriched this project at its initial stages as my doctoral dissertation. To Francine Masiello, my sincere thanks for her careful reading of my work and for her helpful and insightful comments. Multiple discussions of "totality" and "fragmentation" during her graduate seminars have opened up to me a new way of engaging with fiction and historical texts. I owe a significant debt of gratitude to Arturo Arias for being enormously generous with his time and his vast knowledge of the region. Thank you, Arturo, for being a constant source of positive encouragement. Many of the questions raised in this study stem from discussions initiated at Harvard College with my undergraduate advisors, César Salgado and Doris Sommer. I am indebted to both of them for exposing me to current debates about history and literature and the representation of the past through fiction.

I am grateful for fellowship support from the Department of Spanish and Portuguese of the University of California, Berkeley, for the Dissertation-Year Fellowship during the spring of 2004 and the Summer Research Grant during the summer of 2003. I thank the Bancroft Library of the University of California, Berkeley, for granting me the Bancroft Library Study Award during the summer of 2003, and the Graduate Division of the University of California, Berkeley, for the University of California Dissertation-Year Fellowship during the 2002–2003 academic year and the Mentored Research Award for the academic year of 2000–2001.

My gratitude extends to all of the authors who have graciously allowed me to cite their texts in my analysis: Humberto Ak'abal, Manlio Argueta, Arturo Arias, Ernesto Cardenal, Julio Escoto, Victor D. Montejo, and Calixta Gabriel Xiquín. Citations of Ernesto Cardenal's poetry in English have been taken from *The Doubtful Strait / El estrecho dudoso*, translated by John Lyons, with an introduction and glossary by Tamara R. Williams, project coordinator (Bloomington and Indianapolis: Indiana University Press, 1995; copyright 1995 by Indiana University Press, Ernesto Cardenal, and John Lyons; reprinted with the permission of Indiana University Press). My thanks to the University of Oklahoma Press for granting me permission to cite from Victor Montejo's *Voices from Exile: Violence and Survival in Modern Maya History* (copyright 1999 by the University of Oklahoma Press, Norman, Publishing Division of the University). The image on the cover of the book, *Serie de los Solitarios* (2003), is a painting by the Guatemalan artist, Elmar Rojas. It has been kindly provided courtesy of ArtSpace / Virginia Miller Galleries, Coral Gables (Miami), Florida. Mr. Rojas has generously granted me permission to reprint his painting.

An earlier version of the first section of Chapter 6 was previously published online in Spanish in *Istmo: Revista virtual de estudios literarios y culturales centroamericanos*, no. 3, enero-junio 2002, as "El dedo en la llaga: de articulaciones y fluidaridad. La negociación de identidades en Guatemala después de los acuerdos de la paz" ("A Finger in the Wound: On Articulations and Fluidarity. Negotiations of Identity in Guatemala after the Peace Accords"). A Spanish version of the first section of Chapter 4 is forthcoming from the University of El Salvador Press: "La narrativa fragmentada y el anhelo de comunidad en *Caperucita en la zona roja*" ("Fragmentation and the Search for Community in *Caperucita en la zona roja*") in *Desde la hamaca al trono ... y más allá: Lecturas críticas de la obra de Manlio Argueta (From the Hammock to the Throne and Beyond: Critical Readings on the Work of Manlio Argueta)*, edited by Astvaldur Astvaldsson, Linda J. Craft, and Ana Patricia Rodríguez.

I am indebted to several friends and colleagues who have supported me in this process and generously read excerpts of my work, including Jeanne Lopiparo, Kerry Bystrom, Deirdre d'Albertis, Susan Aberth, Melanie Nicholson, Amelia Moser, Cole Heinowitz, Thomas Keenan, Omar Encarnación, Marina van Zuylen, and Jennifer Day. Thank you to Brigitte Shull, Lee Norton, and Rachel Tekula at Palgrave Macmillan and the team at Macmillan Publishing Solutions for guiding me through the publication process. Thank you also to Lisa Rivero for helping me with the index.

I dedicate this book to my family, Juan José, Jo Mary, and Maggie Caso. They have offered me unbounded and unconditional support in all of my endeavors, and have enthusiastically stood by me on the long road that has culminated in this project. Thank you.

INTRODUCTION: COVERING
THE MOUTH OF SILENCE

This study follows the trajectory of Central America in the area's historical fiction of the twentieth century as it has embarked on the painful and complicated project of modernity. In assessing the paths taken toward this end, creative fiction has been a key forum for engaging in critical self-evaluation along the way. The cultural realm in general has often provided a platform from which to supplement and contest historical and political discourses. Given the drawn-out violence and extreme sociopolitical conditions of the region, literature in particular has frequently been in dialogue with historical perspectives replete with charged silences and evasive euphemisms. By paying close attention to the aesthetics of language and the techniques of discourse formation, the study of Central American literature—with a distinct focus on historical fiction—insistently challenges the reader to contend with the implications of the interplay between texts and contexts, as they become inextricably intertwined in the literature of the region.

Fictional texts in the isthmus have repeatedly interrupted and problematized Western master narratives when applied to the singularities of each of the countries addressed. The unique contexts and human experiences conveyed in the plot and reflected in the aesthetics of the texts I examine complicate the implementation of foreign models and discourses about a variety of issues that include the writing of history, the employment of liberal policies in the late nineteenth and early twentieth centuries, the integration into a capitalist world market, the homogenizing tendencies of Marxism, the conflicts between national identities and globalizing forces, and the practice of solidarity. Responding to the preponderance of fictional texts that take on historical issues in the region, this book addresses the central questions: What kinds of stories are told about the past when authors choose the fictional realm to engage in representations of history? Perhaps more importantly, why access memory through fiction?

Having grown up in Guatemala during the violence of the late 1970s and early 1980s, surrounded by the stressful ambiguity of charged silences, while aware and fearful of the potential consequences of language, I have long been interested in strategic choices made when speaking of historical issues or current events. As a student of literature, I am concerned about the broader implications of aesthetic choices, which have led me to ask questions such as: What can be conveyed through fiction that makes it such an appealing vehicle for retelling historical "truths"? What kinds of stories are being told in the face of repression and violence? What forms do they take? What do they reveal in terms of the possibilities for the future that are mapped out in the author's particular view of the past?

The subtitle to this introductory section, "Covering the Mouth of Silence," is a reference to a poem by the Maya K'iché poet Humberto Ak'abal:

Hablo[1]	Kinch'awik[2]	I speak
para taparle	che utz'apixik	to cover
la boca	ri uchi'	the mouth
al silencio.	ri tz'inowik.	of silence.[3]

This poignant sentiment can be read as a template for what all of the texts analyzed in this study are able to achieve in different ways. With a shared legacy of fear and imposed silences, there is much at stake in voicing particular perspectives about a painful and traumatic past, or even about a daunting and complicated present. Nonetheless, the very process of asserting creative voices through literature allows for wounded subjects and silenced societies to reclaim a sense of dignity in the face of impotence, to value their complex subjectivities upon being forced into marginal and abject positions, and to reassert their multifaceted humanity on their own terms.

By assertively claiming a valid place from which to expose silenced perspectives and envisioning spaces of potential action (personal and political), the process of writing and engaging in creative/critical thought becomes a regenerative exercise in the face of violence, fear, and destruction. "Covering the mouth of silence" becomes a way of reclaiming personal agency through the process of naming—even though the stories sometimes belie confusion rather than certainty, they can expose the ineffable precisely as what cannot be easily captured through conventional discourse; they might be told through irreverent mockery and ironic hyperbole instead of aiming for a mimetic realism in order to provoke immediate psychological responses or to reveal inconsistencies in a system that does not work; and at times they can be profoundly disconcerting. Frequently, in fact, fiction serves to expose the open-ended and the unresolved. It thus helps interrupt, in a self-conscious manner, any attempts by other forms of discourse to smooth out inconsistencies in favor of a homogenous recounting of events. Moreover, in the process of such interruptions, literature makes a compelling case for the importance of creative and critical thought as a self-referent example of such an endeavor.

The regenerative effect of fiction thus stems from a thoughtful reappropriation of language to convey an unabashedly partial perspective through the author's own vision of the past. Writing and "telling" in the face of a silencing authority (or even as a way to break out of a paralyzing sense of social complacency) allow an author to trace the mental parameters for potential action and to question (or to reinforce) current modes of collective behavior. Fictional tales that refer to events from actual sociopolitical experiences participate in the creation of meaning through a two-way dynamic that both provides conceptual borders and limits of action by envisioning events within a given set of parameters, and also interrupts, breaks open, and challenges conventional ways in which potential social agency can be imagined and, therefore, experienced. Envisioning scenarios through fiction and poetry thus helps trace the limits and possibilities of behavior through the mapping of mental or psychic spaces, which inevitably inform social interactions beyond the fictional realm. Specifically, alternative or different ways of naming open up new opportunities for personal and social identities to develop within changing perceptions of this abstract, conceptual space that encompasses identities as they can be conceived and expressed through language.[4] Again, within the configurations of this mental geography, it is creativity and critical thought that set the stage for any possibility of change. It is in mapping the contours of this imagined space that the reconfiguration of potentialities for action can take place and collective identities can be defined and reinforced.

Language, memory, and the performance of social identities therefore continuously inform each other, and these interactions can be closely observed in the fictional and poetic renditions of the past that we examine. By studying the aesthetic form and rhetorical strategies of the texts considered in this project it is possible to analyze the sociopolitical dynamics implied in their representation of history. I draw from the critical theories of Michel de Certeau, Néstor García Canclini, Jean-Luc Nancy, Diane Nelson, Hayden White, and Armando Muyolema, among others, to elucidate particular social and power relations that are determined and reproduced by distinct forms of organizing space, language, and memory. Rather than provide a comprehensive listing of texts in which Central American historical themes are conveyed, or presume to capture a sense of regional history as a cohesive whole, I have organized my reflections in terms of suggestive spatial considerations: "the isthmus," "the city," "the nation," and a space for "the Other."

Accordingly, I turn to the polysemous metaphor of "space" as a useful way to structure my analysis of multiple representations of historical memories in twentieth-century Central American literature. This metaphor allows me to address issues of inclusion and exclusion, centers and peripheries, the cultural and sociopolitical implications of geography, the mapping of textual cartographies, and the negotiation of new spaces from which to speak. I have intentionally left open the ambiguity of the term, as various definitions of "space" serve to address the diverse themes and ideas that become interwoven throughout this text.

At times, I refer to space in its most concrete meaning; it is to be taken, quite literally, as *land* to discuss the discrepancies of land ownership that have so often determined socioeconomic relations in the region's history. The term refers as well to the singular geography of the region, both its shape and its location, as a strategic consideration for geopolitical policy and economic gain. The area has often been seen as a potential passageway to riches or to other sources of opportunity—as a way to arrive at the dreams conjured up by the idea of "the Orient" since the sixteenth century, as the bridge between the North and the South for exiles and immigrants searching for safety and economic prosperity, and as an important battleground during the Cold War confrontation between ideologies of the East and the West.

"Space" is also meant to capture both the literal and more figurative aspects of the Central American city as it is conveyed in several of the novels considered. The city comes to represent the place in which aspirations of economic and social modernity are to be applied in the nineteenth and early twentieth centuries to follow models of liberalism that had been developed elsewhere, in Europe. In this case,

I refer to modernity as the movement toward perceived "development" through capital accumulation and new technologies that would facilitate interaction with a broader world market, along with all that this implies. The urban environment of the second half of the twentieth century provides a sense of how the policies of modernization have worked out as they have been implemented locally, with the problems of the city becoming symptomatic of broader social concerns. In the texts I examine, the city repeatedly stands as an attribute associated with the idea of modernity or the narrative of progress as a whole. As such, the way in which the city is represented provides pointed commentary about the consequences of the pursuit of modernity and the desire for progress as defined by Western Enlightenment and capitalistic ideals.

Beyond the city, the relevance of *the nation* has been questioned in recent scholarship concerning culture in the era of late capitalism, given the broader context of an increasingly global dynamic throughout the world. The easy circulation of information, labor, products, people, and ideas has called into question the significance of national borders and the symbols of national sentiment as the basis for individual and collective identity formation. Thus the concept of the nation is another meaning that our metaphor of space/place takes on in the specific inquiry into the importance of local symbols and national identity markers as a form for resisting powerful homogenizing tendencies from abroad.

On a different level, abstract space encompasses a concern with the perspective and the positionality of the authors, the narrators, and the characters involved in relation to the events and the power dynamics described. The vantage point, the place from which one speaks, inevitably shapes the contours of the stories told, significantly affecting what is said and how. As such, the very *space of the page* is directly implicated in the many definitions of our organizing metaphor, and the configuration of language becomes constitutive for envisioning possibilities of action. Throughout this study we shall observe how the arrangement of language on the blank page, the selection of both genre and style, is informed by ideological positions and points of view determined by the author's present circumstances. We will also explore, conversely, "the content of the form," as Hayden White would put it, researching the effects that a text's genre might have on particular representations of the past, as the form helps reveal a distinct vision and an attitude about the events described. A series of short stories, an epic poem, a short lyrical poem, or a historical novel might expose in their very form a set of parameters with which to read the author's own ideological position regarding the subject matter addressed.

Practicing Memory in Central American Literature situates my analysis of the works examined within contemporary discussions about memory and creative literature, urban studies, hybrid identities and *mestizaje* in the hemispere, twentieth-century historical fiction, and inquiries into the continued relevance of the nation in an era of globalization. As part of these discussions, I propose that the place—both ideological and physical—from which one writes about the past affects not only the form of the representation of events (the literary genre, a style of narrative that is either fragmentary or totalizing in scope), but also indicates how one must read the text within a particular regional context. What does it mean, for instance, when an author writes a totalizing tale from the margins of geopolitical power? Why write an epic poem from the perspective of a group that has been denied access to authority within the state? Why does one speak in terms of ethnic "essences" when writing from within a subaltern group that is vying for a collective voice? Why write a difficult, fragmentary text about a social movement in which one believes profoundly? It is precisely at the point of tension between the positions of articulation and the final form of texts such as these, which provide a rereading of conventional history, that the parameters of imagined social identities are questioned and redefined. This study demonstrates how the place from which one speaks affects the form of the text, and how in turn, the form of the text reveals a map of how the future can be imagined and current identities performed.

I am deeply concerned with examining the ways in which spatial dynamics organize language and how language itself determines the outline of possible social geographies at a given time. This project traces the active interplay between language, space, and memory in the continuous process of defining local identities. Ultimately, we return to a recurrent obsession in Latin American literature, positing the perpetual question: *who are we?* This question haunts these texts and provokes further inquiry when rereading the past in the interest of a better future: Where have we gone right or wrong? And, in this light, who do we want to be? The texts analyzed in this book form part of the corpus of narratives that trace the ways in which social identities can be imagined. They participate in the very narration of collective local identities and, in the process, give voice to the tensions, anxieties, exclusions, and silences that have resulted from the complex project of modernization.

This book hopes to illustrate that it is impossible to reduce the area's history into a singular narrative, as each country provides a unique historical set of circumstances. Moreover, even when addressing the same issue, each author has filtered his/her representation of events from a distinct vantage point. The authors I consider include Ernesto Cardenal, Miguel Ángel Asturias, Arturo Arias, Carmen Naranjo, Manlio Argueta, Julio Escoto, Víctor Montejo, Calixta Gabriel Xiquín, and Humberto Ak'abal. Many of the authors included are often considered to be canonical Central American writers; yet in this project their texts are not meant to be representative of a privileged version of the history of their countries of origin. Instead, I have chosen to read their texts because they have been crafted as entertaining and compelling representations of their own perspectives about the events described, and they also fit well into the general questions this book has been organized to address. As such, all of the texts analyzed highlight instances of particular sociopolitical dynamics and distinct experiences that, together, help provide a more complex, nuanced approximation to the region.

My own emphasis on Guatemala is motivated by purely personal reasons. There are many more authors and texts that could have been included in this study (were it not for a lack of space and time) given the considerable number of regional texts that are written about historical matters.[5] I hope to be able to continue pursuing similar queries in future projects that might, for instance, address the role of the isthmus, not only as a link between East and West, but also as an important connection between North and South, by engaging with diverse forms of cultural production that recount experiences of migration to the United States and back to Latin America.

* * *

Thematically, each of the four parts of the book addresses a spatial category that refers to Central America. Part I (The Isthmus)— "A Geography of Dubious Straits: Cartographies of Trauma and Redemption"—approaches *geographical space* on two levels. Metaphorically, I navigate the textual geographies of three works (an epic poem by Ernesto Cardenal, *El estrecho dudoso,* 1966; a series of short stories by Miguel Ángel Asturias, *Week-end en Guatemala,* 1956; and a novel by Arturo Arias, *Después de las bombas,* 1979), and I explore the ways in which the literary genre of these three texts is shaped and informed by the authors' vision of the past while the perspective of their gaze helps chart a particular map toward the future. The form of the epic poem used by Cardenal, for instance, reveals an inherent faith in a utopian resolution of events that informs his perception, as he both portrays historical situations from the colonial period and alludes to comparable, ongoing circumstances in his present within a similar set of parameters. The short stories in Asturias's collection of vignettes manifest a sense of hopeless impotence that renders the narration of history from his vantage point, in the particular moment when he writes them, both tenuous and fragmentary, much like the short stories themselves. Similarly, the genre of the novel used by Arias allows him to tell a story about the past that irreverently undermines the forcefully monological official accounts of history that he writes against.

In addition, in this first part of the book, I explore a more literal version of geographical space when I address the fact that the three texts in this section problematize the way in which the isthmus is conceptualized from abroad, given its particular shape as a link between East and West—as a potential passageway to the dreams and riches of "the Orient" or as a stage for global conflicts of ideology. Part I includes two chapters: Chapter 1, "The Dubious Strait," an analysis of Ernesto Cardenal's *El estrecho dudoso* (*The Doubtful Strait*) and its critique of unresolved issues from the past that are plotted within an inherently optimistic framework for a better future; and Chapter 2, "The Wounds of 1954," is a reading of *Week-end en Guatemala* (*Weekend in Guatemala*) and *Después de las bombas* (*After the Bombs*), by Asturias and Arias, respectively, that focuses on the lingering effects of the Guatemalan coup d'état of 1954 in the memory of the region and its foreign relations with the United States.

Part II (The City)—"The City as Metonymy for the Costs of 'Progress'"—is about *urban space*. I observe the fictional representations of several Central American cities as metonymical commentaries on the effects of the process of modernization—from its incipient stages, through the proliferation of urban resistance movements, and the eventual disenchantment with the myths of progress. Chapter 3, "*El Señor Presidente's* Liberal City and the Modern Scriptural Economy," captures Guatemala City in the early twentieth century, as portrayed in Miguel Ángel Asturias's *El Señor Presidente* (*The President*, 1946). The novel conveys a fictionalized version of a city deeply marked by authoritarian violence and guarded paranoia in a country where projects of modernization have often gone hand-in-hand with long-standing, despotic, dictatorial regimes. In Chapter 4, "The Effects of a Fragmented Narrative: Community and Alienation in the City,"

I point to the reciprocal dynamic between the form and content of two texts, Manlio Argueta's *Caperucita en la zona roja* (*Little Red Riding Hood in the Red Light District*, 1977) and Carmen Naranjo's *Diario de una multitud* (*Diary of a Multitude*, 1974). Each of these fragmentary novels interrupts totalizing discourses—within the Marxist revolutionary movement in El Salvador (in the case of Argueta), or within the capitalist market system of Costa Rica (in that of Naranjo). Argueta's text follows the secret lives of the urban guerrilla in San Salvador during the 1970s, and traces its own boundaries of "insiders" and "outsiders" at a time of extreme political violence. In contrast, Naranjo's *Diario* captures the mundane complexity of the daily routine of urban life in San José to reveal the repressive aspects of conventional bourgeois society.

Part III (The Nation)—"The Nation in a Global Economy"—is about *Rey del Albor, Madrugada* (*Dawn: The King of the First Light of Day*, 1993), written by the Honduran author Julio Escoto. Chapter 5, "Totalizing Narratives Written from the Margin: Julio Escoto's *Rey del Albor, Madrugada*," counterposes a distinct *national space* to a homogenizing one with global reach, and looks to the "nation" as a site of resistance to powerful cultural forces from abroad. In my reading of Escoto's ambitious novel, I analyze the use of a totalizing narrative when writing from a peripheral, nonhegemonic position of resistance.

Part IV (The Other)—"Negotiating Spaces for Cultural Difference"—addresses the current Maya cultural movement in Guatemala, which has turned toward the distant and more recent past to organize a campaign of pan-Maya self-awareness and cultural revitalization. In Chapter 6, "Defining a Space of Shared Cultural Identity: The Pan-Maya Cultural Movement in Guatemala," I look into the appeal for *a space for cultural difference* within the State, examine the role of the non-Mayan intellectual in this process, and read texts that address Mayan authors as critical theorists, anthropologists, novelists, storytellers, and poets.

* * *

Much has been written about the fact that the decades of the 1980s and 1990s brought about a resurgence of the genre of the historical novel in Latin America as a whole.[6] With a notable experimental playfulness in form that recasts the traditional realist or romantic historical novels from the nineteenth and early twentieth centuries, the proliferation of texts identified with the renewed genre by the end of the twentieth century encouraged a rethinking of the very hegemonic versions of the past that previous historical novels had tended to privilege.[7] In fact, the region's new historical novel frequently destabilizes any singular sense of a solid truth that can be grasped and represented artistically, and instead makes evident the need to speak in multiple, plural terms when engaging with history as a referent for literary texts.[8]

By 1991, Fernando Aínsa had listed some of the general characteristics that distinguish this new take on the genre. Used in different combinations by the various authors writing new historical novels, some of the narrative strategies outlined by Aínsa include a rereading of official historiographical discourse to question its legitimacy (to try to give a sense of coherence to the present through a critical reading of the past, or out of a need to recover a sense of origin, or to justify a given identity, to explain oneself or one's people) (18), the deconstruction or "degradation" of the constitutive myths of the nation, the overlap of different time periods in one narrative story, a multiplicity of points of view that make it impossible to access a single historical truth, hyperbole, parody, the use of anachronisms, intertextuality, pastiche, and using fragments of original documentation and writing over other texts as palimpsest to provoke rereadings of events through a recasting of the same words in different contexts.[9]

Aínsa argues that, paradoxically, the ironic treatment and deconstruction of historical figures and historiography itself allow for the recovery of a certain human authenticity of the individuals involved in the events described: "Gracias a la ironía, la 'irrealidad' de los hombres convertidos en símbolos en los manuales de historia recobran su 'realidad' auténtica" (30) ["Thanks to irony, the 'unreality' of the men who have been turned into symbols in history manuals recover their authentic 'reality'"]. The ability to grasp "authentic realities" hidden behind the conventions of official, univocal versions of history seems to be the driving force behind the resurgence of this genre in its renewed form. Moreover, among the principal components of this desired conception of "authenticity" is the notion of a sense of self that could be recognized as collective identity constructs that are more in tune with people's varied experiences, rather than the useful mythology touted by an imposed official rhetoric from above.

In his article "La historia como pretexto de literatura—la nueva novela histórica en Centroamérica," Werner Mackenbach proposes that the new historical novel genre in effect stands against becoming an instrument for national identity construction, as it resists being subsumed to that end: "La *nueva novela histórica* se niega a una funcionalización para la construcción de una identidad nacional, rehúsa el nacionalismo; el debate sobre la heterogeneidad cultural e identidades posnacionales progresivamente se vuelve el centro del discurso literario" (Mackenbach 194) ["The *new historical novel* refuses to be functionalized for the construction of a national identity, it denies nationalism; the debate over cultural heterogeneity and postnational identities has progressively become the center of literary discourse"]. With regard to the new historical novel in Central America specifically, Mackenbach writes that national and collective identities have ceased to maintain the same relevancy as they did in the political and intellectual discussions of the region up through the 1980s:

> La novela histórica centroamericana a finales del siglo XX presenta un doble reto: por un lado, disputa el derecho exclusivo de la historiografía de contar la historia, por el otro, cuestiona la suposición fundamental de la novela histórica tradicional de contar la historia "como realmente fue." A la crisis político-ideológica después de la derrota de las utopías nacionalista-revolucionarias contesta con un canto de cisne de las concepciones de construcción de identidad nacional/colectiva que dominaban el discurso político-intelectual en Centroamérica hasta los años ochenta.
> (Mackenbach 195)

> [The Central American historical novel of the end of the twentieth century presents a double challenge: on the one hand, it disputes historiography's exclusive right to recount history, on the other, it questions the fundamental supposition of the traditional historical novel of recounting history "as it actually was." To the political-ideological crisis that came about after the defeat of the nationalist-revolutionary utopias it responds with a swan song of the conceptions of national/collective identity construction that dominated the political-intellectual discourse in Central America until the 1980s.]

I believe, however, that it is premature to speak of a swan song that announces the end of the continued relevance of national and collective identity constructs within the historical fiction of the isthmus. Our analysis of Julio Escoto's historical novel *Rey del Albor, Madrugada* (1993) helps illustrate the paradoxical dynamic in which current authors from the region might still choose to draw precisely from existing national and collective identity symbols as a site for resisting the powerful and homogenizing forces that are continuously imposed on the region by its all-too-close neighbor to the north, the United States. Mackenbach's assertion that heterogeneity has taken precedence in current cultural debates is certainly true, and yet, what becomes paradoxical is that one cannot completely discount the force of the symbolism of the nation in this process, for in "the local" at a time of rapid expansion of global and multinational networks, one recognizes shared experiences that can bring compatriots together in a joint attempt to resist the overwhelming influences from abroad.

This is not to say that the use of national tropes to make a case for "difference" is not full of its own internal contradictions, nor to propose that the inherent tensions of this discourse are resolved in recent fiction. Instead, I point to the ironic fact that concepts such as national identity and essential notions of collective identity (based, for instance, on shared ethnohistoric characteristics, as in the case of the current pan-Maya cultural movement in Guatemala), both previously associated with homogenizing tendencies, have served Central American thinkers in recent history as a platform to argue for a place to trace the parameters of difference. This brings us back to one of the principal contentions of this book, which is to insist on the fact that *place matters* when writing and reading texts with sociopolitical referents. When writing from a position of disadvantage, it becomes strategic to make use of collective identity constructs or even totalizing narratives as a way to carve out a space for sociocultural agency that resists the powerful forces of homogeneous assimilation.

An important contributor to the wealth of new historical novels in Central America, the Costa Rican / Chilean author Tatiana Lobo, also writes about the continued relevance of the nation and collective identity production in current fiction from Costa Rica:[10]

> En Costa Rica se ha producido un preocupante vacío de identidad. La pregunta, si no somos así, ¿cómo somos? puede ser respondida con la novela sin violentar los sentimientos nacionalistas [...] los mitos son reemplazados por la reflexión. Es por eso que ahora existe un gran interés por la novela histórica, tanto de parte de los autores como de los lectores. Hay una necesidad tremenda de volver atrás y construir otra historia para que una nueva memoria permita encontrar una nueva identidad.   (Lobo 241–42)

> [In Costa Rica an alarming identity vacuum has been produced. The question, if we are not this way, then how are we? can be answered with the novel without damaging nationalist sentiments ... the myths are replaced by reflection. That is why there is currently a great interest

in the historical novel, on behalf of both authors and readers. There is a tremendous need to go back and construct another history so that a new memory will permit us to find a new identity.]

While setting aside some of the discredited national mythology, a moment of careful reflection about the particular complexities of national identities has been ushered in, that is, without discarding the nation as a site for identity construction *per se*. The new historical novel helps in this search for a revised sense of national identity that does not merely echo a hegemonic perception from a position of power, but rather opens up the nation's past to multiple stories of pain, contradictions, violence, exclusions, and a genuine messiness that becomes recognizable, and thus, perhaps manageable. This self-awareness appears to be a necessary condition to decide how to move forward in a more pragmatic, realistic way.

Much like Noé Jitrik considers that Latin America's historical novel of the nineteenth century responded to the need of an individual to define his or her relationship to society and to pursue a broader sense of identity at a time of social transformation and uncertainty,[11] Magdalena Perkowska has analyzed the resurgence of the historical novel in its renewed form in the last decades of the twentieth century as a means to try to make sense of another time of crisis and uncertainty in the hemisphere:

> La explosión de la crisis económica produce incertidumbre y angustia social, mientras pone en duda la eficacia de los gobiernos y programas neoliberales instituidos por ellos. Finalmente, fenómenos de la globalización, tales como la transnacionalización, la crisis del Estado nacional y la fragmentación de las estructuras sociales, relocalizan y desubican las identidades de tal manera que se produce un vacío epistemológico y con él, una necesidad de confrontar o esclarecer las condiciones que lo originan. La crisis de los años ochenta en América Latina es la crisis de una modernidad "incompleta", contra la cual se dirigirá el pensamiento posmoderno.   (Perkowska 31)

> [The explosion of the economic crisis produces uncertainty and social anxiety, while it puts into question the efficacy of the governments and the neoliberal programs instituted by them. Finally, circumstances brought about by globalization, such as transnationalism, the crisis of the national state, and the fragmentation of social structures, resituate and displace identities in such a way that an epistemological vacuum is produced and with it, a need to confront and clarify the conditions that cause it. The crisis of the 1980s in Latin America is the crisis of

an "incomplete" modernity, against which postmodern thinking will
be directed.]

Even at a time characterized by a shift away from extended periods
of authoritarian dictatorships and a turn to redemocratization after
the Central American civil wars, the instability and uncertainty that
comes with enduring waves of political and economic unrest bring
back questions of the individual's role in the broader society, which is
in the middle of a process of transformation, and a need to define a
more anchored sense of identity amid such monumental changes.

By following cultural references about the multiple crises engen-
dered by the implementation of the "incomplete modernity"
described above, we become aware that the focus on historical and
sociopolitical subjects in the literature of Central America is not really
limited to cycles, but is rather a constant throughout the twentieth
century. Moreover, the genre of the historical novel is not the only
form used to represent and reread historical events through literature.
As mentioned previously, I have included short stories, poetry, and
novels in my research about the dynamic between language, memory,
and space in the continuing process of identity construction in times
of transition and turmoil in the isthmus. This is why I have not
centered my attention on the end of the century, nor have I limited
the study to a specific genre, such as the historical novel. Important
scholarship has already begun to be carried out to contribute to the
description and definition of the phenomenon of Latin America's new
historical novel and to discuss its likely causes.

Our focus is on the interplay between form and content when
writing about history and recognizable, sociopolitical events through
poetry and fiction without limiting the parameters of our scope
according to one single genre, for the form itself often contributes
to the elaboration of a particular effect for the reader and informs
the vantage point from which events are meant to be interpreted.
A notable omission from this study, which is undeniably fundamental
to the region, and was particularly so at the height of leftist armed
conflicts in the 1970s and the 1980s, is the *testimonio*. This omission
is not meant to discredit in any way the importance of this genre in
representing actual experiences through writing in times of trauma.
The extensive scholarship on the region's *testimonio* has been thorough and, as such, I have turned instead to the less studied, less
mimetic renditions of the past in literature for my own analysis of the
connection between form and content.

Fiction has clearly become a potent tool to counter imposed silences and to write against a univocal perception of historical events in Central America. Literature, in its many forms, becomes a potential agent for change, as the imaginary realms it stirs up and the permanence of its written words resist the heavy burden of official accounts built upon ever present fear or homogenizing complacency. The poetic phrase "covering the mouth of silence" captures perfectly the intention to cast away any external or self-imposed pressures to accept prescribed versions of truth as a passive (but understandable) act of self-preservation. These words clearly convey the desire to reclaim the creative use of language in a way that refuses to acquiesce to convenient renditions of events or pat explanations that flatten out complex human experiences. By defying the dangerous consequences of speech and insisting on the practice of critical and creative thought—which they in fact exemplify—all texts analyzed in this book participate in this courageous endeavor, each in its own distinct way. These texts form part of the regional corpus that helps to build a sense of community through the regenerative act of telling and recognizing shared experiences, for crafting narratives about the past on the author's own terms initiates a process of healing and maps out new ways of imagining more inclusive possibilities of action in the future. *Practicing Memory in Central American Literature* aspires to draw attention to this community of writers and readers and to acknowledge the multiplicity of stories and voices that deserve the dignity of being heard.

PART I

THE ISTHMUS

A Geography of Dubious Straits: A Literature of Trauma and Redemption

[...] en Centroamérica, las banana *republics, terreno de paso, puente entre dos océanos, traspatio de la seguridad continental [...]*[1]

(*Manlio Argueta*, "Autovaloración Literaria" 32)

It is impossible to write about Central America without taking into account its singular geography. Both the narrow expanse of the isthmus, separating the Pacific and Atlantic oceans, and its close proximity to the United States have determined the keen strategic interests of powerful and wealthy metropolitan centers at different points in history. During the initial moments of contact with imperial Spain in the sixteenth century, the region triggered fantasies of easy transit to the Orient, along with aspirations for the considerable wealth and power that control of such a passageway would entail.[2]

Before long, once its imperial power was well entrenched in the region, ambitions for a water passage were put on hold by the Spanish crown's strategic assessment that connecting the two oceans in the center of its "New World" colonies would be detrimental to the security of its colonial holdings, especially given the nautical capabilities of Great Britain. The area then languished at the margins of New Spain and the more lucrative islands of the Caribbean during much of the seventeenth and eighteenth centuries. It was not until the mid-nineteenth century, with the discovery of gold in California, that a desire to find easy transit between East and West returned international attention to the isthmus. The link between the Atlantic and the Pacific would be forged first by traversing the rivers, lakes, and treacherous land treks of Nicaragua and then by carving out Panama, creating a passable waterway by 1914.

With the Cold War backdrop of most of the twentieth century, the United States' strategic positioning of its hegemonic status in the hemisphere drew attention to the region once again, but this time it was cast in a much different light. Starting in the 1950s, and intensifying after the Cuban Revolution of 1959, Central America provided the stage for global East/West confrontations. Rather than an alluring bridge joining East and West to exploit the promises materialized in the concept of the Orient, or in dreams of California's gold, Central American ground became the stage from which to fend off menacing ideologies that could hamper the status quo in the hemisphere.

These perceptions of the region from abroad—both in terms of potential economic gains stemming from the promise of connecting East and West and the military/commercial objective of regional stability—shape the underlying context of many contemporary Central American literary texts. As can be gleaned from the epigraph cited above from Salvadoran writer Manlio Argueta, Central Americans are well aware of the perceptions of *place* that circulate abroad regarding the isthmus: that is, Central America as a "banana republic," "a terrain to be passed to arrive elsewhere," a "bridge between two oceans," or a "courtyard for continental security." These images are frequently incorporated and problematized in the literature of the region.

Such recurrent representations of Central America in the international imagination have become internalized or reconceptualized from within, as can be seen in the texts of Ernesto Cardenal, Miguel Ángel Asturias, and Arturo Arias analyzed in this section—*El estrecho dudoso* (1966), *Week-end en Guatemala* (1956), and *Después de las bombas* (1979), respectively. In my reading of these texts, I will focus on two extremely suggestive representations of the region: (1) the isthmus as a passageway to the riches of an idealized Orient, as a means to an uncertain, elusive object of desire; and (2) the area as a stage for global antagonisms, specifically the binary battle between communism and Western capitalism. Both standard characterizations of Central America originate from predominantly spatial concerns: the region's *spatial promise*—the ever-elusive interoceanic link—and, conversely, the *spatial perils* it represents—as a menacing entryway for communism and as a catalyst for the disruption of regional stability.

All three texts discussed in Part I turn toward the painful past to suggest a "map" toward a better future.[3] In what Derrida might term the messianic glance at past events, the archive—and for our purposes, the realm of historical fiction—shapes the representation of these events with the promise of hopeful cartographies and the responsibility of possible responses. As all texts to be analyzed in this section were written at the height of the Cold War, with its particular repercussions in the region (in the 1950s, 1960s, and 1970s), the type of maps that are charted for future "liberation" are necessarily framed by the possibilities that could be imagined within the circumstances of the time. At issue is the question of what kinds of stories are being told about the past through these fictional texts and what maps of action are being imagined in the attempt to process and respond to the traumas of history.

CHAPTER 1

THE DUBIOUS STRAIT

Halló el Estrecho en Veragua:
Veragua, en la provincia de Mango,
que limita con Catay ...
Pero el Estrecho era de tierra,
no era de agua.[4]

(*Ernesto Cardenal* 4)

In brief, Nicaragua in the year of 1855 had nothing but location ...
but that location was a prize worthy of the mightiest king's utmost
strivings. To bridge Nicaragua was to marry the oceans. And to
marry the oceans was to control the seas, and to control the seas was
to be Britain herself, or as great as Britain.

(*Laurence Greene* 53)

El Muy Magnífico Señor Pedrarias Dávila
Furor Domini!!!
fue el primer "promotor del progreso" en Nicaragua
y el primer Dictador[5]

(*Ernesto Cardenal* 56)

Ernesto Cardenal organizes his long poem *El estrecho dudoso* (1966)
around the notion that for the Spanish conquerors of the sixteenth
century, the "wealth" to be reaped from the isthmus consisted primarily in the discovery of a potential passageway toward the East,
where innumerable spices and material riches were to be found.[6]
The Nicaraguan poet crafts a collage out of segments of primary
historiographical sources, using the written words of such chroniclers

and religious men as Bernal Díaz del Castillo, Gonzalo Fernández de Oviedo, and Bartolomé de las Casas, and also fragments of prophetic indigenous texts, such as the Mayan *Chilam Balam*, to give an account of the first hundred years of the conquest and colonization of present-day Central America. In his reading of the colonial past, Cardenal simultaneously reflects upon his country's present circumstances and traces a path toward a better future.

The poem begins in 1502, during Columbus's fourth voyage, when he sailed along the coast of the isthmus, still searching for the route to the East. After recounting the subsequent enterprises of the first century of Spanish conquest and occupation—the accounts of multiple European adventurers who dreamt of discovering and controlling the "doubtful or dubious strait" that led to the *Mar del Sur* (the Pacific Ocean), the power struggles between conquerors, the perils and devastation they endured in the process of the search, the oppressive regimes that brought violence and destruction upon the indigenous populations, and the religious men who sought alternative means to incorporate the Amerindians into the Christian Kingdom of God—the poem ends in 1609 with the eruption of the Momotombo volcano and the destruction of the city of León.

While it directly incorporates parts of documents written during the time period described, through its collage structure and the juxtaposition of diverse voices, the poem takes on a critical stance and functions as a powerful commentary upon the events represented.[7] Cardenal's *exteriorista* poetry, with an eye on concrete images from the immediate world around him, combines well with "ready-made" fragments taken from descriptive historical documents. Many of the original sources were meant to represent what chroniclers perceived in their new surroundings in an extremely visual way to spark the imagination of a public back in distant Europe.

Instead of hermetic poems with difficult literary tropes, Cardenal tends to incorporate accessible and sometimes shockingly graphic or recognizably suggestive metaphors that appeal to the imagination of a broader public. In *El estrecho*, he focuses on visual images taken directly from representations of historical events, disturbing and violent ones, at times—such as those of the severed heads of the enemies of Pedrarias Dávila displayed publicly as a warning to potential future detractors in canto v[8]—or figures most likely taken from the accounts of local informants provided to the original chroniclers and documented in turn in their written representations—such as the old woman believed to reside in the crater of the Masaya volcano in canto ix, who demanded that the Spaniards be thrown out of their land, and was mentioned also in Gonzalo Fernández de Oviedo's *Historia General y Natural de las Indias*, compiled between 1492 and 1549.

While his intention to create a more democratic poetry steers him away from difficult metaphors, Cardenal's accessible symbolism, nonetheless, masterfully captures the complexity of the events and relationships described. As Jonathan Cohen puts it when describing the poet's *Epigramas* in the introduction to *With Walker in Nicaragua*, Cardenal has the "ability to condense complex relationships into a single, hard and clear image" (Cardenal, *With Walker in Nicaragua and Other Early Poems, 1949–1954* 12). This direct, yet highly charged and multilayered imagery is exemplified in *El estrecho dudoso*, for instance, in his rendition of the encounter between Gil González and the *cacique* Nicaragua:

> Detrás del palacio de Nicaragua
>   un lago azul.
> Gil González y Nicaragua se sentaron junto al lago.
> El conquistador con ropa de hierro,
>   el cacique casi desnudo. (30)

> [Behind the palace of Nicaragua
> a blue lake.
> Gil González and Nicaragua sat down beside the lake.
> The conquistador in chain mail,
>   the cacique almost naked. (31)]

Much is conveyed through the immediacy of the visual, without the need for superfluous explanation. The contrast between the armored conquistador and the nakedness of the native *cacique* speaks volumes of the discrepancies of force and vulnerability despite the fact that both men are seated side by side by the lake.

As has been widely documented, Cardenal is profoundly influenced by North American and British modernists, particularly by Ezra Pound and the Imagist movement, which sought clarity of expression through the use of precise images and linked techniques derived from the Symbolist movement and Oriental poetry.[9] Like Pound, Cardenal draws from a wide array of documentary texts to capture the sense of "wonderment" witnessed in the sights described, as Cohen puts it:

> Cardenal has used the eye of explorers, travelers, journalists and adventurers for recovering the wonderment and otherness of his world. And, like Pound, he has used documentary sources, crosscutting from

source to source, and making a kind of verse montage that attains a
lyric or epic movement of energy and whose grace lies in the cuts and
seams of the poems.

(Cardenal, *With Walker in Nicaragua and
Other Early Poems, 1949–1954 7*)

From the cuts and seams of the cantos of *El estrecho* emerges a clear
ethical position. The poetic voice manages to construct a critical
stance beyond the text taken from the original sources by careful
placements and omissions, by engaging the senses of sight and sound
to provoke a sense of immediacy, and by alluding to parallel circumstances in Nicaragua's more recent history.

Following, for instance, is an illustration of one approach in Cardenal's critical engagement with an original source—a fragment cited
from a section of Oviedo's *Historia General* (Book XLII, Chapter V),
entitled *El volcán (The Volcano)*, in which Gonzalo Fernández de
Oviedo describes the old woman of the volcano mentioned previously above:

Oí decir a aquel cacique de Lenderi que había él entrado algunas veces
en aquella plaza, donde está el pozo de Masaya, con otros caciques, y
que de aquel pozo salía una mujer muy vieja, desnuda, con la cual ellos
hacían su *monexico* (que quiere decir consejo secreto), y consultaban si
harían guerra o la excusarían […] que después que los cristianos habían
ido a aquella tierra, no quería salir la vieja a dar audiencia a los indios
sino de tarde en tarde o cuasi nunca, y que les decía que los cristianos
eran malos, y que hasta que se fuesen y los echasen de la tierra, no
quería verse con los indios, como solía.

(Anderson, Imbert, and Florit 26)

[I have heard the cazique of Tenderi (Nindiri) say that he has often
gone, in company with other caziques, to the edge of the crater; and
that an old woman, entirely naked, has come forth from it, with whom
they held a *monexico*, or secret council. They consulted her in order to
know if they should make war, or decline or grant a truce with their
enemies ... he added that since the Christians came into the country,
the old woman had appeared only at long intervals; that she had told
them the Christians were wicked; and that she did not wish to have any
communication with the Indians until they had driven the Christians
from their country.][10]

I quote extensively from this passage to compare the use made of
the figure of this old woman by both authors, each to illustrate their
own particular perspectives, inevitably shaped by the context of the

times in which they write. When appropriated by Cardenal, the same woman (through fragments of Oviedo's own text) serves as a means to represent a different interpretation of the ethical position of the Indians and the Spaniards referred to in this anecdote. After the section above, Oviedo proceeds with an extremely detailed description of the physical features of the old woman to evoke from the reader an understanding of his disdain:

> Yo le pregunté que, después que habían habido su concejo con la vieja o menexico, qué se hacía ella, y qué edad tenía o qué disposición; y dijo que bien vieja era y arrugada, y las tetas hasta el ombligo, y el cabello poco y alzado hasta arriba, y los dientes luengos y agudos, como perro, y la color más oscura y negra que los indios, y los ojos hundidos y encendidos; y en fin él la pintaba en sus palabras como debe ser el diablo. (26–27)

> [I asked him what they did after their council with the old woman, and what was her appearance. He replied that she was old and wrinkled; that her breasts hung down over her belly; that her hair was thin and erect; that her teeth were long and sharp as a dog's; her skin of a darker color than Indians ordinarily have; eyes fiery and sunken; in short, he described her as like the devil, which she must have been.]

Oviedo concludes then that the woman, who was so physically unappealing to him and who was said to demand human sacrifices in the crater of the volcano, was clearly an indication that the Indians maintained communication with the devil.[11] Cardenal incorporates this very figure, but through his selection process (inclusions and omissions) and his parenthetical commentary, the effect of the image in *El estrecho* is quite different from Oviedo's conclusions that link the Indians to the devil through her council. Immediately after Cardenal's description of the woman of the volcano, from which he deletes Oviedo's speculation about the connection with the devil, Cardenal goes on to describe (in parentheses) the government of the local indigenous population, led by elders in the community and by votes. By contrast, the poet then describes the infighting, treason, and decapitation of one of the Spanish conquistadores by another. The canto ends with fire spewing out of the Momotombo volcano day and night. The fears that Oviedo originally expressed about the violent sacrifices in the crater of the Masaya volcano that proved to him a link between the Indians and the devil become displaced by the violent behavior of the Spaniards among themselves. Their violence and backstabbing, which contrasts so markedly with the community government of the Indians, seems to feed the fury of the volcano in much the same way that Oviedo originally imagined the savagery of the natives had done before.

The significance of the passage as included in Cardenal's text emerges from the cuts and seams of his montage. Cardenal puts forth an ethical position through the selection of material that he includes and omits from his collage and the placement of one fragment next to the other. It is in the cuts and seams that the collage fragments interact with each other and force the reader to recognize the significance of their connection through contrasts and similarities. In the flow of the sequence of this canto, there is a diametrical contrast between the treason of Hernández de Córdoba and Pedrarias's preventative measures—the decapitation of his enemies (for pursuit of their individual desires at all costs) and the peaceful council of indigenous elders who would rather kill their leader for the good of the community than put the majority in peril. In opposition to Oviedo's original use of the figure of the woman in the volcano, the position of "moral authority" in this instance lies clearly on the side of the indigenous community over the Spaniards. The incorporation of concrete, recognizable images, along with their strategic placement within the poem, triggers potential associations that may likely differ from the intended meaning of the original texts.

The central image of the title given to the long poem is that of *el estrecho dudoso,* translated either as the *doubtful* strait, the *dubious* strait, or the *uncertain* strait. The difficulty of translating the highly suggestive concept of *el estrecho dudoso* points to the complexity of a seemingly simple image. It speaks of an uncertain path, of the dubious nature of failed searches and endeavors, of the repeated presence of foreign powers on Nicaraguan soil both in the Spanish colonial period and again in the mid-nineteenth century in an attempt to link the oceans, cutting through native land for the benefit of amassing wealth and power abroad. The first epigraph that opens this section captures the spirit of the obstructed path and the failed search for the strait in Veragua that is located in the present-day isthmus of Panama. The false, uncertain strait was not made of water; it was obstructed by land. At the same time that Cardenal documents the painful, failed paths of history (like this one in Veragua), he signals the way for a new path, beyond the hardships and disappointments of the dubious strait already traversed.

Much like Ezra Pound, Cardenal is often inspired by a broad array of primary texts.[12] Both poets have resorted to taking fragments of original sources and reworking them to elicit a particular reaction from the montage.[13] It must, however, be noted that Pound's poetic voice is informed by his fascist proclivities, while Cardenal's is geared toward a Leftist reading of events. In *El estrecho,* the combination and juxtaposition of fragments of primary texts produces a collage that forces the reader to face some of the jarring incongruities between diverse versions of events. In this regard, Cardenal's collage has a destabilizing effect similar to that of the avant-garde collages of the European *entre-guerres* movements, which sought to jolt the public out of their uncritical comfort zones with respect to prewar values. Cardenal, however, moves beyond pushing his readers into a more critical stance toward received versions of history, and even beyond shattering some of the historiographical assumptions of the original texts that have been cast as purveyors of a hegemonic, colonizing Truth. In fact, he proceeds to recombine the original texts to produce a new, counterhegemonic but cohesive perspective that falls within the Christian parameters that he espouses as a Liberation Theologist.[14]

As he jolts the reader out of a complacent acceptance of the official history, he also moves on to propose an alternative reading, laying forth the path toward a new, liberating future. Cardenal's position is reflective of the progressive views on social issues of many of the region's Catholic priests in the 1960s. A decisive event in this trajectory (concurrent with the publication of *El estrecho*) was a conference held by Latin American bishops in 1966 in Medellín, Colombia, to discuss how the church could be more active in attaining social change that would significantly benefit the poor. In this way, the spread of Liberation Theology that resulted from the Medellín conference demonstrates the Leftist push within the Catholic Church to bring about social change through active intervention in an unjust political and economic system that marginalized the poor. The poet's accessible style, his questioning of the *status quo* in contemporary Nicaragua, the privileging of a more community-based indigenous sociopolitical system, and his implicit incitement toward militant intervention for radical change, all fit well within the parameters of this widespread religious movement throughout Latin America.

As such, the purpose of Cardenal's critical reading of the area's colonial history is multifold. By situating fragments of primary historical documents within a different context—tied together by the overall theme of the costs of extreme ambition and ultimate failure—the poet destabilizes the version of the past presented by the original authors of the chronicles and, in the process, he lays bare some of the artifices and assumptions that support the historiographical process itself—mainly, the very notion of a disinterested version of history.[15] Moreover, Cardenal's own *interested* and socially engaged reading of events is an attempt to give voice to the silences that mark the primary texts, which in large part continued to have repercussions in the Nicaragua of the 1960s.

When defining the notion of history in *The Writing of History* (1975), Michel de Certeau, much like Hayden White in *Metahistory* (1973), stresses the particular position from which a historical document is written, given that the historian's present circumstances and inclinations inevitably help shape the way in which the past is accessed and represented:

> What we initially call history is nothing more than a narrative [...] When we receive this text, an operation has already been performed: it has eliminated otherness and its dangers in order to retain only those fragments of the past which are locked into the puzzle of a present time, integrated into the stories that an entire society tells during evenings at the fireside. These signs that are arranged into a legend can be analyzed, however, *in another way*.
>
> (de Certeau, *The Writing of History* 287; emphasis mine)

By rereading the colonial texts and exposing the constructed nature of received versions of history, *El estrecho* in fact arranges these "signs" *in another way* so as to retrieve elements that have been marginalized by the texts themselves, resulting in the Freudian "return of the repressed" described by de Certeau in *The Writing of History* (329).[16]

Cardenal repeatedly underscores the insufficiency of a historical text to capture an accurate or complete version of the truth. Blatant inconsistencies between the written word and actual events are comically revealed, for instance, when Gil González Dávila presents Pedrarias with the official royal document conveying instructions from the Spanish monarchy *La cédula real,* which is supposed to give Gil González access to the ships left behind by Vasco Núñez de Balboa upon his death. While on the surface Pedrarias claims to defer respectfully to the written mandate of the Spanish crown and kisses the document with reverence, Cardenal notes in parentheses the fact that he did not follow the royal orders: "(pero no la cumplió)," "(y no la cumplió)" (Cardenal 24) ["(but he did not obey)," "(and he did not obey)" (25)]. Clearly, there is no exact correlation between the official instructions in the written document (what Pedrarias claims that he will do) and his subsequent actions. The blatant gap between writing and lived events is ironically thematized in this passage.

At times Cardenal also points to omissions, inaccuracies, and the conscious manipulation of facts in historical documents in a much more explicit fashion:

> Los guías decían que estaban perdidos
> y que no sabían a dónde iban.
>   Se subían a los árboles
> y no veían desde las copas a un tiro de piedra.
> Se comían los caballos
>   y los indios ya iban comiendo muertos
>   ... y no sólo los indios (un Medrano contó después
> que se había comido los sesos de un Montesinos).
> *No lo cuenta Cortés en las Cartas de Relación.*
>
> (Cardenal 40, emphasis mine)

> [The guides said that they were lost
> and didn't know where they were going.
>   They climbed trees
> and from the treetops could not see a stone's throw.
> They were eating the horses
>   and the Indians were now eating the dead
>   ... and not only the Indians (one Medrano later disclosed
> that he'd eaten the brains of one Montesinos).
> Cortés doesn't mention this in the *Cartas de Relación*. (41)]

In this description of Hernán Cortés's ill-fated travels south toward Nicaragua, the parenthetical commentary attributing instances of cannibalism to the Spaniards provides a version of events that clearly does not appear in Cortés's official account, in his *Cartas de Relación*.[17] As accusations of cannibalism were used as an ethical marker between indigenous communities and Christians, the oral admission of a Medrano having resorted to eating the brains of a Montesinos goes against the grain of the standard written accounts of the journey south according to the Spanish chroniclers. Moreover, the unproblematized representation of the indigenous guides eating the dead along the way may serve as a commentary on the expectations of readers of such accounts, who passively accept conventional stereotypes of "savages" created and perpetuated precisely by these types of chronicles. A passive reader might uncritically accept such an uncontextualized account of Indians devouring human flesh outside of a ritualistic practice, and only be scandalized when a Medrano eats the brains of a Montesinos.

Bernal Díaz del Castillo emerges in *El estrecho* as the defender of
the voices that were marginalized and omitted by the royal historians
who focused their historical narratives on the feats of the expedition
leaders instead of on the daily travails of the Spanish soldiers who
risked their lives alongside them:

> De quinientos cincuenta que pasaron con Cortés
> no quedan vivos más que cinco en toda la Nueva España [...]
> Sus nombres debían estar escritos en letras de oro [...]
> Y ninguno de sus nombres los escribió Gomara,
> ni el doctor Illescas, ni los otros cronistas.
> Sólo del Marqués Cortés hablan esos libros.
> Él fue el único que descubrió y conquistó todo,
> y todos los demás capitanes no cuentan para nada [...]
> Pero las cosas no fueron como las cuenta Gomara ...
> (Cardenal 134)

> [Out of five hundred and fifty who crossed over with Cortés
> no more than five are left alive in the whole of New Spain ...
> Their names should be written in letters of gold ...
> And Gomara wrote down none of their names,
> neither did doctor Illescas, nor the other chroniclers.
> Those books speak only of the Marquis Cortés.
> He alone discovered and conquered everything,
> and all other captains count for nothing ...
> But things were not as Gomara tells them ...   (135)]

While clearly prompted by different motivations, like Bernal Díaz,
Cardenal's task is to fill the gaps of a necessarily incomplete representation and shed light upon the issues from the colony that remain
pertinent during his own lifetime.

AN EPIC OF RESISTANCE

The process of supplementing the gaps of history is affected greatly
by *the kind* of story told about the past. Many have written about
the epic or neo-epic characteristics of *El estrecho dudoso* and also of
the poem's frequent deviations from the classic epic form (*i.e.*, Elías,
Pérez, and Williams). Among the similarities with the traditional epic
are: the organization of the text in twenty-five sections like cantos and
in a style comparable to epic songs; the versification of actual historical events to convey the collective history of Central America (with
a special emphasis on Nicaragua); the pitting of good against evil

personified in the greedy and despotic figures of Pedrarias Dávila, Pedro de Alvarado, Hernán Cortés, et cetera, versus the relatively peaceful strategies of religious leaders such as Bartolomé de las Casas and Antonio de Valdivieso;[18] and the turn toward a distant past in order to define "beginnings" and identify "peak times" in Nicaragua's national history.[19] And yet it can be argued that one of the primary deviations of Cardenal's poem from the classical epic form is fundamental to his project, namely, the critical evaluation of past events described and the pointed parallels with the author's own present.

In fact, when defining the epic genre in *The Dialogic Imagination*, Bakhtin stresses the unbridgeable temporal distance between the epic past and the author's contemporary world:

> The epic past is called the "absolute past" for good reason: it is both monochronic and valorized (hierarchical); it lacks any relativity, that is, any gradual, purely temporal progressions that might connect it with the present. It is walled off absolutely from all subsequent times, and above all from those times in which the singer and his listeners are located. (15–16)

Bakhtin distinctly emphasizes the "complete" and "close-ended" view of history represented in the epic, which, again, maintains a temporal distance and resists a critical evaluation of the events represented:

> By its very nature the epic world of the absolute past is inaccessible to personal experience and does not permit an individual, personal point of view or evaluation. [...] The epic world is an utterly finished thing, not only as an authentic event of the distant past but also on its own terms and by its own standards; it is impossible to change, to re-think, to re-evaluate anything in it. It is completed, conclusive and immutable, as a fact, an idea and a value. This defines absolute epic distance. (16–17)

Ernesto Cardenal's poem, however, has been situated by critics in a particular Latin American epic tradition—including, most notably, Alonso de Ercilla's sixteenth-century *La araucana* and Pablo Neruda's *Canto General* (1950)—that *does*, in fact, bridge the epic distance described by Bakhtin. Unresolved issues that revert back to colonial times must still be addressed in modern (or concurrent, in the case of Ercilla) representations of what necessarily results in a more open-ended perception of history.

In fact, in *Epic and Empire: Politics and Generic Form from Virgil to Milton* (1993), David Quint proposes that open-ended histories have been portrayed in epic poetry as far back as the Roman Empire. Using the example of Lucan's *Pharsalia* in contrast to Virgil's *Aeneid,* Quint argues that the epic genre in itself does not necessarily provide a closed account of history. Rather, the ideological perspective of the poet—that is, is it a story of the victors or of the vanquished?—will determine whether it makes sense to recount history as a linear teleological inevitability (the story of the victor) or as a series of contingent factors that could have turned out differently (the story of the vanquished):

> [...] Virgil's poem attached political meaning to narrative form itself. To the victors belongs epic, with its linear teleology; to the losers belongs romance, with its random or circular wandering. Put another way, the victors experience history as a coherent, end-directed story told by their own power; the losers experience a contingency that they are powerless to shape to their own ends.   (Quint 9)

Lucan writes during the reign of Nero and is in favor of the old oligarchic republic that has given way to the monarchical rule of the Roman emperor. The aesthetic style of his poem reflects his pro-republican leanings. Through a series of digressions, of "random or circular wanderings," that Quint associates with the incorporation of romance into epic poetry, the *Pharsalia* interrupts the closure of Virgil's linear story, a story that had traditionally served as a model for celebrating the foundation of the empire. Remaining within the formal scope of the epic genre, Lucan and his subsequent imitators (Ercilla's *La araucana* and Agrippa d'Aubigné's poem of Huguenot resistance *Les Tragiques* of 1616) resort to digressions of "romance" and inconclusive endings as a way to maintain hope for a more favorable turn in history: "Such epics [Lucan's tradition of the losers' epic] valorize the very contingency and open-endedness that the victors' epic disparages: the defeated hope for a different future to the story that their victors may think they have ended once and for all" (Quint 9). Keeping in mind this long-standing tradition of an epic of resistance, Cardenal's text still begs the question: why select the form of a totalizing epic when crafting a poem that engages both the past and present from a counterhegemonic stance?

One explanation might be found in the apparent homology between several aspects of the epic genre and the worldview shaped by the author's adherence to Liberation Theology.[20] Tamara Williams points to the correspondence between the Christian apocalyptic cycle and the eschatological framework of the poem, in which a supreme, overarching sense of morality separates the heroes from the villains:

> [...] this eschatological framework, by invoking a specific theological imperative, creates a moral space in which all action is judged, or sanctioned, characters are saved or damned according to the will of a Supreme God who militantly intervenes on behalf of "those who are persecuted in the cause of right."
>
> (Williams, "Ernesto Cardenal's *El Estrecho Dudoso*: Reading/Re-Writing History" 113)[21]

She further describes a palpable alliance in Cardenal's text between God and the Amerindians in a struggle "for life and renovation" (Williams, "Ernesto Cardenal's *El Estrecho Dudoso*: Reading/Re-Writing History" 111). The portrayal of indigenous communities in *El estrecho* is often cast as a sociopolitical structure to be aspired to as a sort of model of a socialist communal organization that existed spontaneously, before the violent interruption from the West.[22] Given the light in which it is cast, the lessons to be drawn from history seem to be a warning against the consequences of extreme materialism and authoritarian power, while the desired "goal" would be a turn back to "grass-roots," community living within the realm of a sympathetic Christian God.

When Lukács lists the distinguishing characteristics of the epic, in *The Theory of the Novel,* many of them resonate with some of the basic tenets of Liberation Theology. For instance, Lukács insists upon an inherent "totality" within the epic worldview when he compares it to other literary genres such as drama and the novel:

> Great epic writing gives form to the extensive totality of life, drama to the intensive totality of essence. [...] The epic gives form to a totality of life that is rounded from within; [whereas] the novel seeks, by giving form, to uncover and construct the concealed totality of life. (46-60)

This extensive totality and coherent view of life within the structure of the epic is comparable to the internal coherence of any religious doctrine with a defined moral hierarchy and division of good against evil. In both instances, within the epic worldview and in that espoused by Liberation Theology, the very "extensiveness" of this totality moves the field of action *beyond* a personal, internal struggle against "evil" or injustice and changes it to that of *an entire people.* Correspondingly,

Lukács further notes that "the epic hero is, strictly speaking, never an individual. It is traditionally thought that one of the essential characteristics of the epic is the fact that its theme is not a personal destiny but the destiny of a community" (Lukács 66). The homology between the epic genre and Cardenal's religious intention of collectively empowering the abjected community becomes evident.

Another parallel can be drawn when Lukács writes about the way the epic relies on a sense of cosmic balance, of a certainty of eventually attaining justice:

> The epic world is either a purely childlike one in which the transgression of stable, traditional norms has to entail vengeance which again must be avenged *ad infinitum*, or else it is the perfect theodicy in which crime and punishment lie in the scales of world justice as equal, mutually homogenous weights. (61)

This faith in ultimate justice and in a just balance between crime and punishment can also be applied to Liberation Theology, which counts on a militant God to intercede on behalf of the marginalized, who will eventually be included and avenged after fighting for their own liberation from oppressive circumstances. In his turn toward the past, Cardenal's representation of events in a binary epic, within a closed system of justice, points to the path toward a future in which past and current injustices will finally be resolved.[23] *El estrecho dudoso* can then be read as a map of hope toward a redemptive future and, as such, it makes sense to bridge the epic distance described by Bakhtin as a call to action to readers who can position themselves in solidarity with the "good guys" in the epic battle toward liberation.[24]

To this end, Cardenal metonymically displaces the colonial power of the Spaniards to critique subsequent North American enterprises in the region through his parenthetical commentary in canto x:

> Los indios preguntaron al Demonio
> (¿a los brujos? ¿a las brujas? ¿a la Vieja del Volcán?)
> cómo se verían libres de los españoles
>   y el Demonio les contestó.
> Que él podía libertarlos de los españoles
> "haciendo que los dos mares se juntaran
>   (¿el Canal de Nicaragua?)
> pero entonces perecerían los españoles
>   (¿el canal Norteamericano en Nicaragua?)
> juntamente con los indios." (Cardenal 60)

> [The Indians asked the Demon
>   (male witches? female witches? the
> Old Woman of the Volcano?)
>   how they could be rid of the Spaniards
>   and the Demon replied:
>   That he could free them from the Spaniards
>   "causing the two seas to come together
>   (the Nicaraguan Canal?)
>   but then the Spaniards would perish
>   (the North American Canal in Nicaragua?)
>   along with the Indians."   (61)]

The insinuation is that the endeavor to construct a North American canal in Nicaragua would amount to making a deal with the Devil himself. The joining of the two oceans through Nicaragua would bring the hegemony of a new foreign power to replace the Spaniards in the region.

This type of commentary, which detonates associations with both colonial times and the modern period, can be found throughout Cardenal's text. Williams also notes that through a Bakhtinian double-voicing, Cardenal triggers such indirect dialogues with readers who are familiar with the historical context of Nicaragua.[25] Under a climate of censorship and tangible repercussions for speaking against the Somoza regime, a refracted commentary upon the distant past serves as a thinly veiled mirror for the present situation. In the letter that serves as a prologue to the 1991 version of *El estrecho*, José Coronel Urtecho compares the Pedrarias figure both to the prototypical modern businessman and to the Latin American dictator figure. Despite claiming a friendship with Somoza and remarking that he has even served in the ranks of his government, Coronel Urtecho ventures to point out the difficulty of engaging in a direct critical analysis of the Somoza regime without suffering the consequences:

> [...] se le tiene [a Pedrarias] por precursor o antecedente del dictador hispanoamericano, [...] como [...] el General Zelaya, de quien mi padre fue Ministro, hasta mi amigo el General Somoza, del que yo fui, además de partidario, funcionario de su gobierno—, pero lo peor de todo es que tanto a Pedrarias como a los dictadores y aun ya, según parece, a los mismos hombres de negocios, resulta cada vez más difícil, por no decir imposible, estudiarlos, definirlos, juzgarlos, clasificarlos y discutirlos entre nosotros sin sacar las pistolas o caer a la cárcel, lo cual, precisamente, es una de las causas de que existan Pedrarias y dictadores y hasta posiblemente hombres de negocios.   (31–32)

[... he is considered (Pedrarias) as a precursor or a precedent to the Latin American dictator ... like ... General Zelaya, for whom my father served as a Minister, even my friend General Somoza, for whom I was not only a supporter but also held a post in his government—, but the worst of all is that it has become more and more difficult, if not impossible, to study, define, judge, classify, and discuss amongst ourselves men such as Pedrarias or the dictators, or even, as it would seem these days, the businessmen, without drawing guns or ending up in jail, which is precisely one of the reasons for the existence of a Pedrarias and dictators and maybe even businessmen.]

Even in this climate of vigilant censorship, Cardenal's allusions to his present are many. Among the more notable would be in canto x, where an ironic link is suggested between progress and despotism in the figure of Pedrarias, who is repeatedly displaced into the figure of Somoza. Pedrarias is referred to as the first "promoter of progress" and the first "promoter of commerce" in Nicaragua, but the poet's parenthetical comments inform us that the maximum beneficiary of such progress and commerce is Pedrarias himself, while the costs are paid by the many. Somoza's name rings out explicitly in canto x when the source of the documents listing Pedrarias's commercial enterprises (records of his slave trade) are taken from the "colección Somoza": "¡Dulces nombres en los áridos documentos comerciales de la COLECCIÓN SOMOZA!" (58) ["Sweet names in the arid commercial documents in the Somoza Collection!" (59)]. The entire canto oscillates between records of Pedrarias and parenthetical allusions to the modern world: "la propaganda," "una Huelga General," "el canal Norteamericano en Nicaragua," et cetera. The indication that Pedrarias governs despotically, overstays his time in power, and plans to pass on his ill-begotten leadership to his sons is, again, a wink toward the reader who is familiar with the Somoza regime:

Y ya tenía noventa años y no moría nunca
ni iba a Castilla. Estaba tullido y enfermo
y gobernaba con mano de hierro (monopolios
robos, sobornos, prisiones, espionaje, elecciones
fraudulentas ...)
y no moría [...]

[...] Pedrarias enterrado con todas sus banderas.
Después un Asesinato y un terremoto ...
Un gobernador tirano y sus dos hijos
(dos hermanos tiranos).[26]   (60–62)

[And by now he was ninety and would not die
nor go to Castille. He was crippled and ill
and governed with an iron fist (monopolies
thefts bribes prisons spying fraudulent elections ...)
and he would not die [...]

[...] Pedrarias buried with all his flags.
Later a Murder and an earthquake ...
A tyrannical governor and his two sons
(two brother tyrants). (61–63)]

Beyond the parallels that serve as a critical commentary, Cardenal
indirectly suggests an alternative course of action.
   One of the poet's strategies is to incite a reaction through reflections that clearly resonate with recent painful circumstances:

Se levantó en las sierras un indio
   llamado Lempira ("Señor de las Sierras")
y reunió los indios de 200 pueblos,
y más de 2.000 señores y caballeros conocidos
y los juntó en Piraera ("Sierra de las Neblinas").
Les dijo: que era vergonzoso
que tantos hombres estuvieran en servidumbre
de tan pocos extranjeros, en su propia tierra. (102)

[In the mountains there rose up an Indian
   called Lempira ("Lord of the Sierras")
and he gathered together the Indians from 200 towns,
and more than 2,000 known lords and knights
and he brought them together in Piraera ("Sierra of Mists").
He told them that it was shameful
that so many men should be in servitude
to so few foreigners, in their own land. (103)]

The "embarrassment" or "shame" of a powerful foreign presence in
local territory certainly resonates with the United States' repeated
military intervention in Nicaragua since the U.S.-backed ouster of
the Liberal dictator, José Santos Zelaya, in 1909. The U.S. Marines
maintained a presence in the country from 1912 to 1925 to help
preserve the Conservative Party's rule as well as to ensure the prompt
repayment of Nicaragua's significant debt owed to New York banks.
Shortly after their departure, the U.S. Marines returned to Nicaragua
to supervise a presidential election in 1927 that brought into power
José María Moncada, who was considered a puppet of the United

States even though he was a Liberal (Anderson 150). Augusto César
Sandino, much like Lempira in the citation above, emerged as a leader
of the guerrilla forces who resisted the U.S. Marines in Nicaragua.
Led by Somoza García, the National Guard ultimately succeeded in
assassinating the guerrilla leader in 1934. "Somoza became the master
of Nicaragua from that moment forward" (Woodward 220).

In another telling comparison with the Amerindian communities
during the colonial period, Cardenal insinuates a perilous course
toward future liberation:

> (No se gobernaban por caciques ni por señor ni jefe
> sino por un consejo de ancianos elegidos por votos
> y éstos elegían un capitán general para la guerra
> y cuando moría o lo mataban en la guerra elegían otro
>   —*y a veces ellos mismos lo mataban*
>   *si era perjudicial para la república*—
> y se reunían en la plaza a la sombra de una ceiba:
> aquel consejo de ancianos elegidos por votos.)   (54, emphasis mine)

> [(They were not governed by caciques nor by a lord or chief
> rather by a council of elders elected by votes
> and these elders chose an overall war captain
> and when he died or was killed in battle they chose another
>   —and sometimes they killed him themselves
>   if he was doing harm to the republic—
> and they met in the square under the shade of the ceiba:
> that council of elders was elected by votes.)   (55)]

Referring to the pre-Hispanic indigenous forms of government as
a model to emulate, Cardenal points to the need for a community to
resort to such extremes as killing their own leader if he proves to be
detrimental to the republic as a whole (like the Somozas, for example).
In its reading of the past, *El estrecho dudoso* thus traces a daring road
toward future redemption, perhaps even through the use of "justified"
violence, if necessary.

THE STRAIT AS PALIMPSEST

In charting the map toward the future, the author's strategy is then
to start out by pointing to compelling connections between past
and present injustices. The allusions to the present situation must
also take into consideration an even more subtle link to similarities
that resonate with other moments in Nicaragua's history, including

the nineteenth century. The repetitive, unresolved nature of actual historical occurrences in the region makes it possible to allude to different moments in history simultaneously to make a broader commentary regarding the events described. By referring to recognizable circumstances during the colony that can be associated with subsequent occurrences in the nineteenth century and, more importantly, with the poet's contemporary period, the poem operates as a palimpsest that triggers thematic associations between different "layers" or moments in history.

Therefore, such general themes as foreign intervention and aspirations of material accumulation through local geographic control, and the region as a site of ruthless oppression by leading local strongmen in the name of "order" and "progress," conjure up painful wounds in the collective memory pertaining to several different time periods regarding the entire region at large. Applied specifically to present-day Nicaragua, these general thematic associations simultaneously evoke references from:

(1) **The colony:** the search for the *Mar del Sur*, the despotic rule of Pedrarias Dávila and others, the destruction and subjugation of indigenous communities;
(2) **The nineteenth century:** remarkable figures such as William Walker[27] and Cornelius Vanderbilt;[28] and
(3) **The twentieth century:** unrestrained despotic nepotism and the protection of U.S. interests under the Somoza dictatorship.[29]

The three epigraphs at the beginning of this section (from colonial times, the nineteenth century, and veiled references to the twentieth century) allude to this layered, repetitive course of events. Thematic associations often lead to the conflation of plans for an interoceanic passageway, leading to foreign investment in local infrastructures, frequently leading in turn to foreign political and military intervention, resulting in foreign alliances and support for local authoritarian leaders, or even policies that promote order and progress at the expense of personal rights and liberties. The reason for this conflation becomes evident upon revision of Nicaragua's painful past experiences. It would be difficult, for instance, to read about foreign intervention, in general, and interoceanic traffic in Nicaragua without triggering at least a remote association with two prominent U.S. figures of the nineteenth century: the infamous Tennessee-born filibusterer, William Walker, and the wealthy New York financier, Cornelius Vanderbilt ("The Commodore").

Only a few decades after Central America's independence was declared in 1821, amidst the chaotic turmoil between the Conservative and Liberal political factions, William Walker was lured by Liberal leaders to help the fight for their cause.[30] In June 1855, Walker arrived in Nicaragua with fifty-seven men, mainly mercenaries and freebooters, and soon enlisted thousands of supporters. After emerging as a military commander for the Liberals, Walker became the president of Nicaragua in 1856. As the president, he tried to entice other North Americans to join his troops by offering them large land grants. While in power, he declared English the official language and also legalized slavery—which had been outlawed in Central America, at least nominally, since 1824. In fact, his plan was to annex Nicaragua to the United States as a new slave state. To this end, "through a crash program he sought to Americanize the republic, and through a forced-labor vagrancy law he attempted to provide a peasant work force for the landholders" (Woodward 144). He thus alienated the other Central American republics[31] that were appalled by his plans for annexation; and a coalition was created—garnering the support of the powerful magnate Cornelius Vanderbilt—that ousted Walker from power in 1857.[32]

Walker's intervention in Nicaragua flew in the face of high aspirations for the region expressed during the pursuit of the hemisphere's independence from Spain at the beginning of the century. In Simón Bolívar's famous *Carta de Jamaica* (1815), the champion of Latin American independence speculated about the enormity of the potential to be reaped by Central American nations given their privileged position between the seas:

> Los Estados del istmo de Panamá hasta Guatemala formarán quizás una asociación. Esta magnífica posición entre los dos grandes mares podrá ser con el tiempo el emporio del universo. Sus canales acortarán las distancias del mundo: estrecharán los lazos comerciales de Europa, América y Asia, traerán a tan feliz región los tributos de las cuatro partes del globo. ¡Acaso sólo allí podrá fijarse algún día la capital de la tierra! Como pretendió Constantino que fuese Bizancio la del antiguo hemisferio.   (Varona-Lacey 97)

> [The states of the Isthmus of Panama, as far as Guatemala, will perhaps form a confederation. Because of their magnificent position between two mighty oceans, they may in time become the emporium of the world. Their canals will shorten distances throughout the world, strengthen commercial ties between Europe, America, and Asia, and bring to that happy area tribute from the four quarters of the globe. There some

day, perhaps, the capital of the world may be located—reminiscent of the Emperor Constantine's claim that Byzantium was the capital of the ancient world.][33]

Despite Bolívar's optimistic enthusiasm, the mid-nineteenth century marked the moment in which Spain's colonial grip over the isthmus gave way to new neocolonial, expansionist enterprises under the dual guise of imperial England and the "Manifest Destiny" of the United States.[34] In 1850, the Clayton-Bulwer Treaty was signed to give both British and U.S. investors joint access to collaborate in the construction of a canal route. However, by 1849, Cornelius Vanderbilt had already secured a contract with the government of Nicaragua to construct a passage by way of the San Juan river and Lake Nicaragua. Vanderbilt made a fortune with his steamship and railroad lines, making possible a speedier transit from the East to the West coasts of the United States via Nicaragua at the height of the gold rush in California. However, Bolívar's visions of wealth and strategic power being amassed locally through the provision of transit tributes did not materialize. According to Greene: "[...] with his contract, he [Vanderbilt] received the right to transport passengers across the Isthmus. For this privilege he was to pay to Nicaragua ten thousand dollars annually and ten per cent of his profits. (His accountants saw to it that there were no profits)" (Greene 56–57). Ultimately, once the Panama Canal was opened in 1914, traffic shifted away from Nicaragua to the U.S.-controlled passageway between the seas.[35]

Cardenal's poem thus triggers painful memories that relate to several moments in the history of Nicaragua. To speak of foreign presence and interoceanic traffic conjures up all of these memories at once and signals the urgency that arose, by the 1960s, to try to provoke a change. As evidenced in *El país bajo mi piel* (2001), the autobiography of Gioconda Belli, another prominent Nicaraguan poet, these powerful images continue to circulate in the collective consciousness of many Central Americans.

While telling Belli's own personal history, the image of the canal in Nicaragua appears in her memoir as a painful wound:

En el pasado de mi país, como una herida, existe la memoria de un canal interoceánico que nunca se construyó pero que atravesó y cambió nuestra historia, dándonos desde un presidente norteamericano hasta una estirpe de dictadores que gobernaron durante medio siglo. (22)

[In my country's past there exists, like a wound, the memory of an interoceanic canal that was never built; but which did, however, traverse and change our history, giving us from a North American president to a lineage of dictators who governed for half a century.]

The dubious link between the oceans and its multiple repercussions are still felt today. *El estrecho dudoso* was written as an attempt to alter the course of history represented by the failures and excesses ushered in by the doubtful strait.

As seen above, Cardenal's representation of colonial times triggers an indirect association with similar experiences of foreign intervention and greedy strongmen that seem to be repeated over and over again. The similarities with the author's present allow him to provide a critical reading of events without having to do so directly. His open-ended engagement with history, perceiving the resolutions of past conflicts still looming in the future, permits him to participate through his text in charting the road toward better times. Similarly, a potential liberation from past trauma in Guatemalan history is explored in the texts *Week-end en Guatemala* (1956) by Miguel Ángel Asturias, and *Después de las bombas* (1979) by Arturo Arias, discussed in Chapter 2.

CHAPTER 2

THE WOUNDS OF 1954

Off with your history.

(*Rabindranath Tagore*)[1]

When contemplating the course of history in Central America in the second half of the twentieth century, and analyzing the region's geopolitical relationship with the United States during this period, the *coup d'état* sponsored by the Central Intelligence Agency (CIA) in Guatemala in 1954 looms as a constant reminder of the long-term effects sparked by this controversial act of foreign intervention in local affairs. The traumatic events of 1954 serve as an astounding case of successful propaganda campaigns, calculated information manipulation, and psychological maneuvers in the media and the public sphere, culminating in the ouster of Guatemala's elected leader. The orchestration of incendiary language, alarmist Cold War rhetoric, and graphic images in the media—which operated alongside public relations undertakings on behalf of large corporations invested in the area and on behalf of anticommunist diplomatic sectors in the United States—had the short-term strategic effect of rallying support for the opposition forces and damaging the morale of Guatemala's government-elect. A more long-lasting effect of waging a significant component of the coup against President Jacobo Arbenz in the symbolic realm of alarmist words and images was the extreme polarization of Guatemalan society and the propagation of a particular version of history that fit into Cold War agendas, but ignored the more subtle and enduring impact of the fight against "communism" on the lives of the individuals affected by its consequences.

In *History at the Limit of World-History* (2002), Ranajit Guha, the prominent historian, political economist, and Subaltern Studies scholar from India, writes about the limitations of historiography as a genre in capturing just such subtleties and nuances. Referring to "World-history" in Hegelian terms, Guha notes that much is left out of history when defined from the perspective of Western, state-oriented concerns. He resorts to Rabindranath Tagore's notion of "historicality" to account for what is excluded from historiographical accounts and turns to the field of literature for an engagement with the past that revolves around people's experiences in everyday life: "The noise of World-history and its statist concerns has made historiography insensitive to the sighs and whispers of everyday life" (73). Concerned about the hold of the politics of statism over historical representations of the past, he writes:

> We work within the paradigm it [World-history] has constructed for us and are therefore far too close and committed to it to realize the need for challenge and change. No wonder that our critique has to look elsewhere, over the fence so to say, to neighboring fields of knowledge for inspiration, and finds it in literature, which differs significantly from historiography in dealing with historicality. [...] historicality has not been assimilated to statist concerns in literary representation according to Rabindranath Tagore, the greatest South Asian writer of our age. The past, he believes, renews itself creatively in literature, unlike in academic historiography with its insistence on keeping its narratives tied strictly to public affairs. (5)

The term historicality is meant to include the broader discourse of the "prose of the world," an account of the past that is not confined or powered by statehood and public affairs, but rather is inclusive of the individual and his quotidian encounter with his surroundings. Guha's glance "over the fence" to literature situates his critique of historiography at the limit of language. He is in search of an approach to talk about the past that incorporates creativity to tell the familiar story of the past in a way that will arouse wonder and astonishment and incite a thoughtfulness that goes beyond or even against the grain of "World-history's" foundational project of legitimating the development of the state.

This attempt to renew the past creatively in literature, to provoke a more nuanced reflection of its impact beyond official accounts or geopolitical considerations, is the project of the two fictional texts to be discussed in this chapter: Miguel Ángel Asturias's *Week-end en Guatemala* (1956) and Arturo Arias's *Después de las bombas* (1979), both concerned with the complexity of the events of 1954 and their aftermath during the subsequent decades of military dictatorships. Beyond representing the impact of the coup on the daily lives of individuals in Guatemala for years to come, each text brings to the fore the problematic use of partial historiographical discourse in retelling the events of the past. They demonstrate the contentious rhetoric used to justify the overthrow of President Arbenz, and highlight the precarious nature of words and writing itself at a moment of extreme ideological polarization—with physical repercussions leveled against those daring to voice antihegemonic views regarding the coup after 1954. Both texts shed light on the highly constructed use of language for particular statist or corporate interests, to carry out the government overthrow and beyond, to sustain and authenticate the subsequent polarization that entrenched future military regimes. The urgency of renewing the language of the past becomes painfully evident in the face of silences and blank pages alluded to repeatedly by Arturo Arias's character Max throughout the novel. The blank pages and silences he speaks of serve as place holders for people who have suffered physically the repercussions of telling a story of the past that does not correspond with the official rhetoric of the militarized state instituted as a direct result of the coup.

Under such circumstances, the challenge for writers becomes how to find creative ways to sidestep the danger of voicing their perspective as they fill the silences imposed by the official version of events. Both Asturias and Arias turn to fictional narrative as a way to express the collective sense of anger and frustrating impotence felt when faced with the formidable force of the United States and its heavy-handed foreign policy. A fictional representation of historical events enables both authors to subvert official accounts of the "truth" and renew a language of historical memory that has been emptied of credible meaning. Hence, the authors attempt to regain a sense of agency by connecting signifier and signified on their own terms while they use the process of writing and, at times laughter, as a way to counter both the silence and feelings of impotence left behind "after the bombs."

HISTORICAL CONTEXT[2]

It is worth pausing for a moment, before delving into our reading of the literary texts, to assess the set of circumstances that led to the United States' involvement in Guatemalan affairs. I rely primarily on Stephen Schlesinger and Stephen Kinzer's *Bitter Fruit: The Untold Story of the American Coup in Guatemala* (1982) and Piero Gleijeses'

Shattered Hope: The Guatemalan Revolution and the United States, 1944–1954 (1991) for their behind-the-scenes view of the United Fruit Company (UFCO) and U.S. government agencies. Among the primary points of contention in interpreting and representing the occurrences of 1954, leading to vastly different versions of history, are the extent of communist influence on the Arbenz regime, the support and strength of the opposition forces of "liberation," and the amount of influence of the UFCO within the U.S. government. In the face of opposing assessments and representations of each of these issues, the "spin" given to information was key in the crucial battle of public perception.

Cast as an anticommunist endeavor, the so-called "Operation Success" was allegedly prompted by the perilous communist influence within President Jacobo Arbenz's regime. After a decade of fledgling democracy in Guatemala, from 1944 to 1954, some of the nationalist reforms carried out by the presidents, Juan José Arévalo (1945–1950) and Arbenz (1950–1954), especially the Agrarian Reform Law of 1952, began to distress large U.S. companies, such as UFCO, that had grown accustomed to favorable conditions for their investments in the country under previous military regimes. As many top officials within the U.S. government had close associations or even direct stakes in UFCO and its subsidiaries, particular attention was given to the possibility of a "red scare" in Guatemala.[3] Be it due to the influence of UFCO or be it due to the genuine concerns regarding a growing communist presence, a campaign was launched by the Eisenhower government in conjunction with the CIA to destabilize the Arbenz regime and institute a leader who would be more amenable to American business, creating suitable conditions for the banana company once again.[4]

The official justification for the move against Arbenz was then a concern against communist infiltration so close to the strategic Canal Zone. Although the local communists were allowed to form a legal party under his regime, some argue that internal divisions within the party weakened their cause and that, consequently, the party's influence was minimal. Regardless, among the "red" flags causing concern were the facts that a few members (only four) of the communist party did serve in congress during the Arbenz presidency, that the regime was instituting agrarian reform policies that affected U.S. companies and other large landholders, and that the Swedish freighter *Alfhem* arrived in Guatemala's Atlantic port in May 1954 with a cargo of faulty weapons from Czechoslovakia as a result of the United States' refusal to sell arms to Guatemala since 1948.

Despite these indications, theories of impending communist control in Guatemala have been subsequently discredited by many, including historians Stephen Schlesinger and Stephen Kinzer in *Bitter Fruit: The Untold Story of the American Coup in Guatemala* (1982). Harrison Salisbury puts forth the following questions in the introduction that the authors of *Bitter Fruit* attempt to answer in their text:

> Did [Arbenz] genuinely represent a threat to the United States or was he really only a kind of secondary threat to a leading U.S. monopoly, the United Fruit Company? Did his successors actually provide a firm and reliable base for U.S. policy? Was the whole thing just a charade? [...] Did we not merely repeat in more elaborate, more expensive, more complicated technological form the old pattern of entrusting our interests to greedy colonels, petty dictators who sowed the soil with ingredients in which radical and Communistic sentiment was bound to flourish? (xiii–xiv)

While *Bitter Fruit* tends to emphasize the key role of UFCO in shaping U.S. policy toward Guatemala, Piero Gleijeses' *Shattered Hope: The Guatemalan Revolution and the United States, 1944–1954* argues for a more nuanced reading that differentiates between U.S. policies toward the Arévalo and the Arbenz regimes. While he concedes that during the Arévalo years it was primarily the UFCO representatives that shaped U.S. government attitudes toward Guatemala, he claims that by the time Arbenz was in power the UFCO's role had become "marginal" (Gleijeses 363). Gleijeses contends that the communist influence was not a mere public relations embellishment, and that it was thanks to the party's help that Arbenz was able to bring agrarian reform to the countryside (377).[5] Even so, while Gleijeses argues that Arbenz at times turned to the Communist Party when he could not find enough support for his progressive policies elsewhere, he clarifies that there was never an imminent danger of a communist takeover of the reigns of power.

Even though historians debate about the precise reasons that would prompt a global superpower to launch an attack against a small independent republic without a reasonable threat of domestic danger, the U.S. position can be understood, regardless, in the general terms of *space*. If the Eisenhower government was primarily protecting the corporate concerns of UFCO and its subsidiaries, then the issue comes down, quite literally, to space (*i.e.*, land)—who has the right to own and use uncultivated land in a country with severe land distribution inequities? If, as Gleijeses proposes, the U.S. motivation comes down to a sense of hegemonic entitlement in its own backyard, then geographical proximity in itself provides the impetus for action.

Schlesinger and Kinzer put the Guatemalan land distribution problem in perspective when they point to the fact that:

> In 1950 [...] 2.2 percent of the landowners owned 70 percent of the nation's arable land. Of the roughly four million acres in the hands of these plantation owners, less than one fourth was under cultivation [... and] by far the greatest segment of the economy—an investment of $120 million—was in the hands of American corporations, primarily the United Fruit Company. (50)

The authors of *Bitter Fruit* highlight the fact that Arbenz's strategy was to limit the power of foreign companies through direct competition rather than nationalization (53). By the 1950s the UFCO controlled nearly 40,000 jobs and its investments in Guatemala were valued at $60 million. It also controlled the system of communications through its ownership of telephone and telegraph facilities; administered Puerto Barrios, Guatemala's only port on the Atlantic; and its subsidiary, the International Railways of Central America (IRCA), owned most of the tracks within the country (Schlesinger and Kinzer 12). Much of the country's infrastructure was in foreign hands and, ironically, it was deemed and promoted as a threat to capitalism and democracy when Arbenz intended to create some local competition for the U.S.-owned monopolies in his attempt to transform Guatemala into a "modern capitalist state" (Schlesinger and Kinzer 53).

In response to the implementation of agrarian reform, the UFCO wanted a $16 million compensation for the property seized from them, rather than the $627,572 offered on the basis of UFCO's own valuation for tax purposes (Schlesinger and Kinzer 15). For the first time, the local government was tampering with their business and the North American "banana men" were not willing to comply with the new nationalist reforms. The fruit company hired public relations experts to discredit Arbenz's policies and launched a psychological campaign of persuasion in hopes of galvanizing an opposition and setting the stage in the event of U.S. government intervention against the local leader.

By the late 1940s, UFCO had hired Edward Bernays to create an image that portrayed the company as a progressive, benevolent agent that was building Guatemala's infrastructure and improving the local living standards, while depicting the reformist regimes as hostile to U.S. investments and anti-American in sentiment. Bernays was a successful public relations expert who had previously planned marketing strategies for Procter and Gamble, Crisco, and the American Tobacco Company (80). Curiously, he was Sigmund Freud's nephew and was a noted master in techniques of persuasion and propaganda.[6] His strategies for Guatemala included convincing his many friends in U.S. media circles to publish articles according to his spin on events and hosting various press junkets in which he coordinated the people that the press interviewed. As time progressed and the situation became more pressing for UFCO, more experts were enlisted: "With intimidating financial resources and shrewd planning, the United Fruit Company thus deployed a platoon of lobbyists and publicists at a cost of over a half million dollars a year to convince Americans that something evil was afoot in Guatemala" (Schlesinger and Kinzer 97).

Enormously effective in preparing the terrain against Arbenz, a strategy of information manipulation was central to the June 1954 invasion as well, for the struggle for power was carried out in large part in the arena of conflicting perceptions. On June 17, the "liberation" forces led by Colonel Carlos Castillo Armas, comprising a ragtag group of a few hundred rebels, crossed the Honduran border into Guatemala.[7] This provided the front for the CIA operation to make it seem as though it was a Guatemalan movement that arose spontaneously to oust their president as a result of popular dissatisfaction with his policies. Among the primary devices of persuasion was a radio station based in pro-U.S. Nicaragua, Honduras, and the Dominican Republic—"the Voice of Liberation"—that was used for the express purpose of disseminating misinformation during the course of the insurrection. Directed by the American David Atlee Philips together with three Guatemalans, the "Voice of Liberation" radio transmission was used to spread panic within Guatemala and create a skewed perception of the effectiveness of the antigovernment initiatives. Another component of "Operation Success" consisted of jamming the Guatemalan government's radio messages so that it could not present its own account of occurrences. Importantly, key sectors of the Guatemalan public—the large landowners, the Catholic Church, and all those negatively affected in any way by the recent reforms—were highly receptive to the criticism made by foreign journalists and to the rumors that were rampant.

At the same time, potential supporters of Arbenz were demoralized by the fact that U.S. aircraft, P-47s, were flown over the capital city and other key towns as a form of intimidation. Sporadic bombs were dropped by the planes in strategic areas, "causing little damage but unnerving the populace" (Gleijeses 326). Gleijeses argues that, in the end, it was the belief within the army that the U.S.-backed Castillo Armas's forces would potentially mount a direct offensive against Guatemala if the rebels were defeated that led to their disobedience and betrayal. The perception that it would be preferable to lose to the rebels than to incur the wrath of the United States might explain the fact that the army officers ultimately turned against Arbenz, leading to his eventual resignation on June 27, 1954.

HISTORICALITY IN FICTION

As the controversial events of June 1954 have been represented in vastly different ways, being spun according to powerful vested interests, with particular versions promoted by subsequent military repression, the realm of fiction allows for an in-depth exploration of the themes of incongruent perceptions, language manipulation, and the effects of unfathomable historical occurrences on the psyche of particular individuals in their everyday life. Completed just a year after the insurrection, Miguel Ángel Asturias's *Week-end en Guatemala* is structured in eight distinct vignettes that convey how the events of June 1954 affected several individual characters in a very personal manner. Through their intimate experiences, Asturias reflects upon the frustration of impotence, the arbitrary use of accusations of communism, the manipulation of the press, and the blatant silences in official accounts of history, among many other pertinent issues.

As early as the summer of 1955, when Asturias completes his text, he is able to anticipate and convey the broader implications of interrupting the implementation of the social reforms that were initiated in the democratic decade of 1944–1954. His vignettes indicate how the coup would likely unleash the tremendous hostility and violence inherent within an exclusionary power system that was fearful of labor unions and the indigenous majority. A vague language of "communist" affiliations and a pathological vocabulary of ideological "contamination" are appropriated by anti-Arbenz forces to gloss over much more complex and profoundly entrenched sociopolitical issues particular to Guatemala. In his short stories, Asturias includes various instances in which this vague terminology is appropriated and conveniently used to serve personal interests. The failure of the U.S. government to contextualize such domestic issues and take them into consideration when carrying out the anticommunist offensive would trigger a chain of events that would eventually result in the closing of viable political spaces and lead to a thirty-six-year civil war that would take a toll of over 200,000 lives.[8] In large part, Asturias's text is a poignant lament for lost opportunities, a testament to the repercussions witnessed in the year since the Arbenz coup, and a perceptive warning about the extreme violence and future bloodshed yet to come.

Whereas Cold War rhetoric defined the parameters of foreign and domestic government policies of the 1950s, its binary narrative was applied to particular situations that had little to do with the battle of democracy versus socialism. In the short story entitled "La Galla" ("The Rooster-lady" or "The Cock-lady"), concerning the issue of land reform, Asturias demonstrates the ambiguity of the term "communism" and how it is wielded against entire groups of people on the basis of useful generalizations. La Galla is the owner of a rural town store and the daughter of a despotic landowner who was killed in a previous indigenous uprising. With a personal vendetta against the indigenous community in her town and a family legacy of racism, she settles the score when asked by an old school friend to produce a list of local communists and report it to the mercenary soldiers during the insurrection. This is precisely the type of personal background and lived history that proves decisive in shaping day-to-day actions that "World-history" cannot gauge. Predictably, La Galla accuses all members of the local *cofradía* (religious brotherhood), a community-level Church organization, who were the beneficiaries of the government land distribution program. Even though the *cofradía* is clearly geared toward the worship of God—and communism was seen as "a threat to religion, tradition and conservative values" (CEH)—the fact that its members received the distributed land that was taken away from others was considered by some as an egregious threat that aligned them with the "enemy."

The complicity of the press in shaping a given take on events and circulating it for public consumption is also addressed by Asturias.[9] In an episode where a biased reporter from the magazine *Visiones* interviews Diego Hun Ig, the head of the *cofradía*, and tries to represent him as the leader of the local communists, Diego is unfortunately portrayed by Asturias as too dim-witted to understand what communism even means. The intention of the encounter is to dramatize the discrepancies between rampant fears of ideological indoctrination and the modest plans of those who received the land from the government—highlighting, as well, dishonest representations in the press. Diego is asked if he is a communist and when he asks, in turn, what that is, La Galla's partner, El Pecoso (Freckle-face), replies that "it is free love, having many women, and giving your children to the State" (143, translation mine). Diego replies that he is happily married

but that he does want to send his children to state schools so that
they can learn to read. The journalist proceeds to ask if the land
received will be communal and Diego insists that it will be for private
use. However, the community will share a tractor, a silo, et cetera.
El Pecoso then informs Diego that he is indeed a communist, and
the malicious article published in *Visiones* suggestively speculates that
Diego Hun Ig conducted the interview outside of his house so that
they would not find his Marxist literature, or his pictures of Lenin,
Stalin, and Mao-Tse Tung (147). The polysemous title of the magazine, *Visiones,* speaks to the dubious credibility of the journalist's
investigative reporting, as *visión* in Spanish, like "vision" in English
can refer to the act of seeing or to the act of hallucinating, of the
imaginary perception of an unreal object.[10] The article preys on its
public's worst fears to provoke hallucinations of communism where
it does not, in good faith, apply.

Alongside such blatant distortions of reality, Asturias demonstrates
how the labeling of the indigenous community as "communists"
justifies a level of violence that is encouraged by the state to reverse
the reforms implemented by the revolutionary regimes. For a state
that is fearful of an indigenous majority, Cold War paranoia becomes
a useful means for repressive control in the name of "order." After
the mercenary insurrection, the *cofrades* are either killed or forced
to work on the roads. When Diego is performing forced labor along
with the rest of his family, his young daughters bring him food and
one of them is raped by the overseer:

> El capataz, teniente Cirilo Pilches, persiguió a una de sus hijas, y a
> la fuerza la obtuvo. 'India comunista', le decía, mientras la ultrajaba,
> 'aprendé lo que es el amor libre, eso que tu padre proclamaba, aprendé
> lo que es tener hijos para el Estado, porque tu tata eso era lo que
> quería, que todos ustedes fueran del Estado ... Aquí está tu tractor, tu
> silo, tu sembradora ... [...] todo esto le valió para que lo condecoraran,
> al triunfar sobre sus indefensos paisanos tamboreros, los bombarderos
> gringos.   (147)

> [The foreman, Lieutenant Cirilo Pilches, pursued one of his daughters,
> and got her by force. He would call her a "Communist Indian,"
> while he violated her, "learn what 'free love' means, that term your
> father would proclaim, learn what it means to have children for the State,
> because that's what your daddy wanted, for you to be of the State ... Here
> is your tractor, your silo, your seed drill ... all of this was acknowledged
> when he was decorated publicly, for triumphing over his defenseless,
> drumming compatriots, the gringo bombers.]

Asturias reminds us that the cost of misrepresentation (like equating those who had received redistributed lands from the government with communists) and privileging signs over actual content is paid quite tangibly by the wounded bodies of many innocents who are pulled into the generalized Cold War battle between East and West and the ostensible confrontation of democracy versus communism. His short stories encompass the historicality of the individuals who fall prey to a historical discourse that excludes the complexity of their personal reality. In the hands of subsequent military regimes, the conceptual terminology that shapes the logic of geopolitical and state policies engulfs people in the violence that is implicated in the proliferation of "blank pages" and pregnant silences when referring to the country's traumatic past.

Week-end en Guatemala repeatedly refers back to the theme of discrepant representations of events and of the partial nature—both biased and incomplete—of official accounts of the insurrection and its aftermath. In one of the short stories set farther in the future, entitled "El Bueyón" ("Big Ox"), an indigenous woman tells her incredulous granddaughter about the time when the government had given her family land:

> [...] al final nos entregó un título de la tierra de que nos hacía propietarios, dueños, propiamente dueños, propietarios de tierra propia ... /—Es como un sueño, Nana Caida—observó la nieta que ya iba a la escuela./—Debe estar en la historia ... /—No, eso no está ... /—Entonces, m'hija, lo quitaron. No ponen lo que no les conviene. Pero como se los estoy contando sucedió.   (Asturias 155)

> [... in the end they gave us a land title which made us proprietors, owners, properly property owners, proprietors of our own land ... /—It's like a dream, Nana Caida—observed the granddaughter who already attended school./—It should be in the history books ... /—No, that's not in them ... /—Then, my dear, they took it out. They don't put the things that are not in their own interests. But as I am telling you that is how it happened.]

Only in the words circulated through private storytelling between generations is the memory of nonhegemonic perspectives passed on. That is, in part, the task of the stories told by both Asturias and Arias in their novels—filling the gaps left untold by conventional history.[11]

The violence of self-serving language and distorted representation is taken to a cynical extreme in the story entitled "Cadáveres para la publicidad" ("Corpses for Publicity"). The story opens when hundreds of members of labor unions, many from U.S.-owned companies—"del sindicato de trabajadores del banano, del sindicato de trabajadores ferroviarios, del sindicato de trabajadores portuarios [...]" (172) ["of the union of the banana workers, of the union of the railway workers, of the union of the workers of the ports ... "]—are forced by the mercenary troops to dig a deep hole in the ground and are then executed. This saves the rebel forces the trouble of having to dig mass graves to bury their victims. Jerome McFee, the publicity "master" from New York, then conceives of the idea of using the corpses of the victims in his anticommunist propaganda campaign. Upon previous consultation with the U.S. State Department, the leader of the liberation movement, himself, receives the copyright for the use of the word "corpses" and proceeds to implement McFee's propaganda plan. The bodies of the labor union members who died defending their beliefs are then, appallingly, photographed as victims of the "communists": "¡Así jodidos, los mataron por ser de los sindicatos, acusándolos de 'rojos' y ahora los vienen a retratar, para presentarlos como víctimas de los 'rojos,' es decir, como sus propias víctimas!" (Asturias 183) ["So that's how it is, those son-of-a-guns, they killed them for being in the labor unions, accusing them of being 'reds' and now they come and take their pictures, to present them in public as the victims of the 'reds,' that is to say, as their own victims!"]. Within this contrived framework, the corpses of the murdered union members are thus emptied of the meaning of their life struggle and become *mere signifiers*—to be circulated publicly for the purposes of disinformation (anticommunism) and even profit (capitalism).[12] Again, signs (and bodies) are "spun" to fit into a political narrative that disregards the particular context of their intended significance. What are the stakes of representing history when even the dignity of human corpses is considered fair game in the spin of events? What is the consequence of treating wounded bodies as so-called floating signifiers to be manipulated in the creation of contrived meaning?

In the face of such strategic manipulations, it must have seemed particularly urgent by 1955 to expose the incongruence between official accounts and the lived histories of individuals who went through the coup and were experiencing its consequences. To point out this discrepancy and to supplement it with parallel stories that cut through the fabric of everyday life is certainly one of the immediate projects of the book. Another political project of the series of vignettes is to underline the incongruence in the military disparity between government supporters

and U.S.-backed opposition forces, and to convey the frustrating sense
of impotence resulting from such disparities.

Due mostly to its obvious political stance, *Week-end en Guatemala* has been compared by critics to the author's "banana trilogy"
novels—*Viento fuerte* (1950), *El papa verde* (1954), and *Los ojos de
los enterrados* (1960)—all of which are commentaries on the effects
of UFCO's involvement in Guatemala.[13] At times, the banana trilogy
has been looked upon unfavorably by literary critics who consider
that its anti-imperialist intentions obscure the richness and complexity
of the aesthetic craft that characterizes Asturias's other well-known
novels, such as *Hombres de Maíz* or *El Señor Presidente*. And indeed,
it could be argued that many of the characters in *Week-end* do possess
some oversimplified characteristics that ultimately serve to present a
particular political position. In fact, many characters that support and
participate in the insurrection against the government-elect are given
despicable personal flaws: drunkenness, racist views, the propensity to
rape women and children, et cetera, resulting in an obvious division
between "good" and "evil" according to the ethical position taken
in the text. In part, this lack of nuance may be due to the urgency of
the author's project and may, in itself, be a reflection of the extreme
political polarization of the times.

While some point disparagingly to the "social realist" tendencies
of *Week-end*, others, such as Dante Liano, consider that the author's
linguistic dexterity saves the text, along with the "banana trilogy,"
from reading like a mere political pamphlet:

> [...] el escritor se lanza a la denuncia del imperialismo con la llamada
> "trilogía bananera": [...] un esfuerzo narrativo de considerables dimen-
> siones cuya finalidad determinante es la toma de posición política. Muchos
> críticos tienden a desdeñar este período asturiano, por encontrarlo
> demasiado plegado al "realismo socialista." Igual señalamiento se hace
> a *Week-end en Guatemala*. Quisiera observar sólo una cuestión: aún en
> estas obras, el oficio del maestro y su indiscutible talento lingüístico
> salen a relucir, quizá con menos continuidad que en sus obras de mayor
> empeño artístico, pero siempre con un envidiable dominio del arte de
> novelar y un uso magistral de la lengua española.
> (Liano, *Visión crítica de la literatura guatemalteca* 150–51)

> [... with his so-called "banana trilogy" the author embarks on a
> campaign to denounce Northern imperialism: ... a narrative effort
> of considerable dimensions with an ultimate goal of setting forth a
> political position. Many critics have scorned this period in Asturias's
> writing, finding it too in-line with "socialist realism." The same has

been said about *Week-end en Guatemala*. I would like to make just one
observation: even in these works, the craft of the master and his unargu-
able linguistic talent are evident, perhaps with less continuity than in his
texts with greater artistic efforts, but always with an enviable capability
to narrate a story in the form of a novel and a great mastery of the
Spanish language.]

As I hope to illustrate further below, through a series of haunting
repetitions and rapid cuts between compelling juxtapositions of images
and sounds, the rhythm of the short stories effectively conveys the
characters' extreme psychological distress. Notably, the most prevalent and poignant emotion captured in the stories is the frustration
that stems from a sense of devastating impotence.

I would argue that beyond a masterful use of literary language to
communicate the immediacy of such emotions, a degree of complexity is introduced into the text at a conceptual level as well, especially
when reading the collection of stories in terms of a "roadmap" for the
future. By this I mean that despite the anti-interventionist and clear
political position taken, the potential recourses for resistance are not
as clear-cut as they may seem, but are rather ambivalent at best. This
is true especially when characters opt for a course of violent resistance
in "¡Americanos todos!" ("We are all American!") and in the story
that closes the collection, "Torotumbo." Instead of serving as an
empowering act or a cathartic release for the pent-up sense of impotence, the consequences of violent resistance are quite problematic in
both of these stories. This is true even though the final story seems to
point to organized violent resistance as one of the only options given
the lack of other spaces for opposition.

"¡Americanos todos!" features Milocho, a tourist guide who was
raised in Guatemala and holds U.S. citizenship, and is tormented
after witnessing the death of twenty-nine villagers in a rural town
during the invasion. His Californian girlfriend cruelly enjoys taunting
him about the lack of local resistance to the 1954 attack: "Sí, sí, tus
volcanes son un poco la imagen de la grandeza impotente de ustedes ...
Pero aquí, *darling*, no sólo los volcanes, todos, todos se hicieron
los dormidos cuando asomaron mis aviones" (85) ["Yes, yes, your
volcanoes are a bit the image of your compatriots' impotent greatness ... But here, darling, not only the volcanoes, but everyone,
everyone pretended to be asleep when my planes drew near"]. In the
face of her taunting comments and the pent-up rage he feels for being
so powerless against unfathomable geopolitical events, he resorts to
driving a bus full of tourists on a suicidal jump off a cliff. With a

strange logic of symmetrical justice, Milocho notices that there are twenty-nine North American tourists on his bus, twenty-nine people who are meant to pay for the death of the twenty-nine villagers. However, driving twenty-nine additional innocent people to their death is clearly not an empowering act of bravery, nor is it meant to be in the story. Milocho's desperate and misguided resort to action to counteract his compatriots' inaction only underlines the perpetuation of impotence and suffering.

The vignette that centers on Milocho's tale is a good example of Asturias's technique of conveying the psychological state of his characters through the rhythm of his narrative. When the idea of revenge enters his mind, he takes hold of the bus and his thoughts accelerate as the pace of the bus accelerates around the ravine:

> Iba acelerando, acelerando, acelerando ... veintinueve ... veintinueve ... acelerando ... acelerando ... ya no verán nada ... quítense esos anteojos ... acelerando ... acelerando ... escupan esos chicles, recen ... recen ... acelerando ... acelerando ... su visión era doble. (91)

> [He was accelerating, accelerating, accelerating ... twenty-nine ... twenty-nine ... accelerating ... accelerating ... you won't see anything again ... take off those glasses ... accelerating ... accelerating ... spit out that chewing gum, pray ... pray ... accelerating ... accelerating ... he began seeing double.]

In Milocho's thoughts, the twenty-nine tourists are juxtaposed with the twenty-nine villagers until they merge and cancel each other out in his scheme for justice taken into his own hands:

> ... ya no sólo veía a los turistas, sino a los fusilados ... sobre cada turista iba un fusilado ... le acariciaba la cara ... el fusilado le acariciaba la cara al turista y le decía ... "¡Quítate esos anteojos gringo, ... que dentro de un momento ya no verás nada ... gringo, míranos ... aún es tiempo de que veas ... aún es tiempo de que escupas el chicle y reces ... gringo ... gringo!" (91)

> [... now he not only saw the tourists, but also those who had been executed by the firing squad ... over each tourist, an executed person ... caressing their face ... the executed person caressed the face of the tourist and would tell him ... "Take off those glasses gringo, ... in a moment you won't see a thing ... gringo, look at us ... there's still time for you to see ... there is still time for you to spit out the chewing gum and pray ... gringo ... gringo!"]

The tourists in the bus first feel exhilaration at the speed of the bus, but soon begin to panic when they realize their guide's intentions. The sound of them all plummeting into the abyss reverberates with his impotent scream of desperation.

This same sense of ambivalent unease due to the complex consequences of violence can be gleaned from the last story in the collection, "Torotumbo." Interestingly, both *Week-end en Guatemala* and Arturo Arias's *Después de las bombas* end with a carnival scene, in which power hierarchies are temporarily suspended in the city streets of Guatemala. In both carnival scenarios lie the seeds of future liberation, as understood by each of the authors. The last story in the Asturias compilation ties together three different narrative threads: (1) the rape and murder of a young indigenous child by Estanislao Tamagás, the owner of a disguise store and fervent member of the Committee of Defense against Communism; (2) Tamagás's neighbor, Tizonelli, who has witnessed the murder, uses this knowledge to diffuse the efforts of the anticommunist committee; (3) the family members of the young girl organize a ritual dance, *el baile de tun*, to appease the Devil and deter future evils against their community. All three story lines converge when the indigenous dance spills onto the streets of Guatemala City and members of all the different sectors of society join them in the festivities, reveling in carnival disguises. Taking advantage of the chaos and confusion, the young revolutionary movement stages an offensive against the anticommunist regime. This attack is presented in an ambivalent way, however, because Tizonelli had previously set large quantities of explosives in his neighbor's house, where the meeting of top officials in the anticommunist leadership was set to take place. Rather than generating a sense of euphoria from justified vengeance against the committee's murderous activities, the attack on the meeting is presented in a stressful and conflicted way. Along with Tizonelli, the reader realizes that the flooding of carnival revelers onto Tamagás's street guarantees the injury of many other innocent individuals. Without glorifying its use, the author points to a perceived need to resort to violence to confront the violence of the anticommunist committee, given the limited spaces for resistance.

In her article, "'Torotumbo': una posible interpretación," Rosaura Ortiz Guzmán interprets the *Torotumbo* dance as an allegory of a future revolution:

> Así, el baile del Torotumbo, inicialmente un baile de guerra contra el diablo comenzado por los indios, se convierte en el baile de guerra de

un pueblo que se levanta contra un gobierno represivo. Todos se unen en una sola causa [...] Asturias reúne así al pueblo indígena vejado, tratado como una bestia—cuya representación se da en Natividad Quintunche—y a la población en general—el campesino, los estudiantes, el pueblo—perseguida, encarcelada, asesinada. [...] El cuento, ubicado dentro de su ámbito temporal de un futuro inmediato, es la visión de una revolución armada de base popular que ha de llegar. Además, en este sentido, el cuento ofrece otro mensaje que, evidentemente, niega la revolución pacífica como algo efectivo. (56)

[Thus the dance of the Torotumbo, initially a war dance against the devil started by the Indians, becomes the war dance of a people that rise up against a repressive government. All unite behind a common cause ... in this way, Asturias brings together the humiliated indigenous community, treated like an animal—represented in the character of Natividad Quintunche, with the general population—the peasant, the students, the people—persecuted, jailed, murdered .... The story, situated within the temporal scope of an immediate future, is the vision of a popular-based armed revolution that is to come. Moreover, in this sense, the story provides another message which, evidently, denies the notion of a peaceful revolution as effective.]

In this final scene, Asturias alludes to a possible antidote to the overwhelming sense of impotence and frustration conveyed in his previous stories. In the dance of the *Torotumbo* lies his message of hope and predictions of a future revolution, a rising up against repressive powers as a desperate resort—even though the story also points to an uneasy awareness of the loss of innocent victims caused by the violence that is sure to come.[14] The tone is certainly quite different from a heroic call to action against the "forces of evil" perceived in a clear-cut, Manichean way, or even the more utopian version of a call to battle against the corrupt Somoza dictatorship that can be read in Ernesto Cardenal's *El estrecho dudoso*.

AFTER THE BOMBS

Laughter alone remained uninfected by lies.

(*Mikhail Bakhtin*)[15]

In *Week-end en Guatemala*, Asturias exposes the many ways in which language and images were distorted to fit a particular Cold War narrative in the immediate aftermath of a local battle of "East" against "West," a battle that was itself carried out largely in the realm of disputed perceptions. His text highlights personal perspectives excluded and misrepresented by this narrative, and communicates the devastation of feeling impotent in the face of such discrepancies, especially given the closing of viable political spaces for moderate opposition. Written decades later, Arturo Arias's novel *Después de las bombas* (1979) remembers the events of 1954 and reveals how they impacted the process of engaging with the past for years to come: glaringly blank pages, forced silences, perilous treading through the indisputable danger of words, et cetera.

Arias attempts to offset this course of censored memories and biased representation through the trajectory of his protagonist Máximo and his individual search for meaning and truth. Máximo's coming into his own, maturing both sexually and intellectually by the end of the novel, signals a personal mode of resistance and refusal to accept such repressive silences. The collective feelings of impotence conveyed so poignantly in *Week-end* are counteracted metaphorically in *Después de las bombas* with Max's difficult road to achieve sexual confidence (regaining the ability to feel tangible pleasure in his body) and, more directly, through his thoughtful mastery of language, which paves the way for active sociopolitical engagement.

On yet another level, the author defiantly dissipates any lingering feelings of collective impotence (conveyed so clearly by Asturias in the 1950s) by recontextualizing historical events through laughter. With a sense of humor that is both irreverent and dark, Arturo Arias claims a narrative voice for his protagonist and a tone for his novel that allow for the recasting of traumatic events in such a way that opens the possibility for active and productive engagement with the present, beyond the paralyzing effects of fear.

In his essay "Forms of Time and Chronotope in the Novel," Mikhail Bakhtin describes the liberating effect that laughter can have upon language and its function in challenging established norms of thought:

> There is no aspect of language that cannot be used in a figurative sense. In all these approaches [irony, parody, humor, the joke, various types of the comic and so forth], *the point of view* contained within the word is subject to a reinterpretation, as is the modality of language and the very *relationship of language to the object* and *to the speaker*. A relocation of the levels of language occurs—the making contiguous of what is normally not associated and the distancing of what normally is, a destruction of the familiar and the creation of new matrices, a destruction of linguistic norms for language and thought. (237)

In a long-standing climate of fear, under the authoritarian imposition of discursive restraint regarding the topics of history and politics in post-1954 Guatemala, the task for Arias will be to create an effect upon the reader that not only casts an alternative version of events, but actually breaks open the possibility of multiple interpretations and allows for the polyvalence of words to resurface. As the protagonist reclaims access to his own body and to the critical use of language within a stifling atmosphere, the reader embarks on a parallel journey of rediscovery. Through laughter, parody, exaggeration, incongruent juxtapositions, and a dizzying rhythm that alternates between humor and extreme anxiety, Arturo Arias reifies the monologic discourse of authority and exposes it as a powerful construct (at times to the point of absurdity) with its own limitations—most certainly *not* as an absolute truth. Through his parodic stance, the author submits the official point of view to reinterpretation, engaging in the discursive process put forth by Bakhtin above.

Arias's novel begins during "the time of the bombs," the invasion of June 1954, when Máximo is a small child. His father, a minor government bureaucrat during the Arbenz regime, disappears during the coup, never to be heard from again. His father's disappearance is shrouded in mystery and ominous silence for the young boy, as his mother, at first, resists talking to him about the painful taboo subject. Máximo grows up under the sequence of repressive military regimes that follow the Arbenz overthrow, which provides the backdrop for his journey toward manhood. The child protagonist is intent on finding out any information about his father that he can, but he is repeatedly confronted with heavily charged silences and a frustrating lack of information:

> Pero estaba determinado en aprender. Ya le había preguntado a mucha gente de la calle. Todos pretendían no oírlo o que no sabían. Como si hubieran roto toda conexión con ese tiempo mítico anterior a las bombas quedándoles sólo ese ombligo negro que era la boca abierta sin dientes, sin palabras.   (Arias 43)[16]

> [But he was determined to learn. He had already asked a lot of people in the street. Everybody pretended they didn't hear him or that they didn't know. As though they had broken off all connections with that mythical time before the bombs, leaving them only with that black umbilicus, an open, toothless, wordless mouth.   (40)]

The quest for his father and his own personal identity is intertwined with the need to bridge the silences and gaps in Guatemala's official history. Thus his oedipal search is also the path toward a broader social awareness.

Remembering a formative exchange with a street vagrant when he was a young child, Máximo later ponders the idea of truth put forth in fiction—a type of truth that applies both to the stranger's story and metadiscursively to Arias's novel itself. As Max searches for his father and for an explanation of what had happened during the "time of the bombs" and before, the man on the street tells him a seemingly unrelated story from which he is able to glean a connection to his father, since it sheds light on a broader historical context of power relations in Guatemala:

> El viejo tenía razón. Su cuento me dijo dónde estaba mi padre. Quién era. La verdad en un cuento no es una verdad que vos podés mirar, tocar. Pero es una verdad de todos modos, tan grande, si no más grande, que cualquier otra verdad. (126)[17]

> [The old man was right. His story told me where my father was. Who he was. And truth isn't always a truth you can see and can touch. But remember. It's a truth, anyway, as great if not greater, than any other truth. (118)]

Through the tale of the street vagrant about the battle between the legendary Maya hero Tecún Umán and Pedro de Alvarado, Máximo comes closer to attaining a social awareness that will eventually give him an understanding of his father's progressive plight. Similarly, *Después de las bombas* brings us to a comparable kind of truth through narrative fiction that is not founded upon rigorous recounting of empirical facts, but on an exploration of the deeper implications and consequences, psychological and physical, personal and collective, that came out of the trauma of 1954. Thus, when young Máximo walks through the streets of the capital city and has to step over the dead bodies that are strewn throughout his neighborhood after the incursion, even though the bombs that fell from U.S. planes in June 1954 did not actually result in such levels of carnage, when one thinks of the more than 200,000 people who were killed or "disappeared" during the military regimes that became entrenched after the coup of 1954, then the knowledge that one gleans from Arturo Arias's fictional rendition is not so far from the actual "truth" after all.[18]

Through the occasional accounts of his friends and family members, Max begins to piece together memories of his father and of the ineffable period before the coup. To come to terms with his sense of loss and the confusing experiences of his coming of age, he begins to write in private. From the time he begins to speak as a child, he learns early of both the power and the danger of words: "Había que tener cuidado con lo que uno decía" (18) ["You had to be careful about what you said" (16)]. The perilous consequences of words are reinforced later on, when he witnesses a book burning in the streets and a man being beaten by soldiers for daring to write and read prohibited literature. Max's exposure to books had been nonexistent before this incident, as school was always officially canceled due to "the situation," and the government kept passing him and his classmates from grade to grade by decree, in acknowledgment of "the children's innocence." In a comical stretch toward the absurd, he actually ends up graduating from high school by official decree without ever having set foot on a school campus. His education would have to take place elsewhere.

The streets become his learning ground, particularly after witnessing the violent beating and book burning, which jolt him out of his indifference concerning books. When young Max pleads with the bloody victim of the beatings to tell him where his father is, instinctively suspecting a connection, the man cryptically responds that he should search in the ashes of his burnt books (59). Max's next significant encounter with books is when he bumps into a man on a bicycle returning a set of texts to the library. When the boy asks the man to let him see one of the books, *La búsqueda de la identidad* [*The Quest for Identity*], he is confronted with nothing but blank pages. Much like Max's own search for his uncertain personal identity, the book is apparently blank; and the task of attempting to read (and especially to write) the pages of both, is weighed down by the ever present constraints of a vigilant authoritarian force. The cyclist explains: "Su contenido es ilegal, joven, ilegal de acuerdo con la ley. Uno puede ser fusilado por poseer el contenido de cualquier libro impreso en este siglo" (68) ["Their contents are illegal, young man, illegal under the law. A person can be shot for possessing the contents of any book printed in this century" (63)]. With hyperbolic exaggeration Arias signals the tight restraint placed upon the circulation of texts in Guatemala during this time. Rather than shying away from exposing the censorship of the decades that followed 1954 by participating in the self-censorship that is generated in a climate of fear, Arias exaggerates the facts to such an extent that what is undeniably tragic becomes contextually comical through a process of recognition of truth within parody. The pursuit of knowledge outside of the acceptable limits of the state has a recognizable cost, and Arias brings his readers face-to-face with the imposed limits of knowledge through his use of irreverent humor.

Little by little, despite their inherent danger, Max realizes that words will somehow lead him to his father and to a better understanding of his own place in the confusing world that surrounds him:

> Encontraré a mi padre a través de las palabras. Lo traeré de vuelta a la vida con las palabras. Construiré una catedral de palabras. Crearé al país con mis palabras. En mis palabras encontraré al universo y entenderé el eterno presente a través de mis palabras. En mis palabras encontraré, acabaré, me volveré las palabras mismas, seré palabras, palabras, palabras, encarnaré palabras, palabras, palabras. (141)

> [I'll find my father through words. I'll bring him back to life with words. I will build a cathedral of words. I'll create a country with my words. In my words I'll find the universe and I'll understand the eternal present through my words. In my words, I will find, I will end, I will become the words themselves, become words, words, words, I will incarnate words, words, words. (131)]

Max turns to writing to fill the blank pages in his search for his own identity. Moreover, beyond understanding his present through words and writing, Max intends to bridge the gap between the forgotten past and the future, giving the Word—a potential voice for resistance—back to the Guatemalan people:

> Tenía que reconstruir ese mundo olvidado aunque fuera solamente con palabras. Comunicar la gran mentira que había sido todo después de las bombas. Mantener aquel glorioso pasado vivo y dinámico. Esculpiría las palabras de su mente, las pegaría cuidadosamente, hasta que los conceptos se empezaran a formar, lentamente, los conceptos de aquel mundo que él perdió. Devolverle las palabras al pueblo, llenar los espacios en blanco, los blancos. (117)

> [He had to reconstruct that forgotten world even if it was only with words. To communicate the big lie that everything had been after the bombs. To keep that glorious past alive and vigorous. He would carve the words with his mind, put them together with great care until the concepts began to form, slowly, the concept of that world he had lost. To return words to the people, to fill in the blank spaces, the blanks. (109)]

Words become the only way to move beyond the secrets and the darkness, to summon the absent bodies and faces, like that of his father, through the practice of memory.

In their critical readings of *Después de las bombas,* both Linda Craft (1997) and Dante Liano (1994) mention the importance of recurrent motifs and metaphors in the novel, most notably, the use of soccer to parallel Máximo's path toward social and personal awareness—for he only succeeds in scoring a goal with a tin can in the street gutter when he is fully politically engaged and understands his sociopolitical surroundings (*i.e.,* when his words are finally put to use publicly as a form of resistance). Moreover, the structure of the novel calls for all of the protagonist's self-defining, quirky characteristics (presented as recurrent motifs) to be resolved almost simultaneously toward the end of the text—the skin problem that has plagued him since infancy clears up (scars and all), and as mentioned before, he is able to make a goal in the street gutter for the first time in the novel, and lets go of his ever present pacifier (his *pepe*), which he has carried with him unproblematically up through his adolescence. The culmination of the bildungsroman comes when Máximo reads his literary creation at a public function, where his search for a well-defined personal identity activates the thoughtful responses of others and blends into a collective moment of resistance to passive interpretation. Perhaps paradoxically, it is at the very moment when he comes to fulfill his role in public society that the particularities of his own most distinctive features disappear. In the process of overcoming his awkwardness and finding himself as an individual, he becomes a part of a collective voice of social consciousness.

Another central metaphor, also linked to his intellectually "(re)productive" grasp of language, is Máximo's developing sexuality. As Max embarks on his path to self-awareness (along with the various parallel motifs mentioned above that together mark the climax of his success), his ability to attain a level of comfort with his own body becomes paramount. His self-perception as a sexual being after enduring a traumatic violation in his early adolescence becomes a goal that is inextricably linked to his achieving enough dexterity with writing to be able to effect change in the world that surrounds him—both signaling and overcoming a deep-rooted sense of impotence and frustration.

When Max clumsily begins to write in private, given his self-conscious secrecy, his mother suspects that he is masturbating:

¿Podría Máximo escribir? ¿Tratar de explicarse qué había pasado? ¿De entender? [...] Había empezado a escribir en el más estricto secreto, escondiéndose en esquinas sospechosas, siempre listo para ocultar los lápices al primer sonido de pasos, determinado en no enseñarlo.

Era su vergüenza privada, su manera de combatir, de negar, la experiencia vivida. De vengarse. Su madre sospechaba que se había empezado a masturbar. (101)

[Would Máximo be able to write? To explain what had happened. To understand .... He had begun to write in strictest secrecy, hiding on suspicious corners, always alert to hide his pencils at the first sound of footsteps, determined to keep them from being seen. It was his private shame, his way of fighting, of negating that real-life experience. Of getting revenge. His mother suspected that he had begun to masturbate. (93–94)]

When the adolescent protagonist starts to write, his enthusiasm is not enough to help him express his thoughts. Max laments how words constantly refuse to cooperate (101). In fact, at this early stage, words are not productive for him in the expression of his desires and demands. He is still clumsily struggling to understand how best to use them. His mother's suspicions of private acts of masturbation tie together Max's incipient endeavor to write to a Lacanian interpretation of the phallus as the ultimate signifier of desire.[19] For Lacan, a child's awareness of its mother's desire for another, represented in the figure of the phallus, forces the child to enter the symbolic order and to express himself through language. As Luce Irigaray explains in *This Sex Which is Not One*: "[...] [the mother and child are reintroduced] to the exigencies of the symbolization of desire through language, that is, to the necessity that desire pass by way of a demand" (61). While the Lacanian phallus is not meant to be equated literally with the physical organ of the penis, the assumption of Max's mother that he was masturbating in private establishes a connection within the novel between the protagonist's use of his sexual organ and his writing skills, a link that will hold true for the rest of the text.[20]

Max's first romantic attachment is with Karen Johnson, the daughter of the president of the Monsanto Company in Guatemala and the interim U.S. ambassador. Karen is an exhibitionist who likes to lie in her room naked in front of a television watching shows beamed in directly from San Antonio, Texas, while Max desirously gazes at her, still sucking on his childhood pacifier even though he is already thirteen years old. He can look, but not touch, as she is intent on protecting her virginity.

However, in a violent turn of events that will leave a profound mark on the development of them both, Max and Karen get out of her protected limousine and, as they walk along a neighborhood park, they see several mutilated bodies float across a stream. They then encounter the men with machine guns who were ostensibly responsible for the carnage. In a terribly graphic scene, the armed men force Karen and Max to lose their virginity with each other at gunpoint. Max is traumatized by the rape and is unable to feel comfortable with his incipient sexuality for years to come. The military had momentarily robbed him of any hopes of sexual performance, and fear had rendered him impotent. A parallel can clearly be drawn between Max's struggle to control language on his own terms and the violent incapacitation he suffers under the power of the men with guns. His attempt to overcome both becomes a joint struggle up until the climax of the novel. Max's incapacitation can, in turn, be applied more generally to the restricted nature of language under the vigilant censure of such violently repressive regimes.

His friend Chingolo—a mentor in his discovery of Guatemala's forbidden history and teacher on how to become a proper writer—recommends that he attempt to solve his sexual problems with a visit to his friend Amarena. Described as a woman who "is always willing," Amarena is both the daughter of the American preacher of the Union Church, and is deeply involved with the local prostitutes, "the strongest social group of the entire country" (107). Sure enough, Amarena helps Máximo recover his sense of comfort with his own body, and simultaneously provides an audience (herself) for his reflections about his newly acquired knowledge regarding Guatemala's past. At the same time, he gradually attains his much desired prowess in socially engaged writing. Chingolo explains to his young friend the explicit connection between the materiality of the body and the past (which must be accessed through language): "Un hombre no es más libre de su pasado que de su cuerpo. Hablá" (73) ["A man is no more free of his past than he is of his body. Go ahead. (Speak)" (68)]. Language, the body, and the past are inextricably linked in Max's process of discovery and becoming throughout the novel.

The recurrent imagery of impotence and sexual penetration is also applied to the broader power relations between the United States and Guatemala. In a conversation between Max and Amarena, he reveals to her what he has learned regarding the 1954 coup and angrily laments:

Tu gobierno como la chingada con el nuestro. Y ellos tenían todos los aviones. La úlcera de Mr. Foster Sucks se inflamó esa mañana y él telefoneó a Panamá colérico. Los aviones se elevaron silenciosamente de *la zona del canal, ese cincho de castidad latinoamericano,* echaron gasolina en Nicaragua con las bendiciones de Tacho Somoza y volaban sobre nuestro territorio por la tarde. El 18 de junio. Los aviones ni siquiera tocaron tierra. Dejaron caer su carga maldita y se escabulleron en la oscuridad de la noche. A la mañana siguiente ya se asoleaban otra vez al lado de las puertas de Gatún. *Fue en el canal donde nos desvirgaron y es desde el canal que nos mantienen bien cogidos.* (139, emphasis mine)

[Your government pissed off at ours. And they had all the planes. Mr. Foster Sucks' ulcer flared up that morning and he telephoned Panama in a rage. The planes took off quietly from the Canal Zone, that chastity belt of Latin America, refueled in Nicaragua with Tacho Somoza's blessing, and flew over our territory in the afternoon. June 18th. The planes didn't even touch down. They dropped their infernal load and skipped in the darkness of the night. The next morning they were back sunning themselves next to the Gatun Locks. It was in the Canal that they deflowered us and it's from the Canal that they keep fucking us. (129–30)]

The interoceanic canal has ceased to be the metaphor for hope it had been up through the nineteenth century, as the Panama Canal comes to symbolize U.S. hegemony over the isthmus. The reference is an allusion to the infamous School of the Americas in the Panama Canal Zone, from which the United States provided training to Latin American officers in anticommunist and counterinsurgency techniques.[21] Arias frequently alludes to this in the novel with the sarcastic threat that any transgressors of the status quo will end up with a "scholarship to Panama."

However, while bitingly critical of U.S. foreign policy in 1954, and of the military regimes that followed, the novel is by no means structured as a Manichean political pamphlet that denounces "good" against "evil" in facile or sweeping geographical terms. On the contrary, the author is self-consciously intent on keeping any tinge of dogmatism or sentimentality out of his text. The way Arias stays away from a moralizing stance is through his ironic humor. In *La identidad de la palabra* (1998), Arias situates his text within the Guatemalan literary movement of the 1970s, Irreverentes 70:

Es una narrativa fresca, comprometida políticamente pero no en un sentido dogmático. Más bien con un fuerte rechazo a los rígidos dogmatismos del realismo socialista, muy consciente de la función y elemento lúdico del lenguaje y cargada de un alto contenido humorístico. Es como si todos los escritores jóvenes se hubieran puesto de acuerdo de que el mejor medio de disolver la horrorosa realidad en que vivíamos era la risa. Por medio de la risa, de la parodia, se buscaba edificar un mundo alternativo al mundo oficial de los militares. (194)

[It is a fresh narrative, politically engaged but not in a dogmatic sense. Rather, with a strong rejection of the rigid dogmatisms of social realism,

very aware of the role and comical element of language and charged
with high amounts of humorous content. It's as if all young writers
would have agreed that the best way to dissolve the horrible reality in
which we lived was laughter. Through laughter, through parody, we
tried to build an alternative world to the official military one.]

Arias constructs his satirical account of history by hilariously distort-
ing the names of Guatemala's key political figures: el general Castillo
Cañones (Col. Carlos Castillo Armas), el general Peralta Absurdo
(Col. Enrique Peralta Azurdia), el general Arriando el Bosque (Col.
Rafael Arriaga Bosque), el general Araña Sobrio (Col. Carlos Arana
Osorio), el general Shell Genial Longitud (Gen. Eugenio Kjell
Laugerud García), doña Ventura sin Cueva (Beatriz de la Cueva),
Foster Sucks (John Foster Dulles), et cetera. He playfully provokes a
kinetic sense of urban movement when he chaotically enumerates the
names of city streets: "Llevaban termos y loncheras y se extendían por
cuadras y cuadras desde la Avenida de los Atletas, bajo el puente del fer-
rocarril y pasando por el callejón de los Cojos, la Avenida de la Desventura,
el Paseo del Macho de Pelo en Pecho, Callejón de las Desalojadas,
Plaza del Maíz Molido, y Callecita de los Meados de Gato [...]" (48)
["Thermos bottles and lunch boxes stretched for blocks and blocks
from the Avenue of the Athletes, under the railroad bridge, passing through the Alley of the Lame, the Avenue of Misfortune, the
Boulevard of Hairy-Chested Machos, the Alley of the Dispossessed,
Ground Corn Square, and Cat Piss Lane ... " (44)]. And as the story
progresses, the street names coincide with the action of the plot.

The intensity of military repression becomes both exposed and
diluted through outrageous farcical situations. For instance, the government curfew is maintained as a given constant, and as it moves to
a later or earlier time of night it serves as a thermometer to assess the
political climate. The pretense of democracy is completely discarded
when presidential elections between top military candidates, *el general
Díaz* and *el general Nochez* (General Dayz and General Nightz), are
either settled with a duel or by a wrestling match. Nevertheless, the
violence of the military regimes does not get trivialized. Fragmented,
dismembered human bodies fill the city to a point that Máximo
becomes numbed to their significance. The children, who step over
dead bodies left after the bombs, are only moved by a dead crow on
the street, for which they stage an elaborate funeral. This incongruent
reaction is further developed to the point of becoming grotesque:

El sol ya se escondía cuando el último cuerpo fue transferido al avión. Se
sentían ya las gotas de agua, cuando despegaba el último, dirigiéndose

hacia el sur. Llovía. Serían alrededor de las cuatro de la tarde cuando abrieron las puertas y botaron los cuerpos al Pacífico. De cabeza.

Los estudiantes protestaron el asesinato del cuervo. Hubo mítines y se formaron comités de solidaridad. Se amenazó con manifestaciones. Las facultades se cerraron. Renunciaron los decanos. El cuervo fue embalsamado, reapareciendo en el salón central del Museo de Historia Natural. (38)

[The sun was wreathed in clouds when the last body was loaded onto the plane. The first raindrops were already falling by the time it took off southward. Soon there was a downpour. It must have been about four o'clock when they opened the doors and dumped the bodies into the Pacific. Headfirst.

The students protested the murder of the crow. Meetings were held and solidarity committees formed. Demonstrations were planned. All the schools of the university closed down. Their deans resigned. The crow was embalmed and reappeared in the main hall of the Museum of Natural History.   (Arias, *After the Bombs* 35–36)]

While dead human bodies are being dropped from airplanes and no one is taking any notice, students feel compelled to protest the death of the crow. The Museum of Natural History will mark the memory of the dead crow for posterity but the numerous bodies thrown into the Pacific Ocean sink into the silence of a history that wants to forget them. Along with such jolting incongruities, the levity of the author's irreverent wordplay is counterbalanced most poignantly by the narrative rhythm of psychological distress and anxiety. Through insistent repetitions, parenthetical comments, and random dreamlike associations of ideas, the narrative flow creates a sense of disorientation, lack of control, and overall anxiety.

Much like the final carnival scene in Asturias's story "Torotumbo," Arias's novel ends in chaotic festivities and upheaval in the street. Upon the assassination of a CIA agent, Max crashes in on the funeral and reads a text he has prepared for the occasion—providing the climactic moment when he achieves self-expression and social activism through writing. While his story is too abstract for the military to comprehend its implications, his tale amounts to a call to arms—or at the very least to a call to critical awareness—that makes him a wanted man. Amarena is able to orchestrate an elaborate escape plan that involves a costume party from which he retreats in disguise to the airport, and then to the freedom of exile.

Like "Torotumbo," Arias's novel also imagines liberation through political engagement in a resistance movement. But in Arias's novel, resistance also entails a self-consciously active engagement with creative language to tell a tale that not only captures what differs from state-centered Cold War rhetoric—like *Week-end en Guatemala* does—but is irreverent and clever enough in its farcical delivery to renew the discourse about the past and begin to offset the sense of impotence conveyed so despairingly by Asturias in the immediate aftermath of 1954. Humor then becomes an important resource for diffusing the paralyzing fear generated by a repressive military state, and literature provides a site from which to launch such critiques and "edify alternative worlds," as put by Arias himself.[22]

The imposed silences, blank pages, and feelings of impotence are thus countered by an empowerment and social agency that is achieved through the dexterous, playful use of language that aspires to change the world around us. As Dante Liano notes: "No se trata solamente de la palabra como fuente de conocimiento, sino de la palabra como redención, como artilugio para cambiar la realidad" (69) ["It is not only about the word as a source of knowledge, but the word as redemption, as a way to change reality"]. Words become a vehicle for creation in the face of destruction. On the one hand, words are put at the service of social engagement, but they can also help construct a parallel universe that is a relief from the violence. *Después de las bombas* can then be read as a quest for redemption through Máximo's personal plight. In a place where signs have been under siege, the author has provided a path to reclaim meaning.

In reading the texts of Ernesto Cardenal, Miguel Ángel Asturias, and Arturo Arias together, it becomes evident that an author's present historical circumstances and ideological inclinations demarcate the perspective through which s/he evaluates the past and the possibilities s/he can imagine for the future. Moreover, the generic form with which he chooses to tell the story of the past (epic poetry, short stories, or a novel) is also conditioned by these factors.[23] The genre of the story, in turn, ultimately helps shape the "map" for future action that emerges from representations of the past, delineating the options that can be imagined for resistance and redemption in times of trauma.

It makes sense, for instance, for *El estrecho dudoso* to be structured as an epic poem because, even though at the moment in which it is written the anti-Somoza struggle in Nicaragua has not yet reached any resolution, Cardenal's faith in final justice under God and in the eventual liberation of the oppressed creates a "closed" and totalizing world view that is compatible with the ideology inherent in the epic form.[24]

For Asturias, the staccato short story format of the vignettes in *Week-end en Guatemala* allows him to interrupt the overwhelming discourse of Cold War rhetoric that organizes the geopolitics of the world in the 1950s. He thus reminds his readers of life stories that do not coincide with broad stroke, binary perceptions of Communism versus Capitalism, or East versus West. As opposed to the totalizing and closed epic form, a short story format captures the author's ambivalence about the next step to be taken, and about the uncertain consequences of violent resistance in its fragmentary, unresolved structure. Faced with limited options, armed resistance is ultimately what Asturias prescribes for his characters as a way out of an impossibly repressive situation. Yet the acts of violence in his stories are not represented in a heroic fashion with utopian results. Instead, attempts to *talk back*, to *write back*, *to act* are tenuously presented within the confines of these loosely connected tales of personal trajectories.

In turn, for Arturo Arias in *Después de las bombas* the genre of the novel opens up an arena for destabilizing the authority of the state's monologic narrative of the past, primarily through humor. Arias makes evident the need for a renewal of language, the urgent and desperate desire to be able to speak about the past and imagine a different future, and the need to break away from a stagnant and intolerant discourse while negotiating the complexities of the present. A new language that will allow for thoughtful critique is needed to enable social agency within a deadly system of repression.

To this end, Máximo's path helps provoke awareness in others and enables the activation of multiple meanings of words by exposing the language of power as one discourse among several, despite the risk that this entails. The process of connecting word with thought and triggering action is dissected from start to finish through the trajectory of Max's character. Upon reading his story, "El hombre de la CIA" ("The CIA Man"), Maximo begins to revive, "con palabras verdaderas" or with "real words" (and not the stale, false words of the reigning language of authority that he has come to question as part of his self-education), the moribund languages of literature (156).[25] Among the "real words" that get repeated in Máximo's story (read at the funeral) is the following metaphorical image: "No era en realidad los cadáveres lo que les molestaba, sino la falta de cabezas, genitales, ojos. Es difícil de aceptar la fragmentación en una sociedad que lucha por integrarse" (160) ["It wasn't actually the corpses that bothered them but rather the absence of heads, genitals, eyes. It is hard to accept fragmentation in a society struggling to integrate itself" (149)]. In a climate of violated, fragmented bodies, what becomes difficult to bear for his narrator is the lack of heads (critical thought), genitals (valor), and eyes (self-awareness). These are precisely the social attributes that both authors, Max and Arias, are trying to restore after decades of repression. In the novel, the effects are immediate, as shortly after, at his good-bye party, people spontaneously start reciting poems: "[...] un par de poetas empujaron a Rodri de la mesa y empezaron a recitar poemas que trataban de rimar. Todos estaban sorprendidos. No se habían oído poemas en público desde hacía ya, ¿cuánto tiempo? Las palabras volvían a la vida" (183) ["... a couple of poets pushed Rodri off the table and began reciting poems that tried to rhyme. Everybody was astonished. Poems hadn't been heard in public since how long ago? Words came back to life" (171)]. Correspondingly, Arias's novel itself is testament to a renewed circulation of thoughts publicly through dynamic, provocative words.

The genre of the novel enables Arias to diffuse the image of authority by reifying its familiar discourse and by revealing the brutal consequences of its implementation.[26] As part of this same struggle against the unity of an imposed language of power, the multivocal form of the novel helps the author break open this questionable unity and orchestrate the many self-conscious voices of resistance (or simply signal the other stories / points of view in existence), that is, the reader of prohibited texts, the oral history storyteller, the prostitutes who traffic in bodies and secret information, the farcical basis of public power, the charged intonation of foreign diplomats, et cetera.

What is here clearly different from Asturias is the ability to objectify and satirize the preposterous state of affairs by the late 1970s in hopes of destabilizing imposed perspectives from above that had already begun to lose credibility (at least for some). By attaining some distance (both historical and critical), something that was not entirely possible for Asturias when writing so soon after the events of 1954, Arias makes use of the dialogic multiplicity of languages that structures the form of the novel precisely to question the endurance of an imposed world view. Fittingly, Bakhtin describes the decentering of unitary languages in "Discourse in the Novel":

This verbal-ideological decentering will occur only when a national culture loses its sealed-off and self-sufficient character, when it becomes conscious of itself as only one among *other* cultures and languages [...] Language (or more precisely, languages) will itself become an artistically complete image of a characteristic human way of sensing and seeing the world. Language, no longer conceived as a sacrosanct and solitary embodiment of meaning and truth, becomes merely one of many possible ways to hypothesize meaning. (370)

While the military regime might continue to insist on imposing its perspective for years to come, the genre of the novel provides a site for the struggle for meaning and truth by corroding, decentering, and questioning the credibility of the state's language as an unfailing absolute.

In all of the texts discussed in this section, the geographies of language map out potential sites for future social agency. All three authors are aware of the many stereotypical representations of the region that circulate in the international imagination. For the purposes of their own stories they appropriate and rework such images, remapping the area on their terms. The central image of the dubious strait—the isthmus as the promising link between the seas—is used by Cardenal to demonstrate the repeated excesses of powerful *caudillo* figures throughout Nicaragua's history and the need to imagine a new path that will not merely repeat the failings of the past. Both Guatemalan authors resist the generalizations of an anticommunist narrative used to justify the events of 1954. The image of Central America as a stage for world confrontations in the Cold War is complicated in both *Week-end en Guatemala* and in *Después de las bombas*. Asturias interrupts the simplistic anticommunist rhetoric to demonstrate how language has been egregiously manipulated to make the unfathomable actions of the anti-Arbenz forces comprehensible and even justifiable to many. Arias, in turn, situates language itself as a site of struggle to reclaim the memories erased by the silences and blank pages of history and construct a path of social resistance toward a better future.

PART II

THE CITY

The City as Metonymy for
the Costs of "Progress"

*We must be insistently aware of how space can be made to hide
consequences from us, how relations of power and discipline are
inscribed into the apparently innocent spatiality of social life,
how human geographies become filled with politics and ideology.*

(*Edward Soja 6*)

The modern city both defines and is defined by the sociopolitical
interactions that take place within and beyond its boundaries. Moreover, the city can be read as a physical testament of the marks left by
the pursuit of modernization and the drive for capital accumulation and
new technologies upon the everyday life of its inhabitants. As David
Harvey puts it: "Understanding the rules of capital accumulation
helps understand why our history and our geography take the forms
they do" (122). Part II will turn to several fictional representations
of Central American cities and trace the effects of modernization and
development—from its incipient stages, through the proliferation of
urban resistance movements, to the eventual disenchantment with the
myths of progress—in the following texts: Miguel Ángel Asturias's *El
Señor Presidente* (1946), Manlio Argueta's *Caperucita en la zona roja*
(1977), and Carmen Naranjo's *Diario de una multitud* (1974). These
fictional representations of Guatemala City, Guatemala; San Salvador,
El Salvador; and San José, Costa Rica, respectively, provide various
instances of metonymical commentary on prevalent social concerns,
such as state violence, authoritarianism, pervasive mechanisms of surveillance, urban guerrilla movements, and wider implications of alienation

within the rhythm of everyday life—all of which amount to the price paid by societies for the costly and uneven road to modernity as it is charted in these particular localities. By "metonymical commentary" I mean that the city stands as an attribute associated with the idea of modernity or the narrative of progress as a whole. As such, the way in which the city is represented provides pointed commentary about the consequences of the pursuit of modernity and desire for progress as defined by Western Enlightenment and capitalistic ideals.

In this case, I refer to the tricky and polysemous notion of "modernity" as the movement toward perceived "development" through capital accumulation and new technologies that would facilitate interaction with a broader world market, along with all that this implies. At the turn of the last century, many countries of the isthmus were ushered into the 1900s under the authoritarian leadership of Liberal governments that aspired to pave the way for the expansion of the region's export economies and its full integration into the capitalist world market. This effort involved significant consolidation of land ownership into large plantations that could support the extensive production of coffee and other export crops, requiring an abundant supply of labor. In Guatemala, church properties were seized under the Liberal reforms, along with the purchase of communal and public lands, and in densely populated El Salvador it was primarily communal lands that were expropriated by the state to sustain the shift from subsistence farming to commercial agriculture and the increasingly lucrative production of coffee. With a significantly sparser population, unused public lands in Costa Rica were purchased and smaller farms were created given the relative shortage of labor supply (Cardoso 42).

Many of these efforts relied on building the infrastructure needed to traverse "space" more efficiently—that is, the construction of railroads, reliable roads, and the installation of telegraph networks. National geographies were then parceled out into large plantations. Public and communal territories were edged out to provide more land and more labor for the growers of export economies, and local governments signed concessions with more developed countries for the installation of massive infrastructure. All of this management of space—its ownership and its traversability—is geared toward the potentially lucrative immersion of the region into the broader geography of the global economy. The result is what David Harvey terms a phase of "time-space compression":

> Capital accumulation has always been about speed-up (consider the history of technological innovations in production processes,

marketing, money exchanges) and revolutions in transport and communications (the railroad and telegraph, radio and automobile, jet transport and telecommunications), which have the effect of reducing spatial barriers [...] Our sense of who we are, where we belong and what our obligations encompass—in short, our *identity*— is profoundly affected by our sense of location in space and time [...] Crises of identity [...] arise out of strong phases of time-space compression. (123)

This reduction of spatial barriers goes hand in hand with reassessing one's identity within the new geographies created. All three novels discussed in this section provide an instance of such reassessments at different moments in the push toward progress.

Among the major costs of the drive toward development are the immense disparities it has created. In Guatemala and El Salvador the polarization between landowners and the labor force was much more pronounced than in Costa Rica, where the extent of coffee farming was much more modest than elsewhere in the region. Strong state and military forces were put in place in Guatemala and El Salvador to implement and maintain the export economy and its gains. It soon became clear in both countries that the desire for progress would go hand in hand with force. *El Señor Presidente* provides an account of the onerous effects of such an oppressive regime, even in its attempts to emulate European models of modernity and Liberalism.

Similarly, it becomes evident in El Salvador that *difference*—both in terms of opposition to regime policies and in terms of race—will be dealt with through extreme violence.[1] El Salvador is perpetually haunted by the memory of 1932, when 30,000 people were put to death by General Maximiliano Hernández Martínez in response to a *campesino* uprising. By the 1970s, after a fraudulent presidential election in 1972 when the opposition party coalition was stripped of its victory by the military candidate, many turned to alternative means of making their voices heard:

> [...] in the aftermath of 1972 [...], political involvement no longer meant voting. It meant joining the new popular organizations and lending a new meaning to democracy in action; it meant civil disobedience; and it meant facing the most brutal repression that El Salvador had known since 1932.   (Armstrong and Shenk 73)

Manlio Argueta's *Caperucita en la zona roja* explores the experiences of a group of young adults who decide to become involved with this political struggle and voice their resistance to an unjust system by joining the revolutionary left. What, then, is the response to the effects of "developmentalism" in a country where a strong military state was not set in place to preserve the inequitable gains of a polarized society, as was the case of Guatemala and El Salvador? Carmen Naranjo captures the experience of Costa Rica—where the army was constitutionally abolished in 1950—and she conveys a keen awareness of the myths of "progress" in her novel *Diario de una multitud*. In Costa Rica, as well as in other coffee-oriented export economies, the world crisis of 1929–1930 and the subsequent plummeting of coffee prices resulted in a severe economic paralysis that stirred up civil unrest and the organization of popular movements. These movements were largely geared to middle class concerns and were oriented toward reformist, nationalistic, and democratic goals. The ensuing civil war of 1948 resulted in a push to institute these modernizing reforms, including the dissolution of the national army and the implementation of a wide program for social, educational, financial, economic, and institutional reform. The formation of the social-democratic National Liberation Party that came out of these struggles had a strong influence in Costa Rica's political arena for the next thirty years, up through the 1970s, including the period when Naranjo's novel was published. Her text can be read as a reflection upon a city that has been shaped by the projects of an urban middle class:

> Poner en relieve la aparición de la clase media en Costa Rica no es superficial puesto que es un fenómeno que interesa mucho en el estudio de la obra literaria de Carmen Naranjo. En efecto, en el eje de cambio social y sobre todo en relación con la clase media urbana se sitúa su producción novelesca. [...] El medio que conoce bien y que aparece desde el principio en sus novelas, es el de los funcionarios y de empleados de la ciudad, que muchas veces luchan con una alienación debida a su trabajo, o bien con la trampa de una mediocridad asfixiante.
>
> (Miranda Hevia 34)

> [To highlight the emergence of the middle class in Costa Rica is not superficial, as it is a phenomenon that is of much interest in the studies of Carmen Naranjo's literary work. Actually, her novelistic production is situated in the axis of social change, especially in relation to the urban middle-class ... The environment that she knows well and that appears early on in her novels, is that of government officials and city employees, who oftentimes fight against the alienation brought on by their jobs, or against the trap of an asphyxiating mediocrity.]

Diario de una multitud satirically conveys a sense of monotony and alienation among this urban middle class and warns against the complacent mediocrity perceived in the everyday lives of the characters that inhabit its fictionalized city.

CHAPTER 3

El Señor Presidente's LIBERAL CITY AND THE MODERN SCRIPTURAL ECONOMY

As we contemplate the city represented in Miguel Ángel Asturias's *El Señor Presidente,* our analysis will rely on both the general dynamics of progress and the city, put forth by Michel de Certeau in *The Practice of Everyday Life* (1984), and on the particular implementation of a program intended toward progress and modernization carried out by the Liberal government of Manuel Estrada Cabrera at the turn of the nineteenth century that inspired Asturias's text. De Certeau traces the structural similarities between his notion of *the scriptural economy* and the modern city itself:

> Combining the power of *accumulating* the past and that of making the alterity of the universe *conform* to its models, it [the scriptural economy] is capitalist and conquering. The scientific laboratory and industry [...] are governed by the same schema. And so is the modern city: it is a circumscribed space in which the will to collect and store up an external population and the will to make the countryside conform to urban models are realized. (135)

In the specific case of Asturias's text, the consequences of this capitalist and conquering dynamic of "accumulating" and "conforming" are exacerbated by the strong-handed will and personal vendettas that shape *El Señor Presidente's* dictatorial regime.

De Certeau further defines "revolution" and the concept of "progress" in terms of what he deems the modern scriptural project:

Revolution itself, that "modern" idea, represents the scriptural project at the level of an entire society seeking to *constitute itself* as a blank page with respect to the past, to write itself by itself (that is, to produce itself as its own system) and to produce *a new history* on the model of what it fabricates (and this will be "progress") [...] Today, by an inversion that indicates a threshold in this development has been crossed, the scriptural system moves forward on its own; it is becoming self-moving and technocratic; it transforms the subjects that controlled it into operators of the writing machine that orders and uses them. (135–36)

The inhabitants of the city represented in Miguel Ángel Asturias's *El Señor Presidente* can be perceived precisely as operators being used by such a metaphorical writing machine, a machine that accelerates forward by inscribing the narrative of progress on their bodies and their daily lives with the ink of fear.

The simultaneous forces operating in the novel's fictional city thus include: (1) the forward motion toward progress[2] that in the Guatemala of the end of the nineteenth century was broadly defined by the Liberal party as integration into the world market, and (2) the centripetal forces of a repressive, authoritarian leader. Much like de Certeau's "writing machine" above, Guatemalan state goals of modernization at the turn of the nineteenth century also "ordered" and "used" its citizens to bring about economic and social changes that would make this particular script viable. Estrada Cabrera's regime was meant to perpetuate the reforms instituted during the so-called Liberal *revolution* of 1871 led by Miguel García Granados and Justo Rufino Barrios. The revolution of 1871 implemented the economic restructuring needed to promote the country's export sector (a turn primarily to coffee and bananas) and fully integrate the nation into the capitalist world market (Cardoso 37). As part of this process, emphasis was placed on improving the efficiency of the transportation and communication networks, expropriating church lands, and secularizing the educational system.

The implementation of Liberal reforms in Guatemala was, however, fraught with contradictions. Inspired by European and North American models, these policies were enforced from the top down under the paternalistic leadership of strong-handed *caudillos*. Unlike the revolution described by de Certeau, whereby an entire society seeks to "write itself by itself" and "to produce a new history," the Liberal reforms of the late 1800s were based on models copied from abroad that were imposed by leaders who saw their role as enforcers of a program for progress that was conceptualized elsewhere. While the rhetoric of Liberalism called for a recognition of basic social rights, "the Liberal order" in Central America, as Ciro Cardoso puts it, was quite exclusionary in practice: "The Liberal order, except in Costa Rica, excluded the vast majority of the population, not only from the profits derived from economic growth, but also from any political participation" (66–67). Rhetorical ideals of liberty were also compromised in practice:

> Liberal leaders in Central America shared a positivist ideology. Unlike the old Liberals of the period of independence, even if they did not formally renounce the democratic political ideal, they believed that the national economies of the isthmus had to progress, with the help of strong political and social control, before democracy became feasible.   (Cardoso 62)

Thus, with a positivist notion of the state as a growing organism, the role of the leader was primarily to ensure "order" and "control" until the country was mature enough to exercise a more inclusive democratic system.[3]

SUBVERTING THE CABRERISTA MYTH

[...] Corta y de carácter interino será mi administración, pero no por eso ha de dejar la Historia de pedirme cuenta estricta de los actos que durante ella ejecute [...][4]

(*Manuel Estrada Cabrera* 1898)[5]

En vez del alfabeto, "la Gran Minerva Luminosa" del Protector de la Juventud Estudiosa nos trajo la United Fruit Co., a la que otorgó las iniciales concesiones increíbles que padecemos. [...] "Ella, la cósmica doncella", en su templo de columnas corintias, en nuestro país indígena de olvidada cultura propia, sentiríase muy extraña con el imaginario transplante.[6]

(*Luis Cardoza y Aragón* 359)

The city of Asturias's novel revolves around the ever-present fear perpetuated by the despotic leader's control over even the most private aspects of society. Whereas the repressive means of establishing this pervasive control and its violent physical and psychological consequences are the central focus of the text, the author organizes his narrative around multiple references to the celebratory discourse that propped up the myth of Estrada Cabrera as a promoter of progress during his regime. Even though Asturias does not name him explicitly, *El Señor Presidente* is inspired by the dictatorship of Manuel Estrada Cabrera (1898–1920) and the Guatemalan society of the early 1900s.[7] It took Asturias ten years (1922–1932) to write *El Señor Presidente*, yet the author waited another fourteen years to publish his first novel in 1946 (during the period of relative openness under President Juan José Arévalo's reformist regime). It would certainly have been precarious for Asturias to publish his antidictatorship novel under any government that might have interpreted the text as a subtle attack on the present, given the succession of dictatorships of varying degrees of ruthlessness that were in power from the fall of Estrada Cabrera to the revolution of 1944.

While the author's decision not to give his fictional dictator a particular name gives the character a sense of universality—whereby anyone subject to the despotism of authoritarian regimes can identify him as a familiar type—for the purposes of the first part of our analysis, we will focus on the specificity of recognizable allusions to Manuel Estrada Cabrera and the implementation of his Liberal policies. Throughout *El Señor Presidente* the author satirizes the basic pillars on which Estrada Cabrera built the myth of his own *persona* during his time in power: for instance, the prolific use of Greco-Roman symbolism to promote his cultural programs,[8] an insistent focus on his policies for the improvement of public education, an emphasis on the installation of basic communications infrastructure—the construction of railroads, telegraph, and telephone systems—and the encouragement of foreign investment to finance these policies.[9]

Asturias often makes use of the exaggerated laudatory style of actual *cabrerista* (pro–Estrada Cabrera) rhetoric, exposing its ring of falseness by setting it against the ominous backdrop of a community in constant terror. For instance, the fictional leader is addressed with the (not-so-exaggerated) protocol of a long list of titles: "el Señor Presidente Constitucional de la República, Benemérito de la Patria, Jefe del Gran Partido Liberal, Liberal de Corazón y Protector de la Juventud Estudiosa!" (101–2)[10] ["the Constitutional President of the Republic, Benefactor of his Country, Head of the Great Liberal Party, and Liberal-hearted Protector of Studious Youth!" (97)[11]]. The contradictory tensions of Cabrera's regime can be gleaned from this sequence of nomenclatures as it mocks the notion that the leader of the Liberal party and "protector of the studious youth" (like Cabrera) would be considered a "constitutional president," given the fact that Estrada Cabrera himself repeatedly manipulated the electoral laws of Guatemala to draw out his rule for twenty-two years.[12]

Asturias simulates the tone and language of *cabrerista* writings to lay bare the rhetorical constructs of the leader's mythology during his time. It is this self-perpetuated positive myth that Asturias subverts and transforms into a negative countermyth in *El Señor Presidente*. Note, for example, how he imitates writings such as the following passage from Perfecto Lara's *Divagaciones de un obrero: Homenaje al Excelentísimo Señor Presidente Constitucional de la República Licenciado don Manuel Estrada Cabrera* (1917) (*Digressions of a Laborer: Homage to his Honorable Excellency Mister Manuel Estrada Cabrera Constitutional President of the Republic*), in which Lara exalts the workers' patriotism, calling for a public demonstration to prove the laborers' unquestionable support for the sole candidacy of Estrada Cabrera:

> ¡Obreros guatemaltecos ... los que tengáis en vuestra conciencia la llama del patriotismo y tengáis voluntad en contribuir con vuestra presencia en la presente manifestación, para probar a nuestro ilustre Benemérito, que es el pueblo en masa el que lo aclama como su único Candidato popular, os invito a que os unáis en las filas del artesano honrado y continuéis con nosotros para presentarle nuestra respetuosa adhesión y presentarle el saludo sincero que brota espontáneo del corazón de los hijos del trabajo.   (Lara 30)

> [Guatemalan workers! ... those of you who have the flame of patriotism in your conscience and have the will to contribute with your presence in the present demonstration, to prove to our illustrious Worthy Leader, that it is the people *en masse* who acclaim him as its sole popular Candidate, I invite you to unite in the ranks of the honest artisan and continue with us to present to him our respectful allegiance and present him with a sincere greeting that bursts spontaneously from the heart of the offspring of labor.]

In comparison, Asturias's representation of a flyer made by the committee for the reelection of the fictional president clearly reflects the adulatory tone as well as the pretense of spontaneous and uncontested popular support of the text shown above. By doing so, he sheds a wryly humorous light on such texts and reduces all similar documents to ridicule, thereby subverting their original intent:

> Pronunciar el nombre del Señor Presidente de la República, es alumbrar con las antorchas de la paz los sagrados intereses de la Nación que bajo

su sabio mando ha conquistado y sigue conquistando los inapreciables
beneficios del Progreso en todos los órdenes y del Orden en todos los
progresos!!!! [...]¡ El sólo imaginar a otro que no sea El en tan alta
magistratura es atentatorio contra los Destinos de la Nación, que son
nuestros destinos, y quien tal osara, que no habrá quien, debería ser
recluido por loco peligroso y de no estar loco, juzgado por traidor
a la Patria conforme a nuestras leyes!!! CONCIUDADANOS, LAS
URNAS OS ESPERAN! VOTAD! POR! NUESTRO! CANDIDATO!
QUE! SERA! REELEGIDO! POR! EL! PUEBLO!!! (Asturias 264)

[Citizens: Merely by uttering the name of the President of the
Republic we shed light from the torch of Peace upon those sacred
interests of a Nation which, under his wise rule, has conquered and
will go on conquering the inestimable benefits of Progress in every
sphere, and of Order in every form of Progress!!!! ... Even to imagine any other than Him in this high office amounts to an attempt
upon the Destiny of the Nation (which is our own destiny); and
whoever dares to do so—if any such there be—deserves to be shut
up as a dangerous lunatic, or if he is not mad, tried as a traitor to his
Country according to the law!!! FELLOW CITIZENS, THE BAL-
LOT-BOXES ARE WAITING!!! VOTE!!! FOR!!! OUR!!! CANDI-
DATE!!! WHO!!! WILL!!! BE!!! RE-ELECTED!!! BY!!! THE!!!
PEOPLE!!! (254–55)]

With numerous exclamation signs and capital letters, the document
punctuates the farce of the "voluntary" nature of Guatemala's electoral
process at the time. The explicit threat directed against any possible
dissenters in this excerpt exposes the latent danger behind the written
words of Lara's document—a threat that is more subtle in original
cabrerista texts, yet crucial in the persuasiveness of such publications
(*i.e.,* if you do not support the reelection campaign, you will be
considered a traitor or a dangerous madman).

The specific imagery of modern communications and transport
infrastructure, which characterized Cabrera's reforms, is also frequently adopted by Asturias and used to satirize and subvert the
despot's own self-perpetuated mythological stature. Notably, when
Cara de Angel is spying on the house of the Canales family, he stops
at a small bar across the street and he notices a portrait hanging on
the wall depicting: "un retrato del Señor Presidente, echado a perder
de joven, con ferrocarriles en los hombros, como charreteras, y un
angelito dejándole caer en la cabeza una corona de laurel" (42) ["a
portrait of the President, outrageously rejuvenated, with epaulette-
like railway lines on his shoulders, and a cherub crowning him with
a laurel wreath" (40)]. The figure of a little angel placing a crown of

laurels on the leader's head facetiously presents him as a "champion" or "god" of the railroads; he sports this prominently across his shoulders on epaulettes, reminding the viewer of his inseparable identification with such images of modern infrastructure. Such ironic use of religious imagery to represent the head of the anticlerical Liberal Party has the effect of transforming the president into both a false god and a false Liberal. Moreover, as a reflection of what happens to the *cabrerista* myth throughout the novel, Cara de Angel himself personifies the soiling of a myth when he is introduced into the narrative as an "angelical" apparition in the municipal dump. His very name, Miguel "Angel Face," as opposed to Miguel "Angel," like the author, suggests that he is not truly an angel, but merely wearing an angelical mask, and is actually a hypocrite. Once again, religious imagery is perverted in the depiction of the president's supporter as an angel of a false god.

The angel itself, crowning the notorious provider of Guatemala's modern infrastructure with congratulatory laurels, is reminiscent of Walter Benjamin's description of what he terms the angel of history, blown away by the storm of progress:

> There is a picture by Klee called *Angelus Novus*. It shows an angel who seems about to move away from something he stares at. His eyes are wide, his mouth open, his wings are spread. This is how the angel of history must look. His face is turned toward the past [...] The angel would like to stay, awaken the dead, and make whole what has been smashed. But a storm is blowing from Paradise and has got caught in his wings [...] This storm drives him irresistibly into the future, to which his back is turned, while the pile of debris before him grows toward the sky. What we call progress is *this* storm. (392)

Benjamin's portrayal of the concept of progress as a symbolic storm that pushes toward the future and makes it impossible for the angel of history to mend the destruction and debris that is left in its wake casts an ominous tone of painful awareness that calls attention to the costs demanded by such a path. These significant consequences become visible to the angel of history, who is nonetheless impotent to mend what has been ravaged in the path of the storm. In contrast, the angel with the laurels in the portrait at the *Tus Tep* bar participates with no self-awareness in the championing of the *cabrerista* version of progress with an unquestioned celebration of the process of modernization. By recasting this image within the ironic context of his novel, however, the author is not completely impotent, for even though he, like the angel of history, cannot warn the victims sacrificed along the road toward progress before they fall victims of the storm, he can bring attention to the very fact that such sacrifices and exclusions are part of the problematic path toward modernity.

This complicated vision of progress demonstrates the dark side of the new technologies ushered in by the Liberal president's regime. When referring to the vast network of surveillance that kept El Señor Presidente's enemies under tight control, Asturias also uses the imagery of modern communications infrastructure to insinuate the ambivalent nature of the new technology:

> Todo le pareció fácil antes que ladraran los perros en el bosque monstruoso que separaba al Señor Presidente de sus enemigos, bosque de árboles de orejas que al menor eco se revolvían como agitadas por el huracán [...] Una red de hilos invisibles, *más invisibles que los hilos del telégrafo*, comunicaba cada hoja con el Señor Presidente, atento a lo que pasaba en las vísceras más secretas de los ciudadanos. (41, emphasis mine)

> [Everything seemed easy until the dogs began barking at him in the monstrous wood which separated the President from his enemies, a wood made up of trees with ears which responded to the slightest sound by whirling as if blown by a hurricane ... A network of invisible threads, more invisible than telegraph wires, connected every leaf with the President, enabling him to keep watch on the most secret thoughts of the townspeople. (39)]

Not even the most hidden corners of the city are free from the leader's web of surveillance and information control. In fact, Asturias incorporates modern communications imagery to indicate not only what is said to el Señor Presidente by his vigilant informants, but also as a powerful reminder of what *cannot* be said under the censorship of his regime:

> A las detonaciones y alaridos del *Pelele*, a la fuga de Vásquez y su amigo, mal vestidas de luna corrían las calles por las calles sin saber bien lo que había sucedido y los árboles de la plaza se tronaban los dedos en *la pena de no poder decir* con el viento, *por los hilos telefónicos*, lo que acababa de pasar. (55, emphasis mine)

> [Immediately after the pistol shots, the Zany's yells and the flight of Vasquez and his friend, the streets ran one after the other, all scantily clad in moonlight, and not knowing what had happened, while the trees in the square twisted their fingers together in despair because

they could not announce the event either by means of the wind or the telephone wires. (51)]

When el Pelele is murdered, the threat of silence is imposed even on the city streets themselves.

Another aspect of the *cabrerista* discourse that gets co-opted and subverted in Asturias's narrative is the portrayal of the leader as champion of culture and public education. The author's use of the figure of Minerva is clearly a wink to acknowledge Estrada Cabrera's connection to the Roman goddess of wisdom through his construction of various temples dedicated to the deity and his yearly celebrations of the "Fiestas de Minerva" dedicated to the "studious youth."[13] As William Clary puts it, public celebrations such as the *Minervalias* served as a vehicle for the state "to ritualize and articulate the dream of progress" (668), as well as to "project rationality and scientific development in a period in which the objective was to privilege Eurocentric discourses and get beyond the barbarous condition that was an obstacle to progress" (670, translation mine). In celebrating publicly the copied script for progress conceived abroad, the *Minervalias* illustrate metaphorically the way in which form (appearances) often took precedence over content (significant education reform) in the push toward modernity. As such, these yearly gatherings provided a forum in which many leading intellectual and cultural figures of the time joined their voices to celebrate and legitimize the authority of the leader.[14] At a time in which writing itself is the distinguishing factor between civilization and barbarism, it is significant that the president frequently turned to "men of letters," like Rubén Darío and many others, to put their stamp of approval on his regime (Clary 671).

The figure of Minerva becomes completely vilified in the author's allusion to the goddess in the following exchange between the fictional president and Cara de Angel. The conversation takes place when the President is in a drunken stupor after finding out that Cara de Angel has crossed him by marrying Camila, the daughter of one of his enemies, without his permission:

—Señor Presidente—saludó el favorito, e iba a ponerse a sus órdenes, cuando éste le interrumpió.
—¡"Ni mier ... va"!
—¡De la diosa habla el Señor Presidente!
Su Excelencia se acercó a la mesa a paso de saltacharquitos, y, sin tomar en cuenta el cálido elogio que el favorito hacía de Minerva, le gritó:
—Miguel, el que encontró el alcohol, ¿tú sabes que lo que buscaba era el licor de larga vida ... ? (229)

["Mr. President," the favourite began, but was interrupted before he
   could go on:
"Ni-ni-mierva!"
"Are you referring to the goddess, Mr. President?"
His Excellency went up to the table with a springy gait, and ignoring
   the favourite's eulogy of Minerva, he exclaimed:
"Do you know, Miguel, that the man who discovered alcohol was
   looking for an elixir to produce long life?"   (221)]

By placing Cara de Angel's praise for the Roman goddess in a satirical context, that of a phonetic slippage between Minerva and the
president's insinuated insult *"ni mier ...,"* the author contrasts the
association between the goddess of wisdom and high culture and
the president's crass, drunken antics. The rare physical description of the leader in this scene completes the contrast between the
venerable rhetorical image and the concrete, deplorable person: "Y
carcajeándole continuó persiguiendo la mosca que iba y venía de un
punto a otro, la falda de la camisa al aire, la bragueta abierta, los
zapatos sin abrochar, la boca untada de babas y los ojos de excre-
cencias color de yema de huevo" (231)[15] ["And still roaring with
laughter he went on pursuing the fly as it flew from place to place,
with his shirt-tails coming out of his belt, his fly-buttons undone,
his shoes untied, dribbling at the mouth and with his eyes exuding
a bright yellow rheum" (222)]. Now that Cara de Angel has crossed
him, the empty discourse acknowledging the goddess of wisdom as
a gesture of allegiance is futile. The president's words foretell the
end of his life in the inner circle and mark him as a wanted man.

   The effectiveness of Estrada Cabrera's educational policies is put
into question more directly when a humble woodman mentions to
Cara de Angel how learning to read has led to his wife's frustration
by giving her such unrealistic desires as "having wings": "Después
de todo, somos los pobres los más conformes. ¡Y qué remedio
pues! ... Verdá es que con eso de la escuela los que han aprendido a
'lér' andan influenciados de cosas imposibles. Hasta mi mujer resulta
a veces triste porque dice que quisiera tener alas los domingos" (29)
["After all, we poor men are more resigned than other people. And
what can we do, anyway? It's true that with the schools and all that,
anyone who learns to read gets ideas into his head. Even my wife
gets sad sometimes and says she'd like to have wings on Sundays"
(27)]. His words indicate that as the expectations of the economi-
cally disadvantaged are elevated through education, their destitute
situation becomes even more intolerable than before. The woodman's
frustration speaks to the exclusionary nature of the Liberal order

attested to by Cardoso. What is more, it is questionable whether Estrada Cabrera's much-touted focus on public education actually had any effective results. According to Rafael Arévalo Martínez, the number of people who could not read and write actually rose during his administration,[16] and Gail Martin proposes that his apparent dedication to education was exactly that, *an appearance* that served to promote his own image:

> El régimen utilizaba su aparente dedicación al fomento de la educación pública para demostrar su compromiso con la modernización del país. Pero aquí también las apariencias camuflaban una realidad amarga, con escuelas mal equipadas y maestros escandalosamente mal pagados. Según Luján Muñoz, "su obra educativa, en especial sus escuelas prácticas, fueron más un motivo de propaganda que verdaderas realizaciones pedagógicas." (564)

> [The regime used its apparent dedication to the fostering of public education to demonstrate its commitment to modernizing the country. But here also appearances camouflaged a bitter truth, with poorly equipped schools and scandalously badly paid teachers. According to Luján Muñoz, "his work in the field of education, especially his vocational schools, were more a cause for propaganda than for true pedagogical accomplishments."]

Education was publicly declared a priority, following the positivist ideals of scientific and cultural development. Yet, while the portrayed desire for a more educated populace suggests possibilities of broader economic development and greater social equality, in practice, these goals were clearly not part of the Liberal project as it was implemented by Estrada Cabrera.

UNLIVABLE PLACES AND INEFFABLE EXPERIENCES

Turning back to the fictional world captured by Asturias, the plot of *El Señor Presidente* is triggered by the assassination of Colonel Parrales Sonriente—a character who had carried out the President's vengeful programs against the townspeople who had looked down upon him during the poverty of his childhood. Parrales Sonriente is killed by el Pelele, a homeless man with mental problems who is known around town to get extremely upset when anyone mentions his mother. When Parrales Sonriente approaches him to torment him about her, el Pelele loses control and kills the Colonel in a fit of hysteria. This incident serves the president to get rid of two of his enemies—Eusebio Canales and Abel Carvajal—by accusing them of the crime. The group of mendicants, who slept in the area of the Portal del Señor along with el Pelele, is tortured until they accuse the leader's enemies of the murder. The president's version of events is thus violently written upon the already fragmented bodies of these marginalized individuals—a deaf-mute pregnant woman, a blind man missing both legs—who are threatened, tortured, and even killed to sustain his vengeful plan.

It is Miguel Cara de Angel's responsibility, as the president's right-hand man, to inform Canales that he is being persecuted so that he will try to escape, and the police will then kill him for attempting to flee. In the process of carrying out his mission, Cara de Angel decides to capture Camila, Eusebio Canales's daughter and, in a turn of fate, he falls in love with her. When they marry without the president's permission, Cara de Angel becomes a target of the dictator's wrath. It becomes common knowledge that Cara de Angel has fallen out of favor when the leader tells him to go to Washington, DC, to protect his image as a Liberal leader abroad and to conduct public relations to promote his reelection campaign, for the president does not allow Camila to go abroad with her husband. Once Cara de Angel arrives at the port from which he is supposed to leave, he is captured and incarcerated. Both are cruelly told lies. Camila is told that he escaped and has purposefully lost touch with her. And he is told that, in her abandonment, she has become the president's lover. In fact, she eventually moves to the countryside where she raises her and Cara de Angel's baby, and he dies of sadness and dysentery in the prison cell. Throughout the novel, Asturias describes in detail the physical and psychological agony of living within a system sustained by espionage and torture, while focusing on specific individuals with whom the reader can empathize. The author recreates a claustrophobic atmosphere of paranoia and fear and transports the reader to the onerous, everyday life in Guatemala City at the beginning of the century.

It is telling that el Pelele's visceral obsession with the loss of his mother is the axis of the entire plot of the novel.[17] One can perhaps read in el Pelele's torment "the alterity of the universe" that is made to conform to the models of the city and the scriptural economy according to de Certeau. It is, after all, the violent results of el Pelele's uncontrollable, quasi-oedipal fit of desperate rage that is appropriated and manipulated by el Señor Presidente's web of power to enact his plans for revenge.[18] El Pelele does not even possess access to standard symbolic language to describe or protest his pain: "[…] el grito del idiota era el más triste. Partía el cielo. Era un grito largo, sonsacado, sin acento humano" (10) [" ... the idiot's cry was the saddest of all. It rent the sky. It was a long-drawn-out inhuman wail" (8)]. There is no representational system that can capture the depth of his loss, and, worse still, without a mastery over normative language he is considered an idiot, an easily manipulated rag doll (*un pelele*), inhuman.

The haunting scream evokes the limits of what can be assimilated and represented within the scriptural system. It is the howl of the radically excluded, the abject, as Julia Kristeva describes it:

> It [the abject] is outside, out of the whole of which it seems not to recognise the rules of the game. However, from this exile, the abject does not cease to defy its master. Without making a sign (to him), it provokes a discharge, a convulsion, a cry. [...] Mute protestation of the symptom, the shattering violence of a convulsion, inscribed, it is true, in a symbolic system, but which, without wanting or being able to integrate itself in order to respond, it (ça) reacts, it (ça) abreacts. It (ça) abjects.   (Kristeva, "Approaching Abjection" 126–27)

In el Pelele's guttural cries of pain for his absent mother, one recognizes a comprehensive, piercing lament for the abject—for all that is excluded and made to conform in Asturias's city. Family, nature, and home (that is, the metaphorical nurturing "Mother") all become strained and are transformed by the centripetal urban force that makes the entire capital city revolve around the despot's personal will. The loss of nature and the stress placed on family ties by the dynamics of the urban system are patent costs of the city and of the process of modernization. In this particular case, the conniving manipulation of the violence implicit in this loss serves the president's authoritarian government as a means to control the city's inhabitants as a whole.

The nuclear family unit is repeatedly tested and undermined by fear in a system that is based upon complete adherence and loyalty to the president. Camila's relatives all close the doors of their homes to her once they realize that her father has been branded an enemy of the leader. Moreover, Camila's new family, with her husband and expected child, is also torn apart and becomes a casualty of the president's personal rage. Likewise, when Niña Fedina's husband, Genaro Rodas, tells her about the plans to capture Camila, she feels a moral responsibility to warn her, but she arrives too late. As a result of Niña Fedina's actions, in one of the most graphic and heart-wrenching scenes of the novel, she is taken to jail and is not allowed to feed her crying newborn child while she is being interrogated. Her baby subsequently dies of hunger. The state's security system literally interferes with her ability to be a nurturing mother. Adding insult to injury, the Auditor de Guerra, who had expected that he would be able to sell Camila for 10,000 pesos to a brothel, tries to sell Niña Fedina instead (the destroyed family transforms into a sellable commodity). Niña Fedina becomes hysterical when they try to take her dead child away from her at the brothel. So instead, she is taken to a hospital where she remains to clean clothes for the nuns. Regardless of this turn of fate, her family has already been brutally destroyed.

In his article entitled "La república clausurada: análisis de los espacios opresivos en *El Señor Presidente*," Ricardo Krauel notes that while much has been written by critics about the ways in which temporal manipulations in the novel's narrative create the effect of a never-ending oppressive regime, not enough attention has been placed on the anxiety-provoking representations of spaces in the narrative that help shape the desperation of the novel's atmosphere.[19] In his article, Krauel provides an analysis of the multiple spaces of incarceration within the novel, as well as the representation of hostility encountered in both private and public spaces. The common thread of all three is a sensation of feeling oppressively confined, with a lack of personal control over one's surroundings. The spaces of incarceration are always dark and those within them are portrayed as being disoriented in terms of the passage of time, suffering ultimately from a degraded identity and a loss of a sense of self.

Even domestic spaces that tend to be associated with refuge and solace become hostile: "Las casas particulares a menudo semejan cárceles en tanto que aparecen como ámbitos de reclusión involuntaria y como asilos del miedo" (Krauel 226) ["Private homes often seem like jails inasmuch as they appear like spaces of involuntary reclusion and like asylums from fear"]. In the case of Camila, he points to the fact that her seemingly perpetual confinement erodes her sense of self—much like the prisoners of the novel—especially when she is expecting news from her disappeared husband, and it never arrives:

La sucesión de continuas reclusiones que es la vida de Camila tendrá su punto culminante en el enclaustramiento a que se somete mientras espera recibir noticias de su marido; este enclaustramiento [...] irá despojándola de su identidad, le irá arrebatando sus más elementales atributos como ser humano, hasta dejarla transformada en un objeto desprovisto de valor: "Desapareció de las habitaciones que daban a la

calle sumergida por el peso de la pena, que se la fue jalando hacia el
fondo de la casa. Y es que se sentía un poco cachivache, un poco leña,
un poco carbón, un poco tinaja, un poco basura." (Krauel 227)[20]

[The succession of continuous reclusions that is the life of Camila
will culminate with a self-imposed confinement while she awaits news
from her husband; this seclusion ... will gradually strip her of her
identity, will tear away from her the most elemental human attributes,
until it leaves her transformed into an object without value: "She no
longer frequented the rooms looking onto the street; the weight of
her grief drew her to the back of the house. She thought of herself as
a kitchen utensil, a piece of coal or wood, an earthenware jar, mere
rubbish."]

The traditional association between domestic spaces and comfort
or protection is thus inverted when the inhabitants of the city are
deprived of any sense of personal agency and control over their private lives. The president's deception, his refusal to inform Camila of
her husband's incarceration, is an intentional form of psychological
torture that is aimed precisely at destroying her sense of value and
personal dignity, by making her question the loyalty of her husband.
Her withdrawal into the depths of the house mirrors her depressive
state of mind.

In the way that Camila retreats to the dark depths of the house,
which mirror her depression, it is often the internal state of mind of
Asturias's characters that shapes their perception of the space around
them. This is the case when el Pelele is a fugitive from justice, and in
a dream-like state he experiences his escape with a distorted sense of
his surroundings:

A sus costados pasaban puertas y puertas y puertas y ventanas y puertas y ventanas ... De repente se paraba, con las manos sobre la cara,
defendiéndose de los postes del telégrafo, pero al cerciorarse de que
los palos eran inofensivos se carcajeaba y seguía adelante, como el
que escapa de una prisión cuyos muros de niebla a más correr, más se
alejan. (21)

[He ran aimlessly, with his mouth open and his tongue hanging out,
slobbering and panting, and his arms in the air. Doors and doors and
doors and windows and doors and windows flashed past him. Suddenly
he would stop and put his hands over his face to defend himself
from a telegraph pole, but when he realised it was harmless he burst
out laughing and went on again, like a man escaping from a prison

with walls made of mist, so that the more he ran the further they receded. (19)]

El Pelele's delirious visions of the walls that delimit his entrapment, moving farther and farther away, convey the desperate fact that his situation is inescapable. While running from justice, el Pelele explicitly laments the horrors of the city when he compares it—unfavorably—to a cemetery. The only escape he can conjure up in his mind is to take a train that will take him out of the city, to the mountains and the volcanoes:

> ¡El cementerio es más alegre que la ciudad, más limpio que la ciudad! ¡Ay, qué alegre que los van, ay, a enterrar! [...] Tomaba el tren del guarda para alejarse velozmente de la ciudad, buscando hacia las montañas que hacían cargasillita a los volcanes, más allá de las torres del inalámbrico, más allá de un fuerte de artillería, volován relleno de soldados. (23)

> [The cemetery is gayer than the town and cleaner than the town! Oh what fun! They're going to bury them! ... He took the local train to get away from the town to the mountains as quickly as possible; the mountains would give him a leg-up to the volcanoes, beyond the wireless pylons, beyond the slaughter-house, beyond the artillery fort—a *vol-au-vent* stuffed with soldiers. (21)]

All together, the harsh city streets, the unlivable domestic spaces and, of course, the literal spaces of incarceration contribute the effect of there being no way out of the all-pervasive, never-ending web of power of the dictator. The only type of loyalty that is tolerated by the authoritarian regime is adherence to the leader himself. The result is a destruction of community that strains even the most intimate family ties.

And yet, a glimmer of hope might be read into the fact that despite Cara de Angel's betrayal of the leader, his son—unbeknownst to him—will be raised in the countryside by a loving mother. The day of young Miguel's baptism in a bucolic rural setting marks a dramatic shift in Camila's state of mind:

> Por entre los pinos de sombra caminante, los árboles fruteros de las huertas y los de los campos más altos que las nubes, *aclaró un día en la noche de su pena*; el domingo de Pentecostés, en que recibió su hijo sal, óleo, agua, saliva de cura y nombre de Miguel [...] Las ovejas se entretenían en lamer las crías. *¡Qué sensación tan completa de bienestar de domingo daba aquel ir y venir de la lengua materna por el cuerpo del*

recental, que entremoría los ojos pestañosos al sentir la caricia! [...] Sin saber por qué, como si la vida renaciera en ella, al concluir el repique del bautizo, apretó a su hijo contra su corazón. *El pequeño Miguel creció en el campo, fue hombre de campo, y Camila no volvió a poner los pies en la ciudad.*
(Asturias 287–88, emphasis mine)

[At last a day came which shed light on the dark night of her grief, as she wandered like a shadow between the pines, the orchard fruit-trees and the tall trees in the fields: it was Whit Sunday, when her son was anointed with salt, oil, water and the priest's saliva, and given the name of Miguel. The mocking-birds were caressing each other with their beaks ... the sheep were busy licking their lambs. What a perfect sensation of Sunday well-being the movements of its mother's tongue over its body produced in the suckling lamb, flickering its long-lashed eyes under her caress! ... Without knowing why, she pressed her baby to her heart when the christening chimes had ended, as if life had been renewed in her. Little Miguel grew up in the country and became a country-man. Camila never again set foot in the city. (276–77)]

This turn toward the countryside and return to a pastoral, premodern world as an alternative to the intolerable urban, market-driven present, is a motif that can be found in other Asturias texts. In his analysis of *Hombres de Maíz,* for instance, René Prieto finds that the novel offers an optimistic and "encouraging social model and emphatically postulates a revolutionary course of action that brings the men of maize from chaos to stability by pointing out the intrinsic relationship that exists between human beings and the land" (Prieto 106). As the character of Goyo Yic and his extended family return to the town of Pisigüilito, at the end of *Hombres de Maíz,* Prieto sees the hopeful beginning of a new era that will entail a communitarian commitment to production (as opposed to those who sell corn just for the profit) and a genuine involvement with the traditions of an ancient cultural past (Prieto 107). In both of these important texts, Asturias rejects the vileness of what urban modernity has come to represent in favor of a rural pastoralism that allows for compassion, community, and respect for premodern values.

If one takes the metaphor of "the caring Mother" as representative of all of the nurturing aspects of society that have been strained and made to conform to paternalistic tyranny, then the multiple references to maternal love toward the end of *El Señor Presidente* stand as a hopeful reminder of the permanence of the many voices that have been excluded from the scriptural enterprise (*i.e.*, the

madman, the "savage," the woman),[21] and from the narrative of
"progress" as applied to el Presidente's Liberal regime. One can
hear in the maternal that reemerges at the end of Asturias's novel
the voice of alterity—a heterogeneous voice that has somehow not
been completely silenced by the script of El Presidente's paternalistic tyranny.[22] In the train ride to what he thinks will be his exile,
even though Cara de Angel knows that leaving the country will be
his only hope for liberation, he laments having to be separated from
his homeland:

> Aquella tierra de asidua primavera era *su tierra, su ternura, su madre,*
> y por mucho que resucitara al ir dejando atrás aquellas aldeas, siempre
> estaría muerto entre los vivos, eclipsado entre los hombres de los otros
> países por la presencia invisible de sus árboles en cruz y de sus piedras
> para tumbas.   (275, emphasis mine)

> [Yet this country with its slow-moving springtime was his country, his
> tenderness, his mother; and however much it might put new life into
> him to leave these villages behind, when he was among men of other
> countries he would always be a dead man among the living, eclipsed
> by the invisible presence of these trees and tombstones.   (265)]

The protagonist equates the countryside and the small villages he
sees pass from the train window with the tenderness of his own
mother. He refers again to memories of his mother as an attempt
to escape temporarily the inhuman conditions of his incarceration.
After describing the demeaning conditions under which he is forced
to satisfy his bodily needs, he is able to remind himself of his humanity through memories of Camila and other sweet remembrances that
conjure up his childhood:

> Antojábasele la rosa que por abril y mayo florecía año con año en la
> ventana del comedor donde de niño desayunaba con su madre. [...]
> Las tinieblas se tragaban los murallones como obleas y ya no tardaba el
> bote de los excrementos. ¡Ah, sí la rosa aquélla!   (292)

> [He thought of her as the rose which used to flower every April and
> May in the window of the dining-room where he breakfasted with his
> mother as a child ... The darkness swallowed up the thick walls as if
> they were wafers and soon afterwards the bucket of excrement would
> arrive. Oh for his rose!   (281)]

Even under the most dehumanizing conditions, Cara de Angel grasps
on to his fond memories to maintain his sense of self. The president

cruelly targets this thin source of hope when he hires someone to be incarcerated with him and tell him that Camila has betrayed him by becoming one of the leader's lovers.

The resilient "voice of alterity," nevertheless, perseveres at the end of the novel when the destruction of the city is announced in the Epilogue by a crazy man. Benjamín, the mentally unstable puppet master, runs shouting and singing through the plaza and when he is about to be apprehended by the police his wife pleads on his behalf: "[...] vea que está loco, no se lo lleve ..., no, no le pegue! ... ¡Figúrese cómo estará de loco que dice que vio toda la ciudad tumbada por tierra como el Portal!" (296) ["He is mad, I tell you, don't take him away—no, don't hit him please! He's so mad that he says he can see the whole town laid flat like the Porch!" (286)]. Benjamín foretells the destruction of the entire city, presumably a reference to the earthquakes of 1917 and 1918 that were the catalyst that finally brought down the Estrada Cabrera dictatorship.[23] Thus as Asturias builds his fictional city around actual reference points from the Guatemala City of the turn of the nineteenth century[24]—such as the *Portal del Señor*[25] and the Temple of Minerva—the cataclysmic demolition of its structures by the earthquakes reads as the ultimate revenge of both Nature and God for being left out of the Liberal program geared toward modernity.

As an ultimate indication of the end of the oppressive regime, the student and the sacristan who had been unfairly incarcerated—symbolizing the confinement of intellectual and religious thought—are set free. When the student returns home, the novel closes with his mother's prayer:

> [...] oyó la voz de su madre que llevaba el rosario: —Por los agonizantes y caminantes ... Porque reine la paz entre los Príncipes Cristianos ... Por los que sufren persecución de justicia ... Por los enemigos de la fe católica ... Por las necesidades sin remedio de la Santa Iglesia y nuestras necesidades ... Por las benditas ánimas del Santo Purgatorio ... *Kyrie eleison.* (298)

> [... he heard his mother's voice telling her rosary: "For the dying and for travellers. So that Peace shall reign among Christian rulers. For those who suffer persecution by the law. For the enemies of the Catholic faith. For the desperate needs of the Holy Church and for our own needs ... For the blessed souls of Holy Purgatory ... Kyrie eleison." (287)]

She prays for all of those who have been victimized and persecuted. Upon the destruction of the modern city, the voice of the Mother has the last word.

Along with the character of el Pelele (the "idiot"), as seen above, Asturias is able to convey the limits of symbolic language and to problematize the issue of representing violence itself through another marginal character, Benjamín (the "crazy" puppet master). Immediately following the assassination of el Pelele in the central plaza, Asturias includes a vaudevillian scene between the petit don Benjamín and his overweight wife, playfully called doña *Venjamón*. After hearing the fatal gunshots, the couple peers out of their house to try to find out who was killed. Since Benjamín has not put in his false teeth properly, his wife cannot understand him explain that he has just witnessed the dead body of el Pelele being carried away:

—¡Habla claro, por amor de Dios!
Cuando el titiritero se apeaba los dientes postizos, para hablar movía la
    boca y chupaba como ventosa.
—¡Ah!, ya veo, esperá; ¡ya veo de qué se trata!
—¡Pero, Benjamín, no te entiendo nada!—y casi jirimiqueando—.
    ¿Querés entender que no te entiendo nada?
—¡Ya veo, ya veo! ... ¡Allá, por la esquina del Palacio Arzobispal, se
    está juntando gente!
—Hombre, quitá de la puerta, porque ni ves nada—sos un inútil—ni
    te entiendo una palabra! [...]
—¡Allí ... que llevan la camilla!—fue lo último que dijo don Benjamín.
    (56)

["Don't mumble, for heaven's sake!"
When the puppet-master left his false teeth out, his mouth was drawn
    in and out as he talked, like a suction valve.
"Ah, now I see! Wait a moment! I see what it is!"
"But, Benjamin, I can't understand a thing you say!" she said, almost
    whimpering. "Don't you understand? I can't understand a thing
    you say!"
"I can see now! I can see now! There's a crowd collecting over there
    at the corner of the Archbishop's Palace."
"Come away from the door if you can't see anything—you're no good
    at all! I can't understand a word you say!" ...
"There—they're bringing a stretcher!" was Don Benjamin's final con-
    tribution.   (52)]

While it is impossible for him to communicate to his wife what he is witnessing—a fact that is conveyed in this farcical interaction—he then uses his experience of being a witness to the effects of violence in his puppet show:

Pero su teatro de títeres salió ganancioso de aquel lance singular. Los muñecos se aventuraron por los terrenos de la tragedia, con el llanto goteado de sus ojos de cartón-piedra [...] Don Benjamín creyó que los niños llorarían con aquellas comedias picadas de un sentido de pena y su sorpresa no tuvo límites cuando los vio reír con más ganas, a mandíbula batiente, con más alegría que antes. Los niños reían de ver llorar ... Los niños reían de ver pegar ...   (58)

[But this unusual event brought prosperity to his marionette theatre. The puppets took the tragedy as their theme, with tears oozing drop by drop from their cardboard eyes ... Don Benjamin thought that the painful element in the drama would make the children cry, and his surprise knew no bounds when he saw them laugh more heartily than before, with wide open mouths and happy expressions. The sight of tears made the children laugh. The sight of blows made the children laugh. (53–54)]

The pain of others, materialized in the puppet tragedies, again, becomes a sellable commodity. The more the puppets cry and hit each other, the more the children laugh, and the more money there is to be reaped from the show. Beyond the commodification of pain, this episode might resonate with the author in the sense that his own novel is an attempt to represent the violent and painful experiences of his compatriots, but is also a source of entertainment for his reading public. Benjamín finds an aesthetic outlet to represent violence in puppetry and is surprised to find that he delights the children; the greater the cruelty the greater the laugh. Perhaps Asturias expresses certain complicity with Benjamín by captivating his audience as well with the aesthetics of fear and pain. Asturias provides an extremely comical, almost slapstick exchange between Benjamín and his wife, making the reader laugh before holding up a mirror to his public in the scene of the children laughing at the violent puppet show. The reader then becomes complicit, along with the author, in the complex process of aestheticizing pain.

It is precisely through images such as this one, and quite masterfully, through the rhythms and the sonority of his text, that Asturias attempts to communicate the fear and the violence that permeates his city, beyond what can be captured in a merely descriptive, linear narrative. Perhaps this is why Asturias insists in his article "*El Señor Presidente* como mito" that the novel was first *spoken*, not written. He describes the genesis of the text as surging from conversations with friends in the cafés of Paris, in which the Latin Americans of the group would try to outdo each other with appalling and somber anecdotes about their respective countries to try to counteract the picturesque images of America that appealed to Europeans at the time:

> Es así como nace *El Señor Presidente*, hablado, no escrito. Y como al decirlo me oía, no quedaba satisfecho hasta que me sonaba bien, y tantas veces lo hacía, para que cada vez se oyera mejor, que llegué a saber capítulos enteros de memoria. No fue escrito, al principio, sino hablado. Y esto es importante subrayarlo. Fue deletreado. Era la época del renacer de la palabra, como medio de expresión y de acción mágica. Ciertas palabras. Ciertos sonidos. Hasta producir el encantamiento, el estado hipnótico, el trance.
>
> (Asturias, "*El Señor Presidente* como mito" 473)

> [This is how *El Señor Presidente* is born, spoken, not written. And as I recited it out loud I could hear myself, I was not satisfied until it sounded right to me, and I did it so many times, so that each time it would sound better, that I learned entire chapters by heart. It was not written, at first, but spoken. And this is important to underline. It was spelled out. It was the time of the rebirth of the word, as a form of expression and as a magical act. Certain words. Certain sounds. To produce an enchantment, a hypnotic state, a trance.]

Ineffable experiences—fear itself—must be represented beyond words through a hypnotizing and vertiginous combination of sounds, rhythms, claustrophobic spaces, provocative images, et cetera, invoking reactions that appeal to the instinctual rather than the rational—an instance of "semiotic" signification that Kristeva associates with the maternal.

In fact, Asturias's novel culminates in an onomatopoeic invocation of the Maya-K'iché "Tohil," the god of fire, war, and rain, in a vision that Cara de Angel has when the president gives him the order to go to Washington. Through the repetition of the drum sound "tun"—a word that in K'iché signifies a type of drum—with a *crescendo* that starts with palpitations and a vision of a bonfire out of the president's window. The concatenation of drumbeats and visions of indigenous warriors dancing around the fire explodes into a frenzy of sounds and motion all directed toward the god Tohil, who is demanding human sacrifices, according to the narrator. The episode announces the duplicitous nature of the leader's offer and foretells Cara de Ángel's abduction and eventual death. Although Cara de Ángel himself does not have the presence of mind to make the connection between his vision and his ultimate demise, the link between the disquieting rhythms of the drum, the dance of the warriors, and

his own death becomes clear for the reader in passages such as this:
"Y cada cazador-guerrero tomó una jícara, sin despegársela del aliento
que le repellaba la cara al compás del tún, del retumbo y el tún de los
tumbos y el tún de las tumbas, que le bailaban los ojos a Tohil" (270)
["And each hunter-warrior blew on their gourds without pausing for
breath, to the rhythm of the tom-tom, and the echo and the drum-
ming which set Tohil's eyes dancing" (260)]. The sound of the tun
and the repetitive syllable tun/tum pounds throughout the sentence
in Spanish, eventually morphing into the word for coffins (*tumbas*),
thus rhythmically linking the vision with death.

The "capitalist" and "conquering" forces driving de Certeau's
scriptural economy and the modern city, and even the process of
writing history—which is also dependent on *accumulating* the past
and making it *conform* to a particular narrative—all rely on both
cumulative and necessarily exclusionary mechanisms. However, in
the very act of denouncing the repressive, authoritarian regime, *El
Señor Presidente* provides a forum for the resilient permanence of
those voices excluded and abjected from the Liberal programs geared
toward modernity. While proposing an alternative model that reverts
back to community and compassion, associated with an idealized
rural space, he tells a story of fear and sorrow that emphasizes the
heartless commodification of pain fostered by a profit-oriented system
that forgets about the individuals that comprise it. The novel captures
what gets left out of historiographical discourse, as the story is conveyed on a more visceral level through sounds, spaces, and images
that fall at the margins of normative language. As el Pelele's howl
indicates, words are not enough to convey the extent of the loss felt
in the "absence of the Mother."

CHAPTER 4

THE EFFECTS OF A FRAGMENTED NARRATIVE: COMMUNITY AND ALIENATION IN THE CITY

The reciprocal dynamic between form and content will be central to our reading of two novels set in Central American cities, published in the 1970s: Manlio Argueta's *Caperucita en la zona roja* (1977) and Carmen Naranjo's *Diario de una multitud* (1974). With similar aesthetic intentions, both of these authors resort to the narrative strategy of interweaving disconnected, nonlinear fragments that initially tend to disorient their readers. In Argueta's text, a difficult, fragmentary narrative is used to portray the urban guerrilla movement in San Salvador, while a long series of anonymous fragments is adopted by Naranjo to convey a sense of urban alienation in a fictional rendition of the Costa Rican capital city, San José.

Why would an author deliberately choose to structure his or her text in an obfuscatory way? In these particular instances, I propose that the answer takes us back to de Certeau's useful metaphor of the scriptural economy. The form of these two texts is meant to serve precisely as a way to obstruct and resist the centripetal forces of homogenizing scriptural economies. By this, I mean that the fragmentary narrative in both novels is meant to interrupt homogenizing tendencies of collective ideologies (that are imposed as received models from abroad on local cities by the equivalent of de Certeau's symbolic writing machine). By interrupting the momentum of passively accepted models, the fragmentary form of these novels is meant to provoke a sense of awareness and reflection, each in its own way.

Both authors strongly resist the notion of totalizing versions of history. As such, with their portrayals of the circumstances they explore—the inner workings of armed struggle and the complacency of many members of a consumerist society—they refuse to offer their readers an unproblematized coherence to their stories. Naranjo and Argueta then each attempt to break through the inertia that plagues both capitalist and even revolutionary group mentalities in the societies they depict. Through discomfort, the recognizable simulation of mind-numbing mediocrity, or by generating a sense of confusion, they each intend to engage their readers in making sense of their narratives, thus provoking critical thought. Both novels, therefore, resort to providing metatextual keys to invite their reader to decipher the intention inherent in their difficult, exasperating, or uncomfortably nonlinear form.

To shatter the feeling of being a sort of automaton in a collective system that (in its unchecked extreme) tells you what to think and how to act, these novelists insist on the power of creativity and the need for continual critical evaluation. They both believe in social activism without having to conform indiscriminately to imposed models for social improvement and progress (that is, an unquestioned, top-down vision of revolutionary action or conforming to a particular version of consumer capitalism imagined elsewhere). It is fitting, therefore, that it is novelists / creative writers that remind us through their literature about the fundamental importance of critical thought and creativity in the successful push toward a better future.

FRAGMENTATION AND THE SEARCH FOR COMMUNITY

[...] la culpa fue mía por pensar más de la cuenta.[1]

(*Manlio Argueta*, Caperucita 116–17)

It is the poet's duty to fight against mechanical, schematic thinking.

(*Roque Dalton,* Poetry and Militancy in Latin America 23)

Manlio Argueta's second novel, *Caperucita en la zona roja* (1977),[2] opens with a disorienting string of obfuscations that alerts the reader to the deciphering role she must play in the unfolding of the text. The initial section, *En el bosque* ("In the Forest"), is about the relationship between the protagonist Alfonso (Al, el lobo, el poeta) and Genoveva (Caperucita, Hormiga, Horm, loba), the woman he loves. The narrative begins with a dreamlike confusion of opposites in which presence/absence, proximity/distance, closed spaces / open windows, him/her, facts/imagination all blur together in a convoluted account of their romance. Opening with a rambling, stream-of-consciousness internal monologue, Al ponders leaving Hormiga and the small room (*cuchitril*) in her aunt's house, where he is a border:

> Doña Gracia descansa en su sofá-cama, después de regresar de su caminata cotidiana del mediodía. Irme ahora que no has llegado, linda Hormiga peruana de junco y capulí. Con el pelo cubierto por un pañuelo rojo y asomándose los mechones por la caperuza, los mechones que se van al cielo con el viento que sopla. Perdone que la moleste, cuando toco la puerta (aterrorizado) [...]. (11–12)

> [She is taking a siesta. Doña Gracia that is, Mamma never took a siesta. To leave now because you haven't come, pretty Peruvian Ant of reeds and *capulí* trees, your hair covered with a red scarf and your locks protruding from under your hood, the locks of hair that rise to heaven with the wind that blows. Sorry to bother you, as I knock on the door (terrified) ... (3–4)][3]

The narrative then continues in the gerund, the infinitive, and in the present progressive tenses, creating a slippery notion of when the time of action actually takes place. The effect is to make it seem as though the events narrated are unfolding in the narrator's thoughts as a reverie. It becomes unclear if the narrator Al is pondering how he will carry out his future departure and is visualizing potential scenarios that could transpire, or if he is describing his surroundings as the events take place, or if he is replaying in his mind a set of occurrences from the past.

The dreamlike, almost evanescent quality of the narrative is reinforced by an ambiguity with regard to the presence or absence of the characters (are they physically there or are they being remembered?), and the frequent confusion between narrative voices as the narrator's perspective changes from one character to another unannounced. Even within a paragraph the narrative voice might begin from the perspective of Al and end with that of Hormiga, with no clear indication of the shift from one to the other. The reader eventually becomes familiar with some of the distinguishing traits of the characters that become cues to identify the different narrative voices: Al, the hypochondriacal poet; Caperucita's flowered dresses; Guillermo, the baker; and his envious resentment of his brother Manuel, et cetera.

The difficulty of the text is exacerbated by the fact that the subsections of each chapter are not told in chronological order. This distortion in time effects a fragmented discourse that often contradicts itself. Since the characters speak according to the limited information they possess in a given moment, at times they are forced to contradict themselves later on, when new information becomes available. As the story is not told chronologically, internal inconsistencies within the characters are exposed in a particularly jarring and unsettling fashion. And yet, the focus of the narrative is not necessarily the development of a character from one position to another. Instead, attention is directed to the fleeting moments that are presented as if perceived through a refracted mirror that breaks open a multiplicity of possibilities within the storyline.

In accordance with this notion of multiple interpretations set out for the reader to ponder for himself, even the physical relationship between Al and Hormiga is described in conflicting ways. After a scene in which the couple is playful and sexually at ease with each other, a subsequent scene emphasizes the sexual tension of a relationship that has not yet been consummated. The discrepancy may stem from the difference between the desires and the actual behavior of the characters, a distinction that is not clearly established by the narrative voice. Another explanation for such discrepancies might be a separation between what the characters do and what they say to others in the interest of propriety. A final explanation could lie simply in the order in which the scenes are narrated: perhaps it is only contradictory because the scene in which they deny a sexual encounter is introduced after the description of the scene in which the encounter takes place. Again, all possibilities coexist in a narrative that does not attempt to even out such contradictions into a coherent, linear account.[4]

Perhaps in part because of the difficulty of the novel, there is a disconcerting vacuum of critical articles that engage with this particular text.[5] The lack of critical literature is paradoxical given that *Caperucita* is widely read and is considered by some, including the Salvadoran author Claribel Alegría, to be "Argueta's best novel."[6] Both the difficulty of the text and the notable critical void that surrounds it raise the question: why would Argueta choose to structure a novel about the resistance movement in El Salvador in such a fragmented way, especially in the midst of the country's armed conflict? It would seem that in the polarized, binary backdrop of the Cold War, while rallying support for antigovernment popular organizations, a novel that features a group of young dissenters and their actions of resistance would be more linear and coherent in pointing the way toward a desired future liberation. Why, then, does Argueta resort to a narrative style that resists straight paths, and instead breaks open a multiplicity of possible interpretations within the text? This is the underlying question that frames my reading of *Caperucita*.

Argueta's resistance to flattening out the possibilities of interpretation put forth in his story becomes evident in the first section of the novel—*En el bosque*. From the beginning, the author insists on shattering any sense of stable barriers that separate seemingly contradictory concepts. He thus sets the tone for a narrative that is sustained by such recurrent tensions and ambiguities. In the relationship between Caperucita and Al, a paradoxical dynamic is set forth in which the couple feels more alienated from each other when they are physically near than when they must connect over distances and silences through the intimacy of their thoughts:

> Tenemos grandes diálogos a larga distancia, por la radiografía de la conciencia. (15) [...] Necesito que me dejés a solas porque es la mejor manera de estar con vos. Así te veo más definido y disfruto de tus palabras bonitas. Pero eso no quiere decir que te vayas. (18) [...] Ella se tira en su lugar predilecto, frente a mí, a unos dos pasos, pero tan lejana como si la estuviera viendo con unos prismáticos al revés. (24)

> [We have great long-distance dialogues via radiography of the conscience. (8) ... I need you to leave me alone because it's the best way to be with you. That way I see you as more defined and I enjoy your beautiful words. But that doesn't mean I'm telling you to go. (11) ... She lies down in her favorite place, in front of me, a few steps away, but as far away as if I were seeing her through the wrong end of binoculars. (18)]

This familiar and easily recognizable trope that inverts distance and proximity, alienation and intimacy—that is, feeling even closer to someone when they are far away than when they are physically near—exemplifies the way in which Argueta sets up a series of apparent contradictions to represent with great accuracy the multifaceted complexity of human experience.

In an attempt to capture this complexity, the novel is organized around three distinct images: *the prison cell, the window,* and *the mirror.* These three symbolic figures operate on a physical, literal level and on a more abstract, metaphorical level as well. They figure directly in the plot of the novel, but they also shape the concepts put forth and even the aesthetics of the text.

THE PRISON CELL AND THE DANGERS
OF CRITICAL THOUGHT

As the story progresses, the reader finds out that Al has repeatedly
been subjected to physical enclosure in claustrophobically small
spaces: his room in doña Gracia's house is described as a small
cuchitril (hovel), and as a student activist in El Salvador's resistance
movement he is forced to live in hiding in close quarters with fellow
members of the "underground" urban movement. The reader also
discovers that Al has been incarcerated in Guatemala as a result of
his affiliation with resistance groups, as well as in El Salvador for
being a student activist. Moreover, in a scene that echoes the predicament of the renowned Salvadoran poet Roque Dalton only a
few years before the publication of *Caperucita*, Alfonso is incarcerated by his own colleagues in the resistance group in an ideological feud between the intellectual and the militant factions of the
movement.[7]

The two sections that describe *el bosque,* dealing with the relationship between Hormiga and Al—*En el bosque* ("In the Forest")
and *Otra vez en el bosque* ("Back in the Forest")—are saturated with
descriptions of entrapment, both domestic and emotional:

> Desde la puerta de la cocina Hormiga:/—¿Querés tomarte una taza
> de café con leche?/ Salgo a la puerta y le digo esperá un minuto, mi
> intención es no aceptar, me siento mal del todo, en verdad es una
> enfermedad producida por este cuarto, por estas cuatro paredes que se
> acercan y se alejan cantando, corriendo, aprisionando. (144)

> [From the kitchen door, Ant: "Would you like a cup of coffee with
> cream?" I go to the door and tell her to wait a moment, my intention
> is to turn it down, I feel lousy, it really is a sickness caused by this room,
> by these four walls that close in and move away from me singing, run-
> ning, confining. (169–70)]

Speaking from Al's perspective, the narrator repeatedly describes
the enclosure of four walls and the malaise that is provoked by his
feelings of confinement. This sense of discomfort is comprehensible
on many levels. For one, he lives in a small, dark attic room in doña
Gracia's house where, as an orphan and a student who has been in
trouble with authorities, he must keep a low profile. The text even
makes direct reference to the increased danger the city streets hold
for Al, given the cruel fact that he does not have parents to vouch
for him in case he were to be detained: "—Pobrecito Al, no puede

salir a la calle. / —Porque no tiene padre ni madre" (60) ["Poor Al, he can't go out in the street. / Because he doesn't have a father or a mother" (62)].

Al's frequent sensation of entrapment also refers to the emotional state of his character who, in his early twenties, is juggling the intensity of his passion for Genoveva (who may very well be expecting their child) and his political commitment to the revolutionary cause:

> Alguna vez estaremos sin hacernos preguntas y será cuando ya no nos entendamos, cuando todo se haya perdido en el mundo [...] y nadie sabrá por qué estamos solos. Vos estarás parada frente a la cocina y yo estaré encadenado a la silla en estas cuatro paredes parecidas a nuestros sentimientos. (15)

> [Sometime we shall be together without asking each other questions and that will be when we no longer understand each other, when everything in the world has been lost ... and no one will know why we are alone. You will be standing in front of the kitchen and I will be chained to the chair within these four walls that are like our feelings. (8)]

Both the literally tight living quarters and his disturbing emotions mirror each other in the imagery used to describe them. The symbolism of all four walls closing in on him, the palpable silence brought on by a lack of questions, the solitude tied to the couple's anticipated distancing in the future of his imagination, and the sense of losing a joint purpose along the way can all refer either to a projected fear of domesticity in light of his girlfriend's pregnancy, or also, to Al's personal trajectory within the revolutionary movement, described further below.

As the reader moves from the sections of the text that feature Al and Hormiga's relationship to the subject matter of the majority of the novel—namely, the clandestine operations of a group of young students who participate in El Salvador's opposition movement of the 1960s and 1970s—the discovery of Al's multiple incarcerations opens up another possibility of interpretation for the insistently mentioned enclosed spaces in the initial chapter. Perhaps the reason that the temporal dimensions of the sections in *el bosque* are so ambiguous, and the imagery of the prison cell is so prevalent, is because those sections can be read as the thoughts and memories of Al and Caperucita during his time in prison. In the sections where the narrator's perspective is written from her vantage point, she may be trying to maintain a link to him through her thoughts, despite the necessary distance forced on them by his clandestine operations. Similarly, as the narrator shifts to Al's voice, he conjures up thoughts of her to reconstitute his humanity in the midst of the extreme isolation of his imprisonment.

Nonetheless, even in their absence from each other, the intensity of their intuitive connection enables them to maintain a bond that transcends mere imagination or stale memories. One of the more notable examples appears when Caperucita becomes aware of Al's incarceration through a dream:

> Y luego voy a tu encuentro en un segundo sueño [dreams Caperucita], te miro rodeado de amigos que van a ajusticiarte por traidor a tus ideas, estás encerrado en una celda de tierra, en una jaula para cusucos, bajo por unas escaleras estrechas, para encontrarte y te veo como si fueras tacuazín metido en su cueva [...] Me decís que añorás aquella casa de ladrillos rojos y sentarte en la silla de hierro con hilos plásticos, y me contás que sos un prisionero eterno, y quizás te van a ajusticiar, te van a aplicar las propias leyes en las que vos has creído, pero que dudás si se deben aplicar, el alacrán se come a sus hijos y vice versa. (101)

> [And then I go to meet you in a second dream, I see you surrounded by friends who are going to execute you for betraying their ideals, you are locked in a cell of mud, in a cage for armadillos, I go down several narrow steps, to meet you, and I see you as if you were an opossum in its cave ... You tell me you miss that red brick house and sitting in the iron chair with the woven nylon seat, and you tell me that you are an eternal prisoner, and perhaps they're going to execute you, they're going to apply the same law that you have believed in, but you doubt that it should be applied, the scorpion eats its children and vice versa. (112–13)]

Even in her dreams she remains keenly aware of his predicament, albeit on an intuitive level.[8] Her dream conveys the ironic fact that his participation in the resistance has led him to a prison cell meant for his enemies. In a tricky game of mirrors, he is punished for no longer being equal to who his friends want him to be; he is castigated for treason against his own previous ideas and is denied the possibility of autonomous self-reflection.

The above scene, Hormiga's dream, puts forth one of the underlying themes of the novel: the danger of critical thought. An explicit mention of the precariousness of thought appears when Al observes the victims of police repression against a student protest from the window of a café:

> Me pongo a pensar tonteras. Pensar es un acto fisiológico, sólo que no hay residuales, es encontrarse en esta ventana viendo pasar el entierro

de los estudiantes muertos por la policía. Y me doy cuenta que es terrible (no el entierro) pensar. / Requisitos para convivir en el país: / 1. No pensar. / 2. Ni pensar. / 3. Pensar nada.   (160–61)

[I start thinking nonsense. Thinking is a physiological act, only there is no payoff, it's finding yourself by this window watching the funeral processions of students killed by the police pass by. And I realize that it is horrible (not the burial) to think. / Requirements for living in this country: / 1) Don't think. / 2) Don't even think. / 3) Think nothing.   (189)]

His own personal experience will tragically prove Al's bitterly sarcastic reflections to be correct with regard to the fatal consequences of thoughtful rebellion for the students killed by the police (or even the perceived rebellion inherent in provocative thought itself). Nevertheless, the dangerous repercussions of critical thought in the face of orthodoxy or ideological cohesion do not stem solely from the government or the military establishment trying to maintain a status quo—they are also sadly mirrored by the reaction of his revolutionary colleagues who disagree with his assessments for their group:

Manuel sostiene que la revolución debe hacerse con los cojones, yo digo que debe ponerse un poco—para ser modestos, una migaja—de cerebro, entrar en onda. Es también su problema. Doce años después esa es la divergencia. (114) […] Dos meses de estar en una celda que estaba en principio destinada a nuestros enemigos. Ahora yo soy el enemigo por traidor a la cohesión ideológica […] *Tus teorías sobre las bases sociales son una traición, dice el compañero jefe, poniendo su 45 sobre la mesa. Yo sé que soy un estorbo para los que manejan la tesis de los cojones* […] ¿Vale la pena haber parado en este agujero incomprensible? Me gustaría tirarme a la calle y vivir. Yo mismo escogí este camino que va a dar debajo de la tierra […] Sólo brillan los ojos de la 45. Y mi cerebro sale volando.   (119–20)[9]

[Manuel maintains that the revolution should be made with *cojones*, I say that we should use a little—to be modest, a few scraps of—gray matter, get with it. It's his problem too. Twelve years later that is the difference of opinion. (132) … Two months spent in a cell that was originally intended for our enemies. Now I'm an enemy for breaking with the party line. … *Your theories about the grassroots social base are treason, the compañero in charge says, putting his forty-five down on the table. I know I'm in the way of those who believe in the "cojones" thesis* … Was it worth ending up in this incomprehensible hole? I'd like to go out on the streets and live. I myself chose this path that leads underground … Only the eyes of the forty-five shine. And my brain is blown to bits.   (137–39)]

Fittingly, the tragic consequence of Al's insistence on maintaining the integrity of his own thoughts is to have *his brains* blown out by his *compañeros.*

REFLECTIONS AND REFRACTIONS: THE WINDOW AND THE MIRROR

The multilayered allusion to prison cells and closed spaces—ranging from metaphorical representations of domestic emotions, to Al's living quarters, and his literal incarcerations—is counterbalanced by the equally insistent use of the imagery of *the window.* Interestingly, "the window" itself is not charged with a purely positive signification, as an opposition to enclosure. Instead, it maintains an ambivalent semantic charge, at times signifying the possibility of exits and escapes to alternative spaces, at times indicating deception and exposure to false images. While incarcerated, Al resorts to imagining a window, to transcend the limitations of his cell:

> Ellos me sacan al excusado cuando apenas ha salido el sol, lástima [...] Luego regreso a la celda húmeda, al sótano de mierda. Por algún agu-jerito que me invento veo apagarse las últimas estrellas, buena señal, porque significa que de alguna manera vienes ¡día feliz! con tus ojos de claridad, día envuelto en papel celofán. Mejor me voy a dar vueltas a los cafetales. *Montado en un caballo más hermoso que la luz, una montaña parecía piafando mi caballo, una ola de sangre.* (120)

> [They take me to the john when the sun is barely up, too bad ... Then I return to the humid cell, to this shitty basement. Through any small crack that I invent I watch the last stars fade away, it's a good sign because it means that in some way you are coming—joyous day!—with your bright, clear eyes day wrapped in cellophane paper. Instead, I'd better take a stroll through the coffee farms. *Mounted on a horse more beautiful than light, a mountain appeared pawing at my horse, a wave of blood.* (138)][10]

In the midst of the humiliating circumstances of his imprisonment, Al tries to escape mentally by imagining the relief of light, mobility, and open nature: he visualizes himself riding a horse that is more beautiful than light itself. However, even in his imagination, the figu-rative window that helps his temporary escape turns to a dark vision of bloodshed. From envisioning himself riding this marvelous horse, his thoughts turn to the horse stomping and kicking anxiously, finally conjuring up a disturbing wave of blood. Not even his dreams allow him to escape the violent confines of his incarceration.

Meantime, in a repetitive play between the images of windows and mirrors, Caperucita sees in (through) "the window" the hope of Al's safe return:

> Truenos corriendo sobre los tejados y tu cara más allá del vidrio de la ventana. Me lavo la cara, me veo detrás de la ventana [...]. (86) He aprendido a estar frente a la ventana, pegada al vidrio, estar al otro lado del espejo viendo pasar abajo los cipotes chorreados regresando de la escuela [...] la loquita denfrente [...] haciendo señales hacia mi ventana [...] pegada al vidrio de la ventana [...] Así estoy en la ventana y las otras habitaciones me miran [...] Y yo con mi timba, mi estómago en movimiento, esperando que aparezcás de algún lado y veás para arriba, al tercer piso, buscando detrás de las ventanas y yo abriendo las celosías para mirarte mejor y no estar detrás de un espejo [...]   (92–93)[11]

> [Thunder running along the tiled roofs and your face behind the window pane. I wash my face, I see myself behind the window [...] (94). I've learned to sit in front of the window, glued to the window pane, being on the other side of the mirror watching the drenched children go by as they return home from school...the crazy woman across the street ... waving at my window ... glued to the window pane ... So I am at the window, and other rooms observe me ... And me with my gut, my stomach in motion, waiting for you to show up from somewhere and to look up, to the third floor, looking behind the windows and I opening the shutters to see you better and not be behind a mirror ...   (102–3)].

During her pregnancy, while expecting their daughter Carmina, Caperucita longs for him to come home, to no avail. Much like the images in Al's thoughts above, which unwittingly morph from positive to negative, the window of hope for Hormiga turns into a revealing mirror that shows nothing more than her own solitary reflection.[12]

The confusion of images and blurring between appearance and reality get further complicated with the third organizing figure: the mirror. Again, the symbolism operates on many levels. A mirror is literally significant in the relationship between Al and Caperucita because in doña Gracia's house he used to spy on her when she would look at herself in the mirror (while she was coquettishly aware of his gaze): "Me daba por verme vestida frente al espejo para exhibirme; me mirabas y te miraba [...]" (97) ["I would dress up to look at myself in the mirror so I could exhibit myself; you observed me observing you ..." (107)]. Fittingly, when he goes "underground" Al's good-bye note to her is written with her lipstick on the same mirror in front of which they flirted with each other repeatedly. Hormiga

ponders the painful realization of his vague words written in red on
her mirror: "Good luck, some day we'll see each other."

Y vos qué, te perdés; inexplicablemente desaparecés [reflects Hormiga
upon his departure]. Sólo dejás un adiós con buenas intenciones:
'Buena suerte, algún día nos veremos'. Una mancha de pintura en el
espejo, pintura de mis labios, una buena suerte más filosa que cuchillo
de cocina. Y me veo entre las letras rojas, espiándome a mí misma o
quizás tus ojos están detrás del espejo, pegados al letrero.   (86–87)

[And what about you, you get lost; for no reason you disappear. You
just say a well-intentioned goodbye: "Good luck, someday we'll see
each other again." A paint stain on the mirror, an imprint of my lips,
a "good luck" sharper than a kitchen knife. And I see myself between
the red letters, spying on myself or perhaps your eyes are behind the
mirror, stuck to the sign.   (95)]

Caperucita and Al tend to be so similar that they often see themselves in each other, as in a mirror. At times, even at a distance,
they mirror each other to such an extent that they seem to fuse
into one:

Tu gran enemigo eres tú y yo. La mujer más grande de tus interio-
ridades debo ser yo. La mujer trascendental de mi cuarto soy yo y el
hombre del espejo sos vos. Reina rodeada de fotografías me siento
cuando estoy a solas en compañía de la imagen del espejo. (35) [...]
O será que Hormiga se parece a las imágenes en el aire, sensación de
inexistencia, de algo vago; yo sé que así como te veo así soy yo; como
te miro soy; cuando te derrites, cuando me hablás con voces saliendo
desde adentro de un cajón de frutas, esa es mi voz; *la manera de verte
es mi forma de ser.* La luz que miran mis ojos para otros es sombra,
siempre te da por estar frente a un espejo, al otro lado de mi conciencia
viendo resplandores.   (143, emphasis mine)

[Your big enemy is you and me. The greatest woman inside you should
be me. The transcendent woman of my room is me and the man of the
mirror is you. I feel like a queen surrounded by photographs when I'm
alone in the company of the image in the mirror ... (31) Or could it
be that Ant is like the images in the air, the sensation of nonexistence,
of something vague; I know that the way I see you, that's the way I
am; I see you the way I am; when you melt, when you speak to me
with voices that come from inside a box of fruit, that's my voice; my
way of seeing you is my way of being. The light of my eyes for others
is shadow, you're always in front of the mirror, on the other side of my
conscience, seeing flashes.   (168)]

Al is aware that the way in which he perceives her is a reflection of his own self, thus underlining the contextual and positional tinges that color both an observer's perceptions of other people and notions of "reality" in general. This play of mirrors and refracted reflections is also captured by the aesthetics of the narrative in many ways. Hormiga's thoughts about Al, her connection to him in her reveries, are expressed by her as a parallel life in which his actions mirror hers and at times overlap through dreams. The vertiginous experience of parallel reflections and disorienting repetitions is a frequent rhetorical strategy in the novel. Immediately after describing a scene in which Al gets up from bed with Hormiga to go to the bathroom, he stumbles upon her dogs (they turn out to be imaginary) and he throws them out of the fourth floor window one by one. The next scene is a similar story about a dog in a rich neighborhood home, an imported Saint Bernard from the United States, who is wounded by a worker from the national telecom company, Antel. This type of repetition, with difference, creates the effect of a hall of mirrors in which each scene has a recognizable kernel that rings familiar, but the individual scenes themselves turn out to be quite distinct. The narrative then simulates a hall of fragmented mirrors or a refracted ray of light, through which the storyline is deflected from a linear, straight path. The etymological root of the verb "to refract" is the Latin word *refractus, refringere* meaning to break open, break up, refract. This is precisely what occurs in Argueta's novel; the representation of events is put forth in a way that breaks open a multiplicity of parallel possibilities.

When Al is gearing up to leave Caperucita, he actually compares her behavior to a refracted mirror: "Tu comportamiento es un espejo refractario: todo lo descomponés, todo lo arreglás en favor de nuestra compañía, para después decir cosas que no entendemos; para amenazarnos con dejarnos o de las maldades expresadas con buenas intenciones" (31) ["Your behavior is a refractory mirror: you take everything apart, you arrange everything to improve our relationship, only to say later things that we don't understand; to threaten us with breaking up or the evil things expressed with good intentions" (26–27)]. This phrase could also be read as a metatextual reference to Argueta's narrative style in the novel, creating distortions and including scenes that are difficult to understand in an effort to bridge the distance between Al and Hormiga during their time apart from each other. Shortly after this episode, Caperucita writes letters to Al when he has recently gone "underground," letters to which he will never be able to respond. He does write her "letters," however, in his mind.

In one of them he apologizes for the fragmentary nature of his/their writing: "Perdonémonos por escribir así tan fragmentado [...]" (36) ["Let's forgive ourselves for writing in this fragmented manner ..." (32)]. Again, this can be read as a metatextual, self-conscious reference to the difficult rhetorical style of the novel that brings to the fore the central question driving my analysis of *Caperucita:* why would Argueta choose to structure a novel about the resistance movement in such a fragmented way?.

Perhaps the reason is twofold. Haunted by the recent assassination of Roque Dalton in 1975, Argueta's novel is replete with allusions to the poet's works. As stated previously, the central character, Alfonso, mirrors Dalton's own predicament toward the end of his life. The danger for both of them stemmed from their resistance to merging seamlessly into one monological, homogeneous notion of what it meant to be in the guerrilla groups to which they belonged. Likewise, the text itself also refuses to come together in a pat version of events that smoothes out contradictions and inconsistencies.

One of the results of this refusal in the novel is that the portrayal of Al's death is so confusing that the possibility of him having survived a shot to the head by his colleagues is left open. Several pages after the episode in which he is shot, Argueta includes a scene in which Al is back in the city and he has the recollection of having been shot in the head: "Fue mi primer día distinto en la ciudad, recién venido, recordando vagamente de cuando estuve perdido en la selva y me dieron un balazo en la cabeza, que de milagro estoy vivo. Además, yo era el poeta más importante de mi país y los poetas nunca mueren" (165) ["It was my first different day in the city, newly arrived, remembering vaguely the time I was lost in the jungle and got shot in the head, it's a miracle I'm alive. Besides, I was my country's most important poet and poets never die" (194)]. Since he had been in another situation in which he was in the countryside, on a mission to get food for the resistance troops, where he was being persecuted by security forces and was in danger of being shot, it is not completely clear which episode he is able to escape from when he returns to the city in the citation above. Moreover, he is aware that as an influential poet, much like Dalton, he will never die as long as his ideas circulate and his work is read by others.

The distinct possibility of the poet's unlikely survival seems to be more than metaphorical in the novel as scattered, vague references are made to a longer life for Al. References that appear before the episode in which he is shot, condition the reader to question the finality of his wounds. When he is about to leave Caperucita, he alludes to a specific time frame in which they will find each other again: "Desde lejos te voy a decir adiós y será la última vez que nos veremos hasta encontrarnos treinta años después, ya perecederos y diferentes, pero siempre amantes" (31) ["From afar I will say goodbye to you and it will be the last time we'll see each other until we meet thirty years later, by then dying and different, but always lovers" (27)]. And yet, this specificity may only refer to his desires and not to the actual events that are to take place. Similarly, shortly before the episode in which he is shot there is another very ambiguous reference to someone's death, a description that could be read as Al's own future passing:

Sólo será por unos meses, Genoveva. Vos serás fiel mientras yo viva. Ella que sí. Se me hace un nudo en la garganta. De mesón en mesón, de bus en bus; en la calle te pegan un balazo y punto. Sale tu foto en el periódico, un muerto más, adiós poemas queridos, vida cotidiana. Los muertos en las páginas de los periódicos, un cementerio tipográfico. (116)

[It'll only be for a few months, Genoveva. You'll be faithful as long as I'm alive. You bet she will. A knot forms in my throat. From boardinghouse to boardinghouse, from bus to bus; in the street they put a bullet in you and it's all over. Your photo appears in the newspaper, another dead person, goodbye dear poems, day-to-day life. The dead on the pages of newspapers, a typographic cemetery. (134)]

The vagueness of the use of tú in this segment leaves open the possibility that the poet does in fact survive. Perhaps the use of the second person singular is a self-reflective tú pondering the way in which he might die in the future; maybe it is Caperucita's voice as narrator speculating about his passing, or perhaps the narrator is signaling that this is what actually occurs. The disorienting ambiguity and lack of chronological order allows for a window of hope for the reader to imagine his survival beyond the devastating shot to the head perpetrated by his friends.

IN SEARCH OF COMMUNITY

Another reason for the author to select a fragmented narrative style is that the lack of chronological order allows him to end on a hopeful note of continued brotherhood. In fact, the very last sentence of the novel highlights the group's ongoing missions in the future as well as the enduring memory of Al's "brothers" in the resistance movement: "Esta segunda misión que nos llevaría a otra y otra, recordándolos a todos, mis compañeros, mis hermanos" (202, emphasis mine) ["This second mission, which would lead to another and another, remembering everyone, my *compañeros*, my brothers" (237)]. Despite portraying the serious rift among the group of young dissenters in the novel, *Caperucita* maintains a hopeful tone and a desire for a continued search for community.

The French theorist, Jean-Luc Nancy, provides a particularly useful discussion about the concept of community for reading Argueta's novel. In *The Inoperative Community* (1991), Nancy theorizes the idea of "community" against the notion of people fusing together into a homogeneous essence—a dynamic he associates with fascism. Through his fictional rendering of El Salvador's resistance movement, Argueta also negotiates the fine line between his characters' commitment to a cohesive political cause and the possibility of maintaining difference and thoughtful creativity within it.

Beyond his turn against the potential homogenizing and totalitarian implications of the concept (as a project of fusion), Nancy also writes against the notion of community as a project of production. Instead, he defines community in terms of endeavors of resistance against power. As such, he perceives community, in part, as sharing the recognition of the finitude that defines singular beings—a thoughtful being-in-common without collapsing into an essentializing erasure of difference. For Nancy, the movement toward community is therefore not one of completion, but rather of "interruption, fragmentation, suspension," that exposes such singularities (31).

The ability to highlight singularities and resist collective essentialization within the parameters of political activism would certainly be an appealing goal for Argueta. To wit, in *Caperucita* he searches for a way to reconcile continued participation in a collective movement with his critique of pressures from inside a group to blend into the ideological orthodoxy for the sake of cohesion. Argueta argues for a community that allows for differences, by interrupting the seamless coherence of his own narrative tale. In accordance with Nancy's argument for interruption, fragmentation, and suspension serving to expose the singular within a community of resistance against immanent power, *Caperucita*'s very structure forces the reader to become aware of the implications of difficult, refracted language beyond the novel's basic storyline.

In this sense, Nancy makes the case that literature can have the important political function of resisting "completion" and essential totalities by constantly interrupting totalizing discourses and mythologies through the testing of limits and exposure of particularity:

> "Literary communism" indicates at least the following: that community, in its infinite resistance to everything that would bring it to

completion (in every sense of the word *achever*—which can also mean
"finish off"), signifies an irrepressible political exigency, and that this
exigency in its turn demands something of "literature," the inscription
of our infinite resistance.

(Nancy 81)

Ostensibly, the political exigency of community would then also
involve an articulation of differences along with a common awareness of singular limits. Through this demarcation and articulation of
particularities, the political nature of community would be precisely
in the resistance to a power that would try to absorb differences and
singular beings into a completed, homogenous essence.

While addressing the need to permit self-reflection and critical
thought, Argueta's text stays away from a cynical dismissal of the
effectiveness of popular resistance organizations. On the contrary,
the novel is very much about finding ways to reestablish alternative
communities at a time in which the socioeconomic conditions have
strained social and even family links to the limit. If the text would
have ended with Al's assassination, this endeavor would have surely
been severely undermined. How, then, does one get past the murder
of Al—and Roque Dalton—to continue a fight toward a new, more
inclusive community?

This central concern resurges in other texts subsequently written
by Argueta, such as in his fourth novel, *Cuzcatlán, donde bate la mar
del sur*, published in 1986. The unrelenting faith in brotherhood
(*compañerismo*) as a valued goal for the author, even in the midst
of engaging in a broad social critique, has been noted by Astvaldur
Astvaldsson in his article "Toward a New Humanism: Narrative
Voice, Narrative Structure and Narrative Strategy in Manlio Argueta's
Cuzcatlán, donde bate la mar del sur":

> [...] the book does not just criticize the Right, the oligarchy and their
> imperialist backers but also, albeit more latently, the often brutal meth-
> ods used by the guerrilla fighters in dealing both with the enemy and
> with their own people during the civil war. Yet it does not condemn the
> movement. On the contrary, [...] it suggests that, given the right influ-
> ence, its members will be able to understand that there is a different
> way, informed by the profound history of the people, that can create
> 'un compañerismo eterno.' (613)

Much like in *Caperucita*, even though Argueta denounces the
excesses and misguided methodologies of some who take up arms
with the Left, he does not turn away from endorsing the resistance

movement as a whole. He is able to maintain an optimistic outlook and a desire for the enduring links of an "eternal brotherhood" by insisting upon a space from which to critique the oppressive aspects of society, both outside and within the resistance.[13]

Many of the family links represented in *Caperucita* are strained to the point of destruction due to the severe economic inequities of the country. Al's father is killed, shot in the head from behind, for encouraging people to loot the houses of the rich families who were hoarding all of the corn in the town during a time of severe shortages:

> Meses antes había desaparecido el maíz de la ciudad, pero se sabía que estaba en los graneros de los árabes y otros ricos del pueblo. Papá era ese hombre subido sobre la caja de madera, llamando a asaltar las casas [...] Murieron más de cien personas sólo ese día. Ladrones dijeron, pero todos habían sido honrados hasta que se les ocurrió asaltar las casas. Lo que hace el hambre. (33)

> [Months earlier, the corn had disappeared from town, but it was known that it was in the granaries of the Arabs and the town's other rich people. Papa was the man standing on the wooden crate stirring up the crowd, calling for the looting of their houses ... More than a hundred people died just that day alone. Thieves, they said, but all of them had been honest until they got the idea of attacking homes. What hunger does to people. (29)]

Much later, Alfonso's potential family with Genoveva and their baby girl would be torn apart as well by his desire to continue his father's fight against his country's uneven distribution of wealth by going "underground" and joining the guerrilla.

While Al's father died trying to even out some of the inequalities at the most basic, subsistence level, Guillermo, Manuel's brother, is motivated to collaborate with the security forces to spy on Manuel and his friends as a result of his resentment against the opportunities his brother and other better-off students have had in their access to an education. Envisioning himself to be a poet, Guillermo is forced to make a living as a baker and he thinks that his brother, paradoxically, looks down on him and his proletarian lifestyle even though Manuel is a leader among student organizers. Ironically, Guillermo's eventual resentment and self-loathing for collaborating with the police lead him to alcohol abuse and to his subsequent separation from his wife and children. The police's promises to give him access to an education and to a better future for his children are thwarted by his feelings of guilt for betraying his brother and by his own self-destructive tendencies. The personal sibling tensions that the security forces are able to manipulate in their favor arise precisely from the bitterness created by an unequal access to schools and resources—a resentment that in a given moment proved to be stronger than family ties.

In a prayer that is an allusion to the Hail Mary, the figure of the universal mother is used to demonstrate the strain that poverty and a hostile system puts on women and their families. Following is a fragment of the "prayer for all," *oración por todos:*

Mamá querida. Oración por todos. Mamá llena eres de gracia. Vendedora de los mercados. Mamá comprando botellas de puerta en puerta. Mamá puta. Mamá que corre por las calles con los policías detrás. Mamá, ¿cómo estás? Mamá como todas las cosas cuando son del alma. Mamá buscadora de tesoros en los cajones de basura. Mamá viajando en tren con grandes canastos de frutas maduras. [...] Mamá cortadora de café. [...] Mamá enferma. Mamá Virgen María madre de Dios. [...] Mamá por esas calles oscuras [...] Mamá de la Unión de Pobladores de Tugurios. Mamá descalza. Mamá lista para salir corriendo por siay balazos. Mamá vergona. Cortadora de algodón bajo el sol agrario de la costa. ¿En dónde estás? [...] Mamá suplicadora para que suelten a mi hijo, él no ha hecho nada, cállese vieja puta. [...] Mamá buscando entre los muertos. [...] Mamá devuelvan el cadáver de mi hijo. Mamá hombre, abuela, abuelo, mamá mamá. Tu madre. (65–66)

[Dear Mamma. A prayer for all. Mamma, full of Grace. Vender in the markets. Mamma buying bottles from door to door. Mamma whore. Mamma who runs through the streets pursued by the police. Mamma, how are you? Mamma like all things when they are from the heart. Mamma searcher of treasures in garbage cans. Mamma traveling by train with large baskets of ripe fruit ... Mamma, coffee picker ... Sick Mamma. Mamma Virgin Mary mother of God ... Mamma through those dark streets ... Mamma of the Union of Slum Settlers. Barefoot Mamma. Mamma ready to take off running if there is gunfire. Tough Mamma. Cotton picker beneath the agrarian sun of the coast. Where are you? ... Mamma, pleader so that they will release my son, he has not done anything, shut up you old whore ... Mamma searching among the dead ... Mamma return the body of my son. Mamma man, grandmother, grandfather, mamma mamma. Your mother. (68)]

The mother of those marginalized by poverty and injustice, forced to subsist by selling bottles door to door, picking cotton and coffee in the fields, delving into the trash of others, is also given the grim task of questioning the violent state for her missing children. She is forced to be absent from home and family when she is pulled out to the streets, the markets, and the fields to make a living—*¿En dónde estás?* [Where are you?]—while she is also unfailingly present at the morgue and the security stations when her children are torn away from her by the authoritarian state.[14]

Much like the fairy tale from which it takes its name, the "Little Red Riding Hood," the novel traces the hostility and un-home-like forces that take over familiar places—places that become as dangerous as Little Red Riding Hood's grandmother's house taken over by the duplicitous wolf. Even the alternative, surrogate "family," which Al and his student friends form early on, becomes fatally hostile toward him in the end. In their late teens and early twenties, Al, Manuel, and a group of other young men move in with Manuel's wife, Margó, and their two children in order to operate a small printing press generating "subversive" literature from their home. Their life together in the house at the *colonia El Bosque* is portrayed in a humorous, bohemian fashion. Their playful and irreverent camaraderie is interspersed with everyday chores and responsibilities and the occasional birthday celebration or illness of one of the children. Margó falls into the traditional role of providing food and maintaining order in a house full of young men.

However, once the security forces discover their hideout, thanks to the information provided by Manuel's brother, those who are in the house at the time it is raided are taken prisoners to be interrogated and are never to be heard from again. In his thoughts, Al, as narrator, bids farewell to his fallen brothers, Pichón and Feliciano, with a final appeal to their enduring struggle and brotherhood:

Adiós pueta Pichón, adiós Feliciano impresor, bebedores de atol shuco al final de la avenida Independencia. Amigos de las putas y de los bolitos madrugadores. Para siempre callados, para siempre dormidos. Y mirándonos siempre como miran los muertos. Los que nunca existieron, los invisibles. Un solo golpe al caite, los soldaditos campesinos sin tierra. Con un ojo en la mira del fusil y otro en el corazón del hijo ajeno. *Mis compañeros, mis hermanos.*   (83, emphasis mine)

[Goodbye poet Pichón, goodbye Feliciano printer, drinkers of dark *atole* at the end of Independence Avenue. Friends of the whores and of the early rising drunks. Forever silent, forever asleep. And looking at us always the way the dead do. Those who never existed, the invisible ones. One step forward, march, the small, landless, peasant soldiers. With one eye on their rifle sight and the other on the heart of someone else's son. My *compañeros,* my brothers.   (89–90)]

Manuel and Alfonso manage to escape and decide to take their opposition activities to another level. They both then go into the countryside and train to become active in the armed struggle. With much at stake, the intensity of their strategic divisions dissolves the previous light-hearted camaraderie that had defined their surrogate family nucleus. As noted above, Al ultimately pays for venturing a critical opinion in the midst of this intensity with his own incarceration and a shot to the head.

Even though the small surrogate family of student friends collapses in the end, as a result of severe external and internal pressures, Argueta insists on including instances of collaboration among people in extreme need in the text, as examples of selfless acts that signal the perseverance of community. Early on, the narrator, as Al, stresses the importance of connecting with others, of being aware of their existence as the very definition of being alive; as he puts it: "Sabemos que vivir significa tener conciencia de la existencia de otros" (35) ["We know that to live is to be conscious of the existence of others" (31)]. Correspondingly, at least twice in the novel, complete strangers are willing to risk their personal safety to help young student dissenters in their efforts of resistance against a system that is exclusive and unjust.

In an episode that mirrors actual events from 1975, Argueta describes a student protest in San Salvador from the perspective of Caperucita as a participant.[15] The government armed forces stage an attack against the multitude of demonstrators. In an attempt to escape their bullets, Caperucita and a small group of students decide to jump off a bridge. Drawing directly from the headlines of the time, Argueta further imagines the interaction between the students who narrowly escape and the dwellers of the marginal neighborhoods that border the capital city by following a group of eight students into the shantytowns where they are taken in by the *marginales* and treated with much empathy and kindness:

Nos vamos por el Tutunichapa hacia las *zonas marginales*. O sea que nos escapamos por debajo del puente; otros corrieron también, renqueando, pero vivitos y coleando. Los pobladores *marginales* nos recibieron con baldadas de agua y luego nos prestaron unos trapos sucios para que nos secáramos; y las señoras llorando: ellas no por los gases, sino porque no se les ocurre otra cosa que llorar ¡las pobres! y que entráramos [...] Un grupo de pobladores nos guiaba por veredas, detrás del Externado de San José. Nosotros: si no era peligroso que nos vean juntos, es decir, por ustedes. Y ellos: ¡vale verga! (con perdón señorita). Antes nos tenían en un cuarto y nos dieron un cafecito, éramos ocho estudiantes [...] La gente: que fuéramos saliendo en parejas, primero las mujeres. Yo iba adelante, una viejita de pelo cano dijo que nos iba a guiar. Otras gentes del barrio *marginal* llorando, hasta que salimos al Metrocentro. La ropa ya seca, del agua que nos habían tirado *los marginales* para neutralizar los gases y contra el calor y las lágrimas. (127–28, emphasis mine)

[We go through Tutunichapa towards the marginal areas. I mean that we escaped from under the bridge; others ran too, limping, but alive and moving. The marginal settlers received us with buckets of water and then gave us some dirty rags so we could dry ourselves off; and the women were crying: not because of the gas, but because they couldn't think of anything else to do but cry—the poor things!—and they told us to come in ... A group of settlers leads us along paths, behind the San José Day Academy. We: Wouldn't it be dangerous for them to see us together, I mean, for you guys. And they: What the fuck! Excuse me, miss. Before that they invited us in and served us coffee, there were eight of us students ... the people: that we should leave in pairs, the women first. I went in front, an old woman with gray hair told us she would lead us. Other people from the poor barrio cried, until we reached the Metro Center shopping mall. Our clothing—wet from the water they had thrown on us to neutralize the gas and to fight the heat and our tears ... (148)]

The repetition of the word "marginal" is contrasted by the hospitality with which the students are taken in, and safely guided out of their neighborhood. The people from the poorest, most marginalized areas cry empathic tears for the students who are violently attacked by the state security forces. This episode, inspired by actual events, and extending into the homes of the people from the most destitute barrios, exemplifies the endurance of community in the midst of destitution and violence.

Another brief, but important act of solidarity among strangers takes place when Al is on the train, when he has just left Caperucita, and is about to leave El Salvador. The humble man sitting next to him warns Al that there are security guards on the platform: "Despierta el menesteroso de su sueño con la ventana, me dice: 'Tenga cuidado con los guardias que van sobre la plataforma.' Y me pregunto qué quiere decirme si él no sabe nada de mí. Me responde que todo se nota en mis ojos" (199) ["The indigent awakes from his sleep by the window, he says to me: 'Watch out for the guards on the platform.' And I wonder what he's trying to say to me if he doesn't even know me. He replies that he can see everything in my eyes" (233)]. Without knowing anything about him, the stranger can see in Al's eyes that he is in danger and decides to reach out to him with a protective warning. Thus Argueta maintains a hopeful attitude toward human solidarity and the possibility of connecting with others while, at the same time, advocating the need to allow for difference and critical thought.

In this way, Argueta's *Caperucita* explores an alternative that anticipates Jean-Luc Nancy's concerns for a community that resists absorption into a homogeneous whole. *Caperucita* does not point to a utopian future into which differences disappear, but rather reminds us of the need for constant critical thought and the articulation of different perspectives to resist the dangers of totalizing powers—even within the resistance movement. The fragmentary narrative style of the novel and the constant repetitions, with difference, interrupt our notions (and perhaps desires) for a coherent totality. Nevertheless, the effect of the novel's fragmentary style is hopeful, as it points to the perseverance of community in the awareness of the needs of others and to people's willingness to reach out on each other's behalf. Maintaining his belief in the importance of the resistance movement, Argueta's fragmented narrative, therefore, resists a cohesive ideology and allows for simultaneous and contradictory voices to coexist while still highlighting the importance of sociopolitical solidarity.

FRAGMENTATION AND ALIENATION

La ojeada no estuvo mal, el país progresa,
todos progresamos y la fábula del progreso
tiene un triste final: el de la ausencia siniestra.[16]

(*Carmen Naranjo*, Diario 142)

Se trata de romper lo prosaico con
las mismas armas de lo prosaico.[17]

(*Carmen Naranjo*, Diario 260)

In contrast to Argueta's novel, Costa Rican author and diplomat Carmen Naranjo uses a fragmentary narrative style in *Diario de una multitud* (1974) to create a completely different effect. Fragmentation, in this case, foregrounds the alienation and lack of communication between inhabitants of a city modeled after San José in the 1960s.[18] The novel's form calls attention to the "sinister absence" (*la ausencia siniestra*) that is produced by the fable of progress mentioned in the epigraph above. In part, by denying the reader any in-depth knowledge of its characters, this absence becomes apparent from the start. Rather than present a group of recognizable characters, Naranjo includes snippets of conversations between a multitude of nameless people. Spanning a compressed timeframe of one day, the text captures pieces of conversations and traces of internal monologue reflections of people throughout the city.

The novel is divided into three parts entitled: "Hilos," "Claves," and "Tejidos" ("Strings," "Keys," and "Textiles"). The longest section is the first one, "Hilos," which encompasses over two hundred and twenty pages. "Hilos" captures fragments or loose *strings* of conversations between various unidentified people who represent recognizable types: the corrupt politician, the lecherous old man, the sly businessman, the deadbeat father, the shrewd vendor at the market, the bored adulterer, the vapid housewife, the stingy bourgeois *señora* of the house, et cetera. Many dialogues take place over the telephone, and include quarrels between lovers, gossip among friends, and such everyday interactions. The second part, "Claves," includes short reflections that can be read as metatextual explanations of the effects she is trying to achieve through her fragmentary rhetoric. With a long string of paragraphs, many of which start with the phrases "it's about" or "it's not about" (*se trata de* or *no se trata de*), the author grounds the seemingly random snippets of interactions of the first part into a larger project, with statements such as the following, meant to provide keys to reading the novel:

> Se trata de penetrar las sendas rutinarias con el deseo de una vía subterránea por donde los trenes de la normalidad choquen y los descarrilamientos muestren otras voces, otros gestos, otros rostros. (231) [...] No se trata de señalar héroes y antihéroes, las clasificaciones se pierden cuando el hombre digestivo digiere con humildad la luminosa ceguera de sus días. (242) [...] Se trata de romper lo prosaico con las mismas armas de lo prosaico.   (260)

> [It is about penetrating the routine paths with a desire for a subterranean way through which the trains of normalcy would collide and their derailments would demonstrate other voices, other gestures, other faces ... It is not about pointing out heroes and antiheroes, classifications become lost when the digestive man digests with humility the luminous blindness of his days ... It is about breaking the prosaic with the same weapons of the prosaic.]

Naranjo's novel thus uses the prosaic aspects of everyday life to interrupt its normalcy and reflect upon the implications of the moment without resorting to a story of heroes or empty classifications, or even the expectation of capturing a totalizing sense of "truth." On the contrary, multiple voices coexist in the text without coming together into a cohesive narrative or a pat version of events. The third, and final, part—"Tejidos"—is the only section woven together with a linear plot. It is organized around a student demonstration that gets out of control and results in the chaotic looting and burning of commercial establishments in the center of the city.

Among the major themes that are repeated in the first section is the rapid pace of life, the lack of time, the sense of speed. Often characters express their desire to talk to each other, but it is impossible due to a lack of time:

> [...] Le hablo y me gusta hablar./— A mí también, lamentablemente no siempre tengo tiempo./— El tiempo vendido, la tragedia, no se puede hacer lo que uno quiere (16). [...] Bien, gracias, mire usted, voy a la carrera [...] Sí, corriendo, ya me ve siempre corriendo, no es para menos, hoy estamos de inventario [...] Me interesa mucho, mucho, de verdad, pero voy de carrera, comprende usted, de carrera, tengo una cita, muy importante para mí, he estado sin empleo por más de dos meses, si no agarro este no sé qué me irá a pasar.   (138)

> [... I speak to you and I like to talk./—I do too; unfortunately, I don't always have time./—Time is money, a tragedy, one can't do what one wants ... Well, thanks, look, I'm in a hurry ... Yes, running, you always see me running, it's no wonder, today we have to do the stocktaking ... I'm very interested, very, really, but I'm in a hurry, you understand, in a hurry, I have an appointment, very important for me, I've been jobless for more than two months, if I don't nab this one I don't know what will happen to me.]

Time and energy are taken away from meaningful personal interactions in the constant rush to be somewhere else. Often, priority is given to devoting time for making or spending money to the detriment of taking a moment to converse for the sole sake of engaging, and perhaps even connecting, with someone else.

The numbing effects of this dizzying hurry and the numerous interruptions that seem to come along with it are reflected in the aesthetics of the text—that is, in the interrupted conversations and abrupt changes of plotlines, rapidly shifting from one anonymous character to another. Hence the following *clave*, or key to reading the novel, that appears in the second section:

> No se trata de hacer parábolas ni baladas, la prisa inventó las interrupciones, ya no hay frases completas, todo queda interrumpido, como los

lectores que suspenden la lectura porque sonó el teléfono o sirvieron
la comida, como el que se queda buscando una palabra que no existía
porque no era palabra sino una cara, un gesto, un remolino de cosas
no entendidas. La prisa, la condenada prisa, que deja las bocas abier-
tas y suspende los ojos en el vacío, inmoviliza las manos y nos vuelve
automáticos. La prisa ... hasta los relojes no tienen tiempo para repicar
las horas. (238)

[It is not about making parables nor ballads, haste invented interruptions, there no longer are complete phrases, everything remains interrupted, like readers who suspend their reading because the phone has
rung or the food has been served, like someone who searches for a
word that didn't exist because it was not a word but a face, a gesture,
a whirlwind of things not understood. Haste, damned haste that leaves
open mouths and leaves eyes suspended in a vacuum, immobilizes
hands, and it makes us automatic. Haste ... even clocks don't have time
to chime the hours.]

The form of the novel (that is, incomplete, anonymous, nonlinear
fragments that can be read in no particular order) caters to the lifestyle of the urban reader who is likely to be subjected to the same
type of time constraints and interruptions that come along with the
pace of a modern city—including telephone calls and countless other
unexpected distractions.

Another frequent theme is the association of objects with
their monetary value and the widespread use of the vocabulary
of commercial transactions: "El mundo se ha hecho un enorme
supermercado" (Naranjo 127) ["The world has become an enormous supermarket"]. Superficiality, materialism, and consumerism
permeate the text. The superficial quality of many characters extends
to their two-faced interactions with each other. Many of them are
quite hypocritical when they act one way in front of acquaintances
and then relish in engaging in disparaging rumors behind their back.
Numerous characters, mainly women, spend endless time talking
about discounts, desirable merchandise, and going shopping. Many
of their dialogues revolve around bargaining for a product and trying to
get a good deal at the expense of someone else. Usually, someone
tries to take advantage of the gathering of people in public places to
try to sell a product, regardless of the reason that brings the crowd
together. For instance, in the final section, in the midst of the student
demonstration, there is a vendor trying to sell *empanadas*.

A particularly inappropriate instance in which the vocabulary of
commercial and financial transactions is used in an unusual context is

a conversation between two men where one is giving the other advice
to warn him against "easy" women:

> Una mujer que ha acumulado su castidad, en una especie de cuenta
> de ahorros, lo único que quiere es entregársela a alguien. Sin que
> le ruegue mucho, se le ponga adelante y le diga 'venga, ya llegó su
> hora.' Lo mismo se hace con los ahorros, llega un momento en que
> uno está loco por encontrar algo y gastarlos ... Mantenerla por toda
> la vida, ¿te imaginás lo que es eso? Por toda la vida. Darle todo, desde
> calzones hasta frijoles y arroz, y ella sentada esperando qué le tenés
> de nuevo y si no hay nada te regateará sonrisas, sentirá pereza y dolor de
> cabeza. (112)

[A woman who has garnered her chastity, in a sort of checking account,
all she wants is to give it to someone. Without too much begging,
without having to stand in front of her and say "come on, your time
has come." The same with one's savings, a time comes when one
becomes anxious to find something to spend them on ... To support
her for an entire life, can you imagine what that's like? The rest of your
life. To give her everything, from panties to rice and beans, and her
sitting around waiting to see what new things you've brought her and
if there is nothing she will bargain with smiles, and she will be too tired
and have a headache.]

Any notions of genuine intimacy are shattered when sexual interaction is perceived outright in terms of a commercial transaction, with
terms such as "savings accounts" and "bargaining" clouding over any
trace of sentimental romance or love. In this man's cynical view, the
loss of a woman's virginity and marriage itself are seen by women as
tactical moves to acquire products from men.

Again, Naranjo's strategy is to interrupt the prosaic with the prosaic.
By focusing on everyday interactions that reveal moments in which
priorities seem to be misplaced, she tries to jolt her readers away from
any similarity they might recognize in their own behavior.[19] Whereas
her characters seem to be stuck in the dystopian society portrayed by
Naranjo, it is up to her readers to identify and change the destructive
tendencies signaled by her fictional city. For Alicia Miranda Hevia,
the driving issue of the novel is a matter of identity: "El sentido
principal es el sentido de la identidad, la respuesta a la pregunta:
¿Qué somos? El texto ha sido escrito como intento de respuesta a
esta pregunta" (63) ["The principal meaning is the sense of identity,
the answer to the question: What are we? The text has been written
as an attempt to answer this question"]. However, more than

the question "what/who are we as Costa Ricans at this moment?" Naranjo is trying to provoke an answer to the more pressing and far reaching issue: who do we want to be, given the particular set of circumstances under which we live?

This issue comes up repeatedly in Naranjo's publications and is central to her approach as Costa Rica's minister of culture between 1974 and 1976.[20] During her time in tenure at the Ministry of Culture, Youth, and Sports, Naranjo tried to foster national cultural production by creating the National Theater Company, the Costa Rican Symphony, and the Costa Rican Film Institute. Yet she also explored the question of national identity by challenging her compatriots to face many of her country's social problems, such as deforestation, malnutrition, alcoholism, and poverty. For this, she received much hostile criticism. She was even accused of promoting subversion and was driven to resign from her post in 1976.[21] Nevertheless, during her time in office she emphasized the importance of cultural development alongside economic gains, and she focused on recognizing and stimulating the uniqueness of Costa Rica's cultural production. This becomes clear in Patricia Rubio's account of Naranjo's project as minister:

> The centerpiece of her plan is that cultural development is essential for and the key to economic growth and social improvement, with the understanding that such growth responds to the needs of the population at large, and not primarily to the interests of privileged groups ... At the heart of her thinking lies a concern with securing the cultural identity of the country, which she sees threatened by economic development, for the most part propelled by foreign interests ignorant or impervious to its internal consequences, and implemented by national interest groups.   (Rubio 196)

In a sense, one can read *Diario* as an effort to disrupt the threat to national cultural identity stemming from the homogenizing force of capitalist economic development and strong global—primarily U.S.—influences. By exposing the potential results of a deeply embedded bureaucracy and a market-driven, materialistic society—that is, mainly the passive acceptance of a mechanical routine and a self-centered indifference to the plight of others—the author makes a case for the importance of personal initiative in conjunction with empathy for those around us. At the same time, her project in the novel is to resist the complacent acceptance of foreign models and to pursue actively a unique cultural identity for Costa Rica. In this way, Naranjo's novel performs the function Jean-Luc Nancy attributes to literature.

Namely, the fragmentary text resists "completion" by the essential-izing forces of homogenizing powers—that is, the mind-numbing routine of operating within a bureaucracy, the selfishness implicit in a system driven by personal gain, the predominance of foreign products and tastes, et cetera.

In an interview with Tanya F. Fayen, Naranjo responds to Fayen's comment: "Para mí, sus experimentos narrativos en *Sobrepunto, Camino al mediodía* y *Diario de una multitud* responden a un deseo de crear o representar una conciencia colectiva. ¿Quiere comentar algo al respecto?" (149) ["For me, your narrative experiments in *Sobrepunto, Camino al mediodía* and *Diario de una multitud* respond to a desire to create and represent a collective consciousness. Would you like to say something about this?"]. The author's answer follows:

Mis experiencias en *Sobrepunto, Camino al mediodía* y *Diario de una multitud* aspiran a crear una conciencia colectiva que ayude a mejorar a mujeres y hombres, siempre envuelta dentro de una perspectiva en que en cierta forma la autora reflexiona sobre el poder de la creatividad y lo necesario que es eliminar la hipocresía. Esas obras y otras son valientes, directas, ambiciosas, hechas de una observación lúcida que pretende abrir otros caminos en este mundo tan material y egoísta.

(Naranjo cited in Fayen 149)

[My experiences with *Sobrepunto, Camino al mediodía* and *Diario de una multitud* aspire to create a collective consciousness that can help improve women and men, always wrapped inside of a perspective in which the author reflects about the power of creativity and how nec-essary it is to eliminate hypocrisy. Those works and others are brave, direct, ambitious, made up of a lucid observation that wants to open other roads in this world, which is so material and selfish.]

Central to the entire project of *Diario* is the author's challenge to her readers to dare to be creative thinkers and to break out of their immediate, self-centered concerns. While the author tries to appeal to a "collective consciousness" or "collective awareness" in opposi-tion to social apathy, at the same time, Naranjo insists on the need to promote *difference*, to be creative and to resist passive acceptance of received ideas. In "Claves," the author highlights this concern when she writes: "Si tuviera que hacer diez preguntas básicas para obtener toda la sabiduría del mundo, sólo haría una: ¿Es posible ser diferente?" (253)[22] ["If I had to pose ten basic questions to obtain all of the knowledge of the world, I would pose only one: Is it possible to be different?"].

One of the most profound criticisms that the author puts forth in the representation of her fictional city is an overall sense of inertia and complacency. Lazy defaulting to mediocrity and routine keeps people from daring to be different or challenging the comfort of fixed ideas:

> No se encuentra aquí un solo hombre auténtico, real, que crea en su misión, es más que aún la tenga. Un hombre comprometido con la verdad, su propia verdad, con un destino hecho por él mismo. Todos, absolutamente todos están dentro del sistema [...] Un sistema que analizado no es nada, un movimiento inerte que se mueve porque mañana es otro día y hay que levantarse temprano para andar por ahí medio dormido, con palabras y gestos muertos, pero con traje muy presentable [...] Un sistema cuya única habilidad es la defensa a como haya lugar [...] La defensa del status quo, que nada cambie [...] (173–74)

> [You can't find one single authentic, real man here, who believes in his mission, or who even has one. A man committed to the truth, his own truth, with a destiny he has forged by himself. Everyone, absolutely everyone is inside the system ... A system, which once analyzed is nothing, an inert movement that moves because tomorrow is another day and you have to get up early to go around half asleep, with dead words and gestures, but with a very presentable suit ... A system that only has the ability to defend itself by any means necessary ... the defense of the status quo, so that nothing changes ...]

This lack of personal initiative and uncritical complacency within an automatizing system is then ironically set against the image of Costa Rica that is generally promoted both within the country and abroad. In several sections, and from many different perspectives, Naranjo insists that attaining relative economic prosperity and having a sense of exemplary "democracy," "freedom," and "peace"—clear markers of Costa Rican self-identity with respect to its neighbors—does not mean that one should be complacent and self-satisfied:

> Estamos progresando, en términos asombrosos y en beneficios palpables para la mayoría. El ingreso per cápita nos ha puesto sobre muchos países [...] En todo caso, un buen panorama, horizontes de amplitud, desarrollo, incremento, actividad, creatividad industrial y comercial, confianza del capital extranjero, participación del capital nacional, democracia, libertad, paz. [...] *Pero los alcances logrados nos obligan a superarnos, siempre dentro del ambiente tradicional del país.* (204–5, emphasis mine)

[We are progressing, in astonishing terms and with palpable benefits for the majority. Our income per capita has placed us above many countries ... In any case, a good outlook, ample horizons, development, increase, activity, industrial and commercial creativity, foreign capital confidence, national capital participation, democracy, liberty, peace ... But the accomplishments attained force us to better ourselves, always within the traditional atmosphere of the country.]

Similarly, through the words of a foreign tourist in *Diario*, Naranjo questions what one does with "liberty" when one is fortunate enough to live in a society in which it is actually viable. The tourist mentions the positive attributes he had heard about Costa Rica that motivated his trip: "[...] había oído cosas maravillosas: la paz, el respeto al ser humano, la libertad, la belleza de los paisajes, la hospitalidad de la gente, la seguridad, la naturaleza verde y tropical, la elegancia de las mujeres" (85) ["... I had heard wonderful things: about peace, the respect for humanity, liberty, the beauty of the scenery, the hospitality of the people, the safety, the green and tropical natural surroundings, the elegance of the women"]. He then wonders why during his visit he never heard anyone venture any controversial opinions given the liberty professed as the country's principal attribute, especially compared to the repressive silences imposed by the authoritarian military regimes of its neighbors:

Comprendo que en algunas oportunidades se presentarán situaciones que exijan la exposición de opiniones crudas, profundamente controversiales, y el sostenimiento de puntos actualmente prohibidos en otras tierras. De seguro aquí se podrán exponer, sólo que a mí no me ha tocado verlo. (87)

[I understand that on occasion situations would arise that would demand the expression of crude opinions, profoundly controversial, and the exposition of points actually prohibited in other lands. Surely they can be expressed here, except that I haven't seen it.]

Through this character, the author challenges the self-satisfied notion that "liberty" is an end in itself. What one does with it, by daring to be creatively thoughtful and, at times, controversial, is ultimately what matters.

When read alongside *El Señor Presidente* and *Caperucita en la zona roja* it is interesting to note that in *Diario de una multitud* the author *does not* turn to the idealized figure of a nurturing woman as a palliative to the problems of society. On the contrary, Naranjo portrays the women in her novel as being very much a part of the problem. Whereas Asturias, in particular, offers the metaphor of the nurturing mother and the utopian countryside as an alternative to the repressive author-itarian city, and Argueta, to a lesser extent, includes the prayer to the "universal mother" confronting the ruthless and violent state and the character of Margó who cooks for the young student revolutionaries, Naranjo offers no such feminine solace from the evils she denounces. The contrast between idealized expectations of strong, yet nurturing women (from Asturias and Argueta) and a more raw and worldly female perspective, can be observed in an episode of *Diario* in which a prostitute is being interviewed by a female social worker. Dissolving any sentimental trappings associated with women's participation in society, the prostitute explains quite brutally that she is not only comfort-able with the line of work in which she has chosen to make a living, but that the true hypocrites are the bourgeois women who also use their bodies for profit under the pretense of propriety (123–24). By presenting women with many flaws alongside the men of her novel, Naranjo does not exempt them from her call to engage in more criti-cal thought and creative personal initiatives. While being very much a part of the problem, Naranjo charges her women readers with the responsibility of also being very much a part of the solution.

Another notable comparison between *El Señor Presidente*, *Caperu-cita*, and *Diario de una multitud* is found at the ending of Naranjo's novel. While Asturias's text ends with the prayer of the student's mother for all those who are oppressed by the authoritarian regime, and Argueta's novel ends with a call to continued "brotherhood" in the struggle against injustice, the final words of *Diario de una multitud* are: "Están asustando, no es con nosotros" (297) ["They are fright-ening people, it's not with us (meaning in effect, we are off the hook, it does not involve us)"]. Thus concludes the final section, "Tejidos," centered on a student protest that turns into complete chaos. The story line is about a group of students who organize an antigovernment pro-test to promote social awareness that brings together an accumulation of people in the center of the city for reasons quite separate from the ideological and political intentions of the organizers: most people converge to hear the musical bands that were hired to draw a crowd, some are vendors taking advantage of the gathering, some are petty thieves trying to capitalize on a prime pickpocketing scenario, others are simply curious bystanders.

"Tejidos" opens with a tone of ironic absurdity when instead of a sense of idealistic solidarity or political commitment there is a confrontation between the students and a man who has accidentally damaged one of their protest signs during his walk in the park to relieve his chronic flatulence. This dynamic of antagonistic absurdity increases into a *crescendo* as the congregation of people becomes restless in a sequence of miscommunications and acts of vandalism. People begin pushing each other and screaming, confusing the sounds of festive firecrackers with gunshots; as the chaos increases, rocks are thrown at store windows, and the looting begins. Amidst the fires and the anarchy, the movement of the crowd, significantly, is directed toward the central market as voices scream out: "No perdás tiempo, vamos hacia el mercado. Buena idea. Hagamos del mercado una fortaleza" (279) ["Don't waste time, let's go toward the market. Let's make the market a fortress"]. Metaphorically as well as literally, the masses gravitate toward the market, looting and setting fires to everything along the way. The confusion eventually dies out, and the official account of occurrences on television is that there was only a small disturbance in the center of the city that is now under control. In truth, the disorder simply collapses within itself, as everyone is out to acquire as much as they can and then run away from the breakout of violence in hopes of self-preservation.

When mention was made previously that a group of students was thinking of distributing political pamphlets to promote social awareness—before the demonstration ever takes place, in one of the fragments in "Hilos"—the reaction of a politician in power was not to turn the police against them. Instead, his cynical plan was to try to appeal to the students' personal interests by offering them fellowships and respected positions in order to diffuse their opposition: "A los de la hojita, conforme a la lista de nombres que tengo, becas, algunos puestecitos que están libres, nombramientos en comités, y la historia de siempre, por la boca muere el pez" (205) ["As far as those with the leaflets, according to the list of names that I have, scholarships, a couple of positions that are free, committee memberships and the same story as usual ..."]. When the student demonstration actually takes place, it degenerates into a frenzy of lawless consumption with the masses symbolically (and literally) pushing toward the central market. Again, personal greed takes over any efforts toward building social awareness.

In "Claves," Naranjo anticipates the collapse of the master narratives later theorized by postmodern critics: "¿Es ésta la mejor época para nacer y morir? Las grandes ideologías están muriendo, sobre el peso de millones de cadáveres que todavía abren sus ojos, sus espantados ojos ante una muerte sin sentido" (235) ["Is this the best age to be born and die? The great ideologies are dying, over the weight of millions of dead bodies that continue to open their eyes, their frightened eyes confronted with a meaningless death"]. The final episode of the novel provides a worst-case scenario of what the implications of this statement could be. With a lack of clear political commitment to a cause or any motivating factor beyond personal well-being, what takes over the absence of meaning weighing over the memory of those who have died before us? In a state of complete apathy and self-centered greed, not even the people who escaped with stolen goods are able to enjoy their booty. Couples are portrayed digging holes in their yards and houses to hide the items that they hoarded so that their neighbors do not disclose to the authorities that they are among the thieves. When the police are heard pursuing potential participants in the looting, the novel ends with the words cited previously: "Están asustando, no es con nosotros" (297). Complete apathy. "It's not with us." It has nothing to do with us. Why should we be concerned? *That* is the question.

   This ending contrasts quite dramatically with Manlio Argueta's call for brotherhood at the end of *Caperucita*. While Argueta attempts to salvage the possibility of community within the resistance in the face of Alfonso's betrayal by his revolutionary colleagues, Naranjo demonstrates the breakdown of community brought about by the extremes of complacency and lack of concern for others. However, both texts share important structural similarities. Both authors use fragmentary narrative styles from within the discourses that they are critiquing to interrupt their homogenizing tendencies. Naranjo resists the negative consequences of capitalism from within the system. She operates within the state apparatus as a diplomat and a minister. Her project is not a call to revolution and her perspective is not a Marxist one. However, she interrupts the numbing forces of a market economy that enable one to forget about those who are marginalized by the system, and insists on a critical and thoughtful participation in this system by all. Argueta also makes a case for critical thought within the homogenizing force of a revolutionary struggle. Maintaining his belief in the importance of the resistance movement, Argueta's fragmented narrative resists a cohesive ideology and allows for simultaneous and contradictory voices to coexist, while still highlighting the importance of sociopolitical solidarity.

PART III

THE NATION
THE NATION IN A GLOBAL ECONOMY

CHAPTER 5

TOTALIZING NARRATIVES WRITTEN FROM THE MARGIN: JULIO ESCOTO'S *REY DEL ALBOR, MADRUGADA*

> *El escritor Rafael Heliodoro Valle afirmó que la historia*
> *de Honduras podía ser escrita en una lágrima ...*[1]
>
> (*Julio Escoto* 11)

How can the main preoccupations of an era be captured through the perspective of a small, often marginalized country like Honduras? What does it mean when a totalizing version of history is composed from the disadvantaged periphery, rather than from an established power (which can often justify its entrenched authority through coherent narratives of the past, conveniently pointing to a "logical" explanation of a position of advantage through stories of cohesive totalities)? How does a totalizing narrative of history fit in a post-modern world that has declared the collapse of the master narratives of modernity? Does the position from which a totalizing voice is expressed—the margin or the center—make a difference in its overall effect? Can an author successfully resort to tongue-in-cheek warnings against outrageous conspiracy theories and ominous "master plans" of U.S. world domination (through calculated cultural homogenization) to make a case for national identity at a time of intense globalization and porous national borders? Honduran author Julio Escoto addresses all of these themes in his ambitious novel *Rey del Albor, Madrugada* (1993).

The primary plotline of Julio Escoto's text is set at a critical juncture for world history in general. The action of the majority of the novel takes place in 1989—when the world at large is riveted by the unfolding consequences of Soviet policies of *glasnost* and *perestroika*, the Berlin wall is about to come down, and all nations are becoming increasingly interconnected through economic, technological, and cultural channels. Setting his text at the cusp of such universal changes, the Honduran author explores the repercussions of this shifting global environment on Honduras, in particular, and Latin America as a whole, especially given the continued presence of U.S. Marines and the U.S.-supported Contras on Honduran soil, perpetuating the struggle of capitalism against the socialist regime in Nicaragua just when the binary world backdrop is about to change.

The main events of the novel are also framed by the upcoming five-hundred-year benchmark in 1992 of the arrival of the Spaniards in the hemisphere. This gives way to a rigorous exploration of the roots of Honduran national identity and all of its cultural components from the point of arrival of the Spaniards through the present horizon of the late 1980s. *Rey del Albor, Madrugada* is organized aesthetically to address both of these contextual forces—the fall of the Soviet Union and its ramifications in Central America and the quincentennial anniversary of the Spanish conquest—by dividing the text into two distinct, yet loosely interconnected, narrative lines: the present events of 1989, and a series of independent, short stories that date back in descending order from the 1970s to the late 1400s, marking significant instances in Honduras's past. The contemporary story is shaped in the form of a suspenseful detective or spy mystery novel, organized in episodic installments.[2] And, as the suspense of the main plot thickens, the reader's desire for answers to increasingly intricate questions is delayed by interspersing the shorter, historical subplots that are themselves triggered by related comments or thematic references in the main story.

The central question underlying our analysis of both plotlines as a whole is, again, why resort to a totalizing discourse when writing from the margins? In previous chapters we have found that totalizing perspectives often tend to be implemented when writing from a place of power—as in the case of Virgil's classical epic poetry, or in the case of official versions of history promulgated by military dictatorships and authoritarian regimes. When organizing a narrative about the past, stories that are told as if events fit logically into a linear, coherent—perhaps even inevitable—totality often tend to be voiced from a position of strength. As discussed in Chapter 1, even within the generic parameters of the classical epic poem, David Quint differentiates between the story of the victor, which recounts history as a linear teleological inevitability, and the story of the vanquished, which portrays history as a series of contingent factors that could have turned out differently. Why tell a tale of coherent continuity when speaking from a place of nonhegemonic disadvantage?

While not always voiced from a position of power, totalizing perspectives also serve the author who has faith in the cohesive logic of events progressing toward a redemptive goal within a set ideological framework (such as emancipating political movements or religious doctrines)—as in the case of Ernesto Cardenal's *El estrecho dudoso*. Conversely, fragmentary discourses tend to interrupt overly simplistic or fundamentalist, homogenizing perspectives. They often point to a discontinuity that can be disorienting, but can also break open the possibilities of action and representation.

And yet, with *Madrugada*, Escoto attempts to critique hegemonic and homogenizing foreign forces while composing a narrative of totality. His novel evokes the history of the entire hemisphere over the last five hundred years in a mystifying tale of interconnected intrigues and conspiracies centered on the experiences of Honduras. The past and present are portrayed as inextricably connected; all aspects of society are shown to be affected by top-down manipulations from abroad; and the shared experiences of a painful and complicated past hold the key to facing the future through a united national consciousness that is inclusive of all cultures that have come together on Honduran soil (with all ethnicities presumed to have wanted to endure the process of such unions).

In the midst of disorienting changes taking place on a global scale, Escoto resorts to the modern concept of "the nation" as the ground for imagined communities and a deep tradition of shared history to carve out a space from which to survive in a new world order and confront the overwhelming hegemonic influences of the United States. His novel captures universal anxieties about how the United States will handle its position as the sole "superpower" in a post–Cold War era and how to address recent technologies that bring North American cultural influences into the homes of the entire world. The author draws from local tradition, interethnic negotiations, and history to employ mechanisms that interrupt such forces and situate Honduras's distinguishable place at the dawn of a new era.

THE "TRUTH" BEHIND THE SCENES:
A DETECTIVE'S QUEST

¿Cuál sería una clave suprema,
la llave maestra que abriría todos los secretos?[3]

(*Julio Escoto* 405)

The plotline situated in the novel's present (1989) begins with a rally of the Honduran opposition (the *Comité por la paz* or "Committee for Peace") in which the leaders of the group acknowledge the existence of a "secret history" in Honduras of which most people are unaware—namely, the extent of their own government's involvement in the war against Nicaragua and the Sandinista regime.[4] The Committee threatens to disclose this information to create a public uproar and garner local and international support for their cause. In order to counteract their efforts, the president of Honduras resolves to hire a good public relations firm and a credible historian.

After the president consults with U.S. representatives, the Agency for International Development delegate Mahoney selects Quentin H. Jones for the job, a well-respected African American professor from the history department at Cornell University. Mahoney then informs the president that Honduras will be paying for the project through loans it will have to repay to the United States. In brief, the project consists of writing a comprehensive text about Honduran history that will dilute anti-U.S. sentiments and diffuse the shock effect of the information released by the opposition. The final product is scheduled to be presented in time for the quincentennial celebrations.[5]

From the start, it becomes clear that whoever manages the means of distribution of information most effectively is in control of what the general public will perceive to be the "truth"—an assertion that would seem to make a case for a relativistic perception of history. Yet another seemingly contradictory notion of history emerges as well early on in the text. This parallel notion that conceives of history in more absolutist terms supposes there is a veiled reality behind the scenes, a truth that can be discovered, or a hidden "master plan" that needs to be disclosed in the interest of the majority being deceived by the public spin of events.

This is where the "detective" element comes in. The historian-as-detective must discern what is actually happening behind the semblance of reality, identifying the series of past events that have shaped the context of the present situation. Both perceptions of history combine logically when situated within a paranoid environment in which it is believed that both local and foreign governments are secretly acting with agendas that do not benefit the average citizen—what initially seemed "relativistic" is only the superficial mask with which a set of events are strategically presented, and the underlying truth is still deemed to be a stable, coherent entity that needs to be discerned, despite the obfuscations set in place by the powers that be.

It is no wonder that such a theory of top-down conspiracies would arise given the past tribulations of the isthmus. But a particularly recent event would color the memories of the region with regard to its relations with the United States. By the late 1980s and early 1990s, when *Madrugada* was being composed, the unfathomable Iran-Contra scandal was unveiled to the world. The multiple conspiracy plots that Professor Quentin Jones is to unearth in the course of the novel thus take on an eerily recognizable, if outrageous, pattern within the context of the (then) recent disclosure of the Iran-Contra affair.[6] In this climate, the government as an institution becomes suspect. With the introduction of the short historical stories in Escoto's text, where instances of violent oppression and creative opposition tend to repeat themselves over and over again at different junctures in the nation's past, the broader notion of "empire" and its duplicitous leadership as the ultimate enemy surfaces as a central theme in *Madrugada*. The dynamic between strategies of domination and resistance throughout Honduran history becomes the moving force that pushes forward the plot of the novel and connects its disparate story lines.

Several events frame the set of questions that Professor Jones, and the reader alongside him, will need to uncover and resolve in order to approximate the underlying truth beneath the surface: from the outset, with the announcement at the rally of the Committee for Peace, questions begin to emerge about the country's deep involvement in the Contra war, indicating the existence of controversial government secrets that would likely scandalize the general public. Then, Professor Jones receives a phone call from the Honduran guerrillas by which they express an interest in revealing to him important information that would, at the very least, provide a counterhegemonic perspective regarding the country's history (and perhaps even reveal a shocking plan with which the United States intends to secure its hegemony in the new, post-Cold War world order). Additionally, the professor makes a discovery by accident when trying to set up his Internet account: he downloads classified information from the American Embassy computer network that reveals to him that there is much more to his project than he has been led to believe.

Professor Quentin H. Jones shares at least one of the key characteristics attributed to the detective hero figure, according to the conventional traits outlined by Larry N. Landrum, Pat Browne, and Ray B. Browne in the introduction of *Dimensions of Detective Fiction*—namely, the condition of being cast as an "outsider." In accordance with generic conventions:

> [...] the fictional detective's motivations, most of his acts and his conscious image of the world exist outside established authority, legal procedure and enforcement. He also lives on the fringes of crime, which area [sic] is usually pictured as a somewhat dirty mirror of the moral or legal authority structure or indeed a part of it. As the central dynamic image of the story, the detective understands and often experiences the distribution and ranges of power within both of these systems. As an outsider the detective avoids both assimilation and entrapment by them.   (Landrum, Browne, and Browne 4)

Whereas Professor Jones is very much an *insider* in a privileged world, in the sense that he is an academic employed at a prestigious university in the United States, he is also an *outsider* in many ways. As far as his project in Honduras, he proves to be an outsider in both obvious and more subtle senses. For one, the professor has never been to Honduras before he embarks on this project. While portrayed as politically progressive, he does not succumb to knee-jerk ideological reactions to the circumstances he encounters while doing his research. Instead, he employs a more rational approach to evaluating the information he receives, much like the empirical Sherlock Holmes figure of the late nineteenth and early twentieth centuries. He refuses to engage in and exclusive alliance with either side of the Honduran "establishment vs. opposition divide" and he is open to information that might reflect negatively on his own country's policies in the region in the interest of finding out the truth.

Nevertheless, he becomes extremely angry when he feels that he is being manipulated by any of the interested parties. When he meets with the leadership of the guerrillas, for instance, he does not take kindly to the practical joke played on him when one of the commanders pretends to have a thick Russian accent and greets him as his "comrade." He refuses to be a pawn in the machinations of a Soviet-backed resistance group, just as he avoids taking an uncritical pro-U.S. stance.[7] Like the conventional detective hero described above, in the interest of maintaining an objective analytical distance, Jones remains on the fringes and does not adhere to any of the delineated ideological camps. Moreover, beyond ideology, it is suggested that his ethnicity—he is an African American—makes him more sensitive to experiences of marginalization on a more subtle level, an attribute that becomes key as he discovers some of the underlying plans for cultural homogenization that will be revealed to him later on in the text.

In hopes of approximating a balanced perspective, Jones agrees to meet with members of the opposition and eventually with the entire leadership of the guerrillas. What is more, after they tell him of a series of secret documents in their possession—documents that disclose a Machiavellian plan that outlines the United States' masterful policies toward Honduras and all of Latin America in the long term—he agrees to help them circulate the information internationally:

[...] Lo haré [...] Acababa de firmar su adhesión a la autonomía de Honduras, al inevitable enfrentamiento con su propio gobierno y quizás a la maligna sonrisa de la muerte, con la que coquetearía durante un tiempo. En su repentina osadía no lo impulsaban razones políticas, las que en el fondo despreciaba. Tampoco la atracción del peligro, estaba dispuesto a cambiar cualquier aventura por una sala cómoda y tibia repleta de libros. Menos aún que en el subconsciente le brillara la luminosidad idealista de su vocación por el amor a la humanidad, antes era necesario saber a cuál parte de la humanidad beneficiaba. *Lo inducían sólo unos razonables motivos éticos por descubrir la verdad.* Nada que no fuera eso tenía la fuerza suficiente para obligarlo a mover un solo dedo.
(Escoto 343–44, emphasis mine)

[... I will do it ... He had just signed his support for the autonomy of Honduras, for the inevitable confrontation with his own government and perhaps an encounter with the evil smile of death, with which he would flirt for a while. It was not political reasons that drove his sudden audacity, as he held them in profound contempt. Nor was it an attraction to danger; he was willing to trade any adventure for a comfortable and cozy living room full of books. He was motivated even less by a purported idealist luminosity of his vocation or a love for humanity that might be shining in his subconscious; before it was necessary to know which part of humanity would benefit from it. He was led solely by the ethical and reasonable goal of discovering the truth. Nothing other than that had enough strength to force him to move even one finger.]

Jones reluctantly puts himself in dangerous and unorthodox situations in the interest of his search for truth. Like the classical detectives described by Landrum, Browne, and Browne, for the professor "personal morality supersedes formal legal procedures" (4). What impulses him in his perilous quest is his own ethical allegiance to an essential notion of a liberating truth.

In his trajectory as historian and detective in Honduras, Jones encounters the name "Madrugada," or dawn, repeatedly. For one, Madrugada is the code name of the downloaded secret embassy file, and Jones and his assistant Erika become intent on discovering the password that will declassify the rest of the document fortuitously in their possession. When the president of Honduras had first met Professor Jones, the name Madrugada had also come up. It is the name of the project that Jones was hired for, the sanitized history text, and it refers as well to the last Mayan king of Copán, who died in the year 992, according to the novel. When given his instructions, the link between both is explained as the reconnection of an interrupted history between the precolonial past and the present: "El señor presidente desea enlazar aquella historia interrumpida con la actual. Ese es el nombre con que se identifica su proyecto" (Escoto 32) ["The President wants to link that interrupted history with the current one. That is the name used to refer to your project"]. The president explains to Jones that his mission, in a sense, is one of regeneration through myth, and of laying the ground for a new society released from its painful memories of violence:

> Una vez que los hondureños olvidaran su pasado trágico infestado de violencia, de la fuerza de potencias extrañas, de gobiernos bastardos y de rebeliones, se podría comenzar a construir una sociedad nueva partiendo de cero [...] como acostumbraba hacerlo cada gobernante de la civilización Maya cuando llegaba al poder, a él le tocaría derribar lo viejo, reconstruir la historia e inventar la realidad.[8]   (21)

> [Once Hondurans have forgotten their tragic past, infested with violence, with the force of foreign powers, of bastard, illegitimate governments and rebellions, a new society could be built starting from scratch ... as each ruler would tend to do when he came to power in the ancient Maya civilization, it would be up to him to destroy the old, to reconstruct history and invent reality.]

The fact that the Mayan king died in 992, and Jones's text was to be launched in 1992, with both sharing the same name and being separated by exactly one thousand years, gives an indication of the millenarian, almost mystical, correspondence that past and present events begin to acquire at this stage in the novel, a correspondence that will become more astounding as the story progresses.

"Madrugada" comes up again in an entirely different setting, in the meeting between Jones and the guerrilla leadership in the old mine shafts below the capital city of Tegucigalpa.[9] The guerrilla leaders tell Jones that they identify with Madrugada as a ruler who had tried to imagine a new empire of peace in the midst of a society in shambles, during the decadence and downfall of the ancient Maya civilization:

> Quisiéramos resucitar la voluntad del soberano Madrugada de Copán que fue capaz de imaginar un nuevo imperio de paz mientras su sociedad se le estaba cayendo a pedazos y se le venía desmembrando... Pretendía un nuevo amanecer, un nuevo hombre [...] nosotros somos también hijos de Madrugada y 18 Conejo, no sólo sus descendientes nacionales sino sus herederos y sus continuadores [...] (341)

> [We would like to resurrect the will of Madrugada, sovereign of Copán, who was capable of imagining a new empire of peace while his society was falling to pieces and was coming undone ... He aspired a new dawn, a new man ... we are also children of Madrugada and 18 Rabbit, not only their national descendants but also their inheritors and their followers ...]

In the face of a new, post-Cold War world order, Hondurans are struggling to forge ahead by coming to terms with their past. For the opposition movement, this endeavor is inextricably linked with recovering a sense of cohesion through their national identity, in all of its particularities:

> Nosotros no es que aspiremos ni pretendamos comunizar al país [...] queremos darle vuelta a esto, ponerlo en su exacto lugar, recuperar nuestro ser nacional y sentirnos orgullosos de considerarnos centro americanos y hondureños [...] Buscamos gozar el orgullo de ser mestizos[10] [...] hemos llegado a la madurez suficiente para entender que carecemos de la disponibilidad para cambiar el pasado pero que conservamos la que nos permite modelar el futuro. (340)

> [It's not that we aspire to communize the country ... we want to turn this thing around, to put it in its exact place, to recover our national being and to feel proud of being Honduran and Central American ... We're seeking pride in being *mestizos* ... we have reached enough maturity to understand that we lack the capability to change the past but that we still have the capacity to shape the future.]

Both the Honduran establishment and the opposition seek the opportunity of a new dawn in their country with the help of the history professor. For the president, a diluted historical narrative will provide a conflict-free "page" on which to write a new beginning where Hondurans will be conditioned and prepared to be integrated into the future enterprises imagined by the United States:

> [...] después de haber vivido en Honduras toda mi vida comprendo que el futuro es anglo-sajón [...] La tecnología, la ciencia, la política y el saber nos inclinan cada vez más hacia los pueblos que dominan el mundo y esos son los sajones. Yo lo que deseo es dar un salto y evitarnos el rodeo: si un día vamos a formar parte de una gran nación americana hay que comenzar a educarse para ello.   (31)

> [... after having lived in Honduras my entire life I understand that the future is Anglo-Saxon ... Technology, sciences, politics, and knowledge all bring us closer and closer to the countries that dominate the world and these are Anglo. What I hope to do is to take a leap and get straight to the point: if one day we are going to be part of a great American nation, then we have to educate ourselves for that event.]

Conversely, for the guerrilla, greater awareness of Honduras's past and its long-term relationship with the United States as a world power will provide a more accurate picture from which to resist assimilation and plan for the future. As the name keeps coming up, Jones realizes that deciphering the multifaceted meaning of "Madrugada" will hold the key to discovering the hidden truths for which he has been searching. The prevalence of the term resonates with the awareness expressed by all of the dawn of uncertain new beginnings and the end of an era.

The uncanny precision, with which all components of the story seem to fit together neatly, is illustrated most evocatively through the symbolic figure of the Mayan Altar Q of Copán. Without revealing too much for future readers, the figure of Altar Q, in which all sixteen dynastic leaders of Copán are portrayed sequentially, will prove invaluable in unlocking the mysteries encrypted on Professor Jones's computer hard drive. The Altar was built by Yax-Pac, the Mayan name for Madrugada, and depicts all sixteen leaders following Yax-Kuk-Mo', the founder of the dynasty. With Madrugada, the sixteenth in line, facing the dynastic founder in the front of the altar, the past and the present literally sit face-to-face in the portrayal:

> Ese pueblo que estaba en decadencia, que se venía desmoronando a poquitos durante más de un siglo aún tuvo el hálito social, la voluntad

de unión que le subyacía en su interior como para retratar a todos los soberanos de su historia en el Altar Q, un gran monolito en cuyas cuatro caras se reconcilian por fin el presente y el pasado. Debió ser en ese momento final, en el despeñadero, como un gran ahogo colectivo, como una enorme brazada de reconciliación.   (Escoto 405–6)

[That society that was in decay, which was falling apart little by little for more than a century, still had in its last social breath the desire for union, which remained deep within, to carve in Altar Q the portraits of all of their rulers in their history, a great monolith on whose four faces the present and the past finally reconcile. That final moment must have been, on the precipice, like a big collective extinguishing, like an enormous stroke of reconciliation.]

In a vertiginous series of mystifying connections, the secret code that opens the computer's cybernetic mysteries of present-day Honduras lies hidden in the message chiseled into the Mayan altar centuries earlier. At the time of its original creation, an evocation of local dynastic pride and unity is sought in the conciliatory embrace between past and present, while simultaneously, the altar was built with full awareness of their society's imminent demise. Ironically, this symbolic image of local pride and perseverance would be used to encrypt the U.S. government's plan to transform and homogenize the local, national culture of modern-day Honduras to sustain its own leverage in a competitive global arena.

Without fully capturing the intricate complexity of the secret master plan engineered by the leadership of the United States in the novel, Jones's findings can be summarized roughly as follows: by the turn of the millennium, the United States will conspire to turn Honduras and all of Central America into a vast colonial satellite to sustain its economic enterprises. Anticipating the downfall of the United States if a series of events were to occur all at once—including heightened economic competition from Japan, intensified Islamic fundamentalist groups threatening access to limited oil supplies in the Middle East, and the failure of the drug war—the U.S. government has concocted a series of widespread conspiracies that would result in the annexation of Central America and the eventual use of all of Latin America as its exclusive terrain to compete and remain afloat as a superpower in the new world order. The tactic to achieve such control is multi-pronged, involving cultural, educational, and religious assimilation as a first step. Preceding this phase is an attempt to "de-Hispanicize" the culture, and make it more amenable to integrate with the Anglo components of U.S. society. In a post-Cold War scenario, rather than turn the region against Russia or other socialist republics, the new goal is to strengthen the colonial Spanish Black Legend to turn people away from their traditional, historical roots and prepare the citizens of Central America to assimilate more easily to the proverbial "American way of life."

With the primary plot of the novel situated on the cusp of global transformations of great magnitude (the collapse of the Soviet Union, the onset of neoliberal economic policies throughout the hemisphere, the opening of economic and political borders to new free trade alliances, the new technologies of the "information super-highway," along with many other policies with globalizing effects implemented toward the end of the twentieth century), it follows that Escoto would plot the historical events he imagines pertaining to his country into a giant conspiracy, where one can visualize a logic—albeit a paranoid, "evil empire" logic—behind the scenes of a disorienting world. Ironically, envisioning the flow of events as an organized master plot, with a coherent purpose and internal ratio-nale, is perhaps oddly preferable to being thrust into the frightening unknown.

The aesthetic form of the detective novel also responds to anxieties relating to the potential chaos of the unknown and a desire to find order within the trajectory of a "truth" finding mission. In his article, "The Detective Story as a Historical Source," William O. Aydelotte argues that the conventions of the detective story genre often appeal to the reader's desire for a reassuring sense of order:

> I suggest that the widespread and sustained popularity of detective stories is principally due to the very elements which make them unre-alistic, to their conventions [...] They are wish-fulfillment fantasies designed to produce certain agreeable sensations in the reader [...] By studying the fantasies contained in this literature, one may gather a description of its readers, in terms of their unsatisfied motivational drives [...] The detective story presents a view of life which is agree-able and reassuring [...] it persuades the reader that the world it describes is simple and understandable, that it is meaningful, and that it is secure.   (Aydelotte 68–70)

In a region intensely affected by the binary Cold War divisions, where U.S. Marines and illegally funded Contra forces were still conspicu-ously present, where the resistance forces had not been organized into drawn-out, perceptible armed conflicts as they had in previous decades in neighboring El Salvador, Guatemala, or Nicaragua, and proponents of local social movements were still struggling to define their concrete goals and their means to achieve them, it must have been overwhelming to imagine the unknown direction the country's future would take amidst the global changes transforming all familiar frames of reference. This is particularly the case in a country residing under the shadow of an increasingly powerful neighbor like the United States that already wielded such palpable influence over all aspects of Honduran society.[11]

To configure this uneasy climate of transformation into the narrative of a detective story implies that the reassuring familiarity of generic conventions will help make sense of this transition, at least in its fictional enactment. The complexity of current geopolitics is simplified into an identifiable problem with a concrete solution, a characteristic that Aydelotte also attributes to the detective story as a genre:

> [...] the simplification of the problem is matched by a corresponding simplification of the solution. Here we come to one of the most universal conventions of the *genre*, the essential clue, the unique significant detail that unlocks the mystery [...] in the unreal world of the detective story, we depart from the intricate currents of causation in life as we know it, and find instead that a whole elaborate plot may be unraveled by discovering the one relevant detail. Furthermore, the factual nature of this detail lends an air of concreteness to the solution: we are led to feel it is the only solution, inevitable, unique, completely certain.
> (Aydelotte 70)

This generic aspect of detective fiction is incorporated by Escoto by making the outcome of events contingent on Professor Jones being able to decipher the secret code of the encrypted Madrugada document on his computer and on the capacity of the guerrilla leadership to transfer a set of their incriminating documents to him so that he can reveal their contents to the world.

The story line that transpires in 1989 does not follow Jones beyond his trip out of Honduras, but the implication is that he will find the documents of the guerrilla waiting for him in a safe deposit box in Jamaica and will follow through on his promise to reveal their contents publicly.[12] Generic conventions condition the reader to assume that once the historian/detective makes the secret plans of the United States public, the result will be one that solves or at least ameliorates the problem revealed. In this sense, the form of the contemporary plot is inherently optimistic, setting the reader up for a positive resolution, implying in this case that public knowledge is empowering against the secret machinations of vast "imperial" forces and covert

government leadership. Somehow, if ordinary people only knew what
the government was planning for the future, they would be able to do
something to change it. What is more, if ordinary citizens were aware
of how their own uncritical consumption of homogenizing foreign
media and numerous other products and ideas might ultimately lead
to their cultural demise as a worst-case scenario, perhaps they would
be more reticent to participate in the potential "erasure" of their own
unique society.

Since Escoto's narrative tone in the 1989 story line remains faithful to the internal logic of the plot, it is hard to tell if the far-fetched
conspiracy theories are meant to be humorous, if they should be
taken at face value as a commentary on the postcolonial "imperial"
designs of the United States, if they are a manifestation of general
paranoia and malaise about what is actually going on behind geopolitical appearances in the wake of the Iran-Contra scandal, or if they
should be taken as a tongue-in-cheek aesthetic exaggeration of the
extreme power the United States has in the isthmus, and Honduras
in particular, while pondering what the implications of that hegemonic power would entail with the end of the Cold War. However,
when the modern-day conspiracy theories are read in conjunction
with the interspersed historical stories, the way in which the short
stories are organized and the themes they represent provide a clue
about how to read the contemporary adventures of Professor Jones
in Honduras.

Each of the nine independent historical vignettes is presented in a
distinct form, varying from the political diary of a journalist during
a siege of Tegucigalpa in 1924, to the narration of the thoughts of a
slave, Mateu Casanga, traveling from Africa to the mines of Honduras
on a Portuguese ship in 1621, or the recollection of the arrival of the
Spaniards from the perspective of the Amerindians in the last chapter,
"La memoria de nosotros (1495)." Yet, even though each unique
historical vignette is written in a different style, their notable thematic
and aesthetic similarities invite the reader to interpret the 1989 story
according to the tone set by the overlapping aspects of the short stories
with the main text. It would seem that in the repetition of several
general themes and the very way in which history is represented, the
strategic form of the historical chapters and of the main story line
holds the key to deciphering the novel as a cohesive unit.

As such, when Jones elaborates on the function of secret codes as
"masks" that are ultimately intended to reveal rather than to hide,
his comments may be applied metatextually to the aesthetic form
of the novel as a secret code that must be interpreted—as a mask

that will reveal its content upon discovering and understanding the architecture of its creation. When contemplating the secret code that might help unravel the mysteries of Madrugada, Jones says to his assistant Erika:

> Uniendo la semiótica con la historia había llegado a entender el colorido de los signos y la trascendencia de los lenguajes con que el ser humano metamorfoseaba sus sentimientos y sus intenciones, encuadernándolos tras la apariencia de las máscaras y la simulación [...] Los códigos secretos eran otra cosa, un laberinto, la voluntad de un hombre que anteponía frente a los demás la máscara no para ocultar sino para revelar. La máscara era el código, la señal, la clave; *conociendo la arquitectura de la máscara se descubría el contenido.* (63–64, emphasis mine)

> [By combining semiotics with history he had come to understand the colorful nature of signs and the transcendence of the languages with which humans morph their feelings and their intentions, hiding them behind the appearances of masks and simulation ... Secret codes were something else entirely, a labyrinth, the will of one man who placed a mask before others, not to hide but in order to reveal. The mask was the code, the signal, the key; by understanding the architecture of the mask, one could discover the content.]

While the author maintains the tone of his main plot as adventurous, but realistic, it will take comparing and contrasting the unfolding of history in the short tales to comprehend fully the intent and the content behind the realist "architecture" of *Madrugada*'s contemporary narrative.

History as a Spiral of Resistance and Domination

La historia no viaja en círculos, se desplaza en espiral.
Siempre hay un nuevo estrato que estudiar, otras circunstancias
a las cuales hay que encontrarles su propia profundidad ... [13]

(*Julio Escoto* 466)

The driving theme that recurs throughout the novel is the dynamic between forces of domination and resistance at different moments in history. While the text is centered on the Honduran experience of these recurrent clashes, the nine historical chapters of the novel (written as independent short stories) do not tend to feature actual historical protagonists. Instead, they are often organized around fictional characters and composites of actual people and places. The effect of this is to emphasize the repetitive dynamic of domination and resistance itself over the significance of any individual actor. Another consequence of emphasizing the process over individual characters is to underline the similarities of these formative historical instances with other Latin American countries.

Paradoxically, in telling a story that searches for the unique roots of Honduran national identity, the author evokes broader regional similarities, adding to the overall totalizing grasp of *Madrugada*'s historical perspective. The combined history of the hemisphere is told through the centrality of the Honduran experience. At the same time, in the face of globalizing and homogenizing tendencies at the end of the century, the turn to specific periods over the past five hundred years is meant to make a case for the rich complexity of a distinct and multicultural national subject formed as a result of this long process.

In presenting instances of both resistance and domination, the independent short stories that make up the novel's historical chapters, focus on how the parameters for "progress" in Honduras are delineated by specific collisions and negotiations of enclaves of power. In addition, a particular emphasis is placed on the perseverance of those who repeatedly attempt to carry out social improvements in the midst of overwhelming constraints in the historical chapters that take place in the postindependence period.

In fact, the chapter that deals with the elaboration of the declaration of independence of Central America in 1821, "Los mismos (Septiembre 21, 1821)," portrays the document itself as a constraint to social change. Under Spain's colonial rule, the territory of present day Honduras was part of the Captaincy General of Guatemala. In the 1810s, many in the creole aristocracy of the region had joined forces in opposition to Captain General José de Bustamante's policies, which had directly threatened their economic stronghold. Aware of the revolutionary movements stirring throughout the hemisphere, and particularly concerned with the possibility that Mexico's Agustín de Iturbide would send troops to liberate Central America and annex the region to the Mexican Empire or, perhaps worse, that local popular organizers would beat them to it, the creole elite of Guatemala drafted the Declaration of Independence *(Acta de Independencia de Centro América)* on September 15, 1821, in hopes of maintaining control of the process of separation from Spain while preserving a strong economic and social position.[14] "In 1821 creoles of the Captaincy General declared their independence from Spain, frankly acknowledging that they took the step to prevent 'the dreadful consequences resulting in case Independence was proclaimed by the people themselves'" (Euraque 1).[15]

Escoto captures the restrictive spirit of the Declaration of Independence of Central America in the chapter "Los mismos (Septiembre 21, 1821)," when a landed aristocrat reads a transcript of the official document in the newspaper, six days after it is signed:

> [...] la independencia había sido ejecutada para que el populacho no se apoderase de ella [...] El documento mandaba que se mantuviera a la fe Católica *"pura e inalterable"* y que se respetase como había sido por siglos la religiosidad y a los ministros eclesiásticos y regulares, *"protegiéndoles en sus personas y propiedades."*[16] Los prelados asumían además una nueva obligación, exhortar a la fraternidad y la concordia–lo que significaba pacificar a los disolutos y afrancesados–y sofocar aquellas pasiones individuales que pudieran dividir los ánimos y originar funestas consecuencias [...] Todo había cambiado y [...] también todo permanecía igual. Gobernaban los mismos, sus mismos. (234–35)

> [... independence had been carried out so that the common masses would not take hold of it ... The document ordered that the Catholic faith remain "pure and inalterable," that religion be respected as it had been practiced for centuries, and that the ecclesiastical and regular ministers be "protected in their persons and in their properties." Additionally, the prelates would assume a new obligation, to encourage fraternity and harmony—so as to appease the dissolute and the French sympathizers—and to suppress those individual passions that might divide people's states of mind and provoke disastrous consequences ... Everything had changed and ... also everything remained the same. The same people governed; his same people.]

Satisfied with the wording of the document, as it promises to preserve his position of wealth and power, the aristocrat plans a celebratory mass and a party to commemorate the moment. Ironically, the very document that breaks the bonds with imperial Spain also limits the scope of those who will benefit from the new independence by closing spaces for radical, redistributive change.

Attempts for progressive social change are also thwarted by entrenched powers in the mid-twentieth century in the chapter entitled "Un silencio blanco (1963)." This chapter takes us into a Cabinet meeting of President Manuel Velasco's reformist regime in which the members of the Cabinet are trying to outline the details of a plan for a new agrarian reform policy. In the discussion, it becomes clear that the military defenders of the interests of large landowners and representatives of previous dictatorships will impede any bold policies that include the formation of agrarian leagues for small landowners to organize and voice their particular concerns.

Beyond confrontations of local political factions, the meeting provides an opportunity for the characters to speculate about the ulterior motivations that the U.S. president John F. Kennedy might have for funding and fostering more progressive policies in the area through the Alliance for Progress. Always looking for the "real" reason behind government policies, someone in the meeting explains his take on U.S. foreign policy:

> ¿Por qué ahora los gringos se han vuelto repentinamente liberales y progresistas? ¡Porque nos tienen miedo! [...] Ellos saben que ya pasó la época de la segunda guerra mundial, cuando sembraron toda aquella cáfila de dictadores caribeños para que el fascismo no tuviera pegue en el pueblo [...] pero ahora es diferente [...] si no propugnan por una revolución pacífica en América, bajo su control, llegará entonces la revolución violenta, la del tipo de Cuba [...]   (167)

> [Why are the gringos all of a sudden liberal and progressive? Because they are afraid of us! ... They know that the second World War period is over, when they were able to put in place that whole pack of Caribbean dictators so that fascism would not take hold over the people ... but now it's different ... if they don't advocate a peaceful revolution in America, under their control, then the violent revolution will arrive, like the one in Cuba ...]

Behind the wrangling of how to carry out a redistribution of lands locally, looms the perpetual presence of a hegemonic neighbor who is portrayed as having the ultimate voice in delineating the Honduran government's scope of action. In the citation above, the United States appears as a virtual puppeteer, setting up dictatorships and instituting strategically progressive reforms at its whim. To have the funding to carry out its modest reforms, Honduras must follow the basic parameters set by the United States, and the Velasco government understands these tangible limitations: "¡o hacemos alguna revolución a la gringa o no hacemos ninguna" (169)! ["We either have a revolution under the auspices of the gringos or we don't have one at all!"] Like all of the historical chapters on the postindependence period, the story regarding the implementation of new agrarian reform demonstrates the attempt to carry out social improvements in the midst of overwhelming constraints.

The influential, hegemonic hand of the United States that looms behind the discussions of agrarian reform is also present in the two other postindependence historical chapters: "Diario de la Guerra: El Sitio en Tegucigalpa (1924)" and, less obviously, in "Amanecer en Olancho (1974)." In the former, a forty-five day siege of the capital city by revolutionary forces calls for the arrival of two hundred U.S. Marines and diplomat Sumner Welles to help resolve the conflict. While the opposition forces ultimately succeed in taking over Tegucigalpa, the chapter, structured as a war diary written by a local journalist, includes critical commentary on the disproportionate number of U.S. troops sent to Honduras—an observation that becomes all the more considerable for readers who are aware of the continued presence of U.S. Marines in the fight against the neighboring Sandinista regime many decades later.[17] The diary's entry for March 19, 1924, reads:

> [...] entran a la capital al paso militar 200 marinos norteamericanos del crucero *Milwaukee*; viene con ellos un camión lleno de armas y pertrechos de guerra [...] El Poder Ejecutivo Provisional [...] hace una protesta al Ministro de Estados Unidos por el desembarque de tropas norteamericanas en territorio hondureño [...] El número de marinos arriba expresado no corresponde a la noticia recibida [...] el Consejo de Ministros manifiesta su sorpresa por este desembarco y venida de ese cuerpo de soldados a la capital y en consecuencia lo considera como un agravio a la soberanía e independencia del país. (204)

> [... two hundred U.S. marines from the *Milwaukee* ship march into the capital; they bring with them a truck full of arms and war supplies ... The Provisional Executive Power ... protests to the United States' Minister against the arrival of North American troops to Honduran territory ... The number of marines mentioned above does not correspond to the news that was received ... the Council of Ministers manifests its surprise at the arrival of the group of soldiers to the capital and, consequently, considers it an affront to national sovereignty and the independence of the country.]

When the U.S. troops leave Honduras upon the resolution of the conflict a month and a half later, the journalist writes in his diary:

> Nosotros [referring to journalist Mario Rivas de Cantruy and his Honduran compatriots soon after the siege] celebramos que hayan desaparecido los motivos que, en la mente del Gobierno de Estados Unidos pudieron haber existido para justificar la presencia de esas tropas en la capital de Honduras, y abrigamos la esperanza de que

el Gobierno de Washington no volverá a encontrar ocasión para
considerar necesario el desembarque de tropas suyas en tierras hon-
dureñas. (217)

[We (referring to journalist Mario Rivas de Cantruy and his Honduran
compatriots soon after the siege) celebrate that the motives for the
siege that could have existed in the mind of the U.S. government to
justify the presence of those troops in the capital of Honduras have
disappeared, and we embrace the hope that the government in Washington will not find another occasion to consider it necessary to send
its troops to Honduran lands.]

The modern-day reader can fully appreciate the sour note behind
these wistful words of hope for greater national autonomy in the
future. Much like in other historical chapters that allude to the
broader issues addressed in the main story line, this fictional diary
entry about the siege of Tegucigalpa in the early 1920s presents an
opportunity to include double-voiced criticism about the country's
situation at the end of the twentieth century. Moreover, the constant
reference to the United States' hegemonic presence in the region is a
way to condition the reader to the fact that the subsequent conspiracy
theories were not born in a vacuum.

Even a historical chapter that does not speak of U.S. involvement
in Honduras directly, "Amanecer en Olancho (1974)," is in dialogue
with the previous contemporary chapter that triggers it in a way
that brings the looming hand of intervention back into the frame of
reference. A clear contrast is established between Father McKenzie,
a Catholic activist in the early 1970s, and the religious conversion
component of the Madrugada conspiracy. With the preconception
that some factions within the Catholic Church in Latin America have
become involved with the promotion of social change from the grass
roots, Father Miguel explains to Professor Jones (in the chapter that
immediately precedes the one featuring Father McKenzie's murder
in 1974) that there is an elaborate and centralized effort coordinated
from the United States to steer people away from Catholicism toward
any other denomination that would be more amenable to the capitalist system. This will then pave the way for the ultimate realization of
the Madrugada conspiracy for cultural domination.

In this way, the historical chapters are set up, in part, to construct
a cumulative backdrop in which some of the outrageous claims of
elaborate master plans and conspiracies become more feasible, illus-
trating the long-standing dynamic of foreign hegemonic control over
all aspects of society. The five preindependence chapters also maintain

the theme of creative resistance and systemic domination within the confines of the Spanish empire. At times, the references to "empire" are clear allegories for Honduras's contemporary position vis-à-vis the world powers of the Cold War.[18] History is thus cast as a continuous power play between empires and super powers, constantly vying for a bigger piece of the pie.

Interwoven in this "top-down" perception of history as being coordinated and manipulated by institutions of power and the metropolis, another key theme takes precedence in the five colonial chapters: namely, the encounter of all ethnic elements that will eventually combine to become the unique, Honduran national subject. Each of the colonial chapters features instances of first encounters and eventual miscegenation or *mestizaje*. The act of retracing multiple encounters of the distinct ethnic and cultural components that will unite over five hundred years draws from the depth and complexity of these interactions to make a case for shared national experience as a basis for identity formation over the impending globalizing forces pushing toward a shift to "the American way of life" that is described in the 1989 plotline.

Foundational Fictions: Reasserting National Identity in the Midst of Globalization

Las naciones y las etnias siguen existiendo. Están dejando de ser para las mayorías las principales productoras de cohesión social. Pero el problema no parece ser el riesgo de que las arrase la globalización, sino entender cómo se reconstruyen las identidades étnicas, regionales y nacionales en procesos globalizados de segmentación e hibridación intercultural.[19]

(*Néstor García Canclini*, Consumidores y ciudadanos *129–30*)

In an era when a case can no longer be made for homogenous national subjects, and multicultural "hybridities" must be accounted for, Néstor García Canclini argues against nineteenth century Romanticism or even Nationalism as ideological sources for constructing a cohesive identity, in his text *Consumidores y ciudadanos: conflictos multiculturales de la globalización* (1995):

Vimos el agotamiento del romanticismo y el nacionalismo como bases ideológicas de la conceptualización sobre la identidad. Ya no podemos considerar a los miembros de cada sociedad como perteneciendo a una sola cultura homogénea y teniendo por lo tanto una única identidad distintiva y coherente. La transnacionalización de la economía y de

los símbolos ha quitado la verosimilitud a ese modo de legitimar las
identidades. (184)

[We saw the debilitation of Romanticism and Nationalism as ideological bases for conceptualizing identity. We can no longer consider the
members of each society as belonging to only one homogenous culture
and having a sole identity that is distinctive and coherent. The transna-
tionalization of the economy and of symbols in general has taken away
the verisimilitude of that way of legitimizing identities.]

In *Madrugada*, nevertheless, Julio Escoto reverts to the national
identity card to focus on a long process of ethnic negotiations
that have taken place through time on Honduran soil. His novel
attempts to trace the complexity of these negotiations through the
series of interspersed, historical chapters. Often times, these short
chapters echo the format, reproduce the content, or capture the
tone of archival documentation, chronicles, or historical fiction
that has been used to construct the textual representation of the
region that was to become Honduras—for instance, to illustrate the
fact that the underlying spirit of Central America's declaration of
independence was to limit the scope of its "revolutionary" repercussions, as mentioned above, one of the short chapters includes
fragments of the document, read in the newspaper by a fictional
character who is a *criollo* landowner, and is about to celebrate his
own personal position of power preserved precisely by the way the
declaration was framed.

The chapters that take place in the preindependence period incorporate many moments of first encounters between the different ethnic
groups that were to come together in modern-day Honduras. Escoto
imagines what this experience must have been like for African slaves
or indigenous communities, writing from a point of enunciation
that strives to capture their perspectives—as in the chapter "Mateu
Casanga" that follows Casanga from Africa to become a slave in
Honduras, or "La memoria de nosotros" that narrates the arrival
of the Spaniards as perceived by the indigenous communities of the
region. When read together, all of the interspersed historical chapters
participate in the author's project of fostering a national consciousness that incorporates all of the cultural components that have come
together on Honduran soil, recognizing a long legacy of shared
experiences. As a whole, the novel makes a case for a multicultural
national identity construct that is used to interrupt the premise set in
the main story line of aggressive, homogenizing, and assimilationist
tendencies being imposed from abroad. In this way, Escoto's novel

can be read as an attempt to conjure up national pride, arguing for local distinctiveness as a strategy of resistance.

Our reading of *Madrugada* will keep in mind García Canclini's reservations about the use of nationalism to generate coherent identities, particularly in terms of Julio Escoto's own awareness of some of the pitfalls of looking within national borders for fostering notions of a collective sense of self in the late twentieth century. In general, García Canclini denounces the renewal of discourses organized around nationalism, regionalisms, and ethnicity as often reductive, flat, and even fundamentalist in nature. He claims that such discourses frequently fail to consider the dynamic negotiations and fluctuating changes that shape the process of identity constructions as a historical practice:

El reavivamiento de nacionalismos, regionalismos y etnicismos en esta última curva del siglo XX pretende reducir el *trabajo histórico* de la construcción y readaptación incesante de las identidades a la simple exaltación de tradiciones locales. El fundamentalismo belicista con que actúan muchos movimientos [...] anula todo espacio de transacción. Para tales sectores la identidad no es algo que se pueda negociar; sencillamente se afirma y se defiende. (185)

[The rebirth of nationalisms, regionalisms and ethnicisms in this last curve of the twentieth century intends to reduce the *historical work* of the incessant construction and re-adaptation of identities to the simple exaltation of local traditions. The belligerent fundamentalism with which many movements tend to act ... annuls all spaces of transaction. For such sectors identity is not something that can be negotiated, it is simply affirmed and defended.]

In contrast to this type of reductive defense of traditional identity markers, condemned by García Canclini in the citation above, Escoto emphasizes the points of tension and negotiation over centuries of colonial rule. Most of the historical chapters demonstrate the extreme levels of initial distrust between different ethnic groups— the Amerindians, the slaves of African descent, the British pirates, the Spaniards—and the many forms of bridging those initial misgivings through collaboration, through violence, through rape, through marriages of convenience, et cetera. Much like the repeated theme of resistance and domination, the emphasis on cultural and ethnic identity negotiations over the years is placed more on the process than on individual historical actors.[20]

García Canclini might call this appeal to nationalism "fundamentalist" or "essentialist," as he perceives identities constantly in negotiation and in flux *up through and including the present times,* when the Internet, satellite and cable television, and the prolific movie industry from the United States provide a plethora of new "ingredients" to add to the hybrid mix of identity "transactions"—new elements that are frequently set in a binary opposition between the "Anglo" cultural tradition versus the "Spanish and *mestizo* historical tradition" in Escoto's text. But the overwhelming hegemony of the United States in modern Honduran society highlighted in Escoto's novel demonstrates how identity negotiations are too uneven. Therefore, the appeal in *Madrugada* to preserve national tastes, practices,[21] and cultural particularities cultivated over time are meant, in a way, to give a sense of leverage and a space for choice rather than being swallowed up whole into a system portrayed in the novel as imagined elsewhere for the express purposes of establishing a "capitalist colony" in the United States' backyard.[22]

In the words of Linda Craft: "Julio Escoto's *Rey del Albor, Madrugada* literally picks up the pieces of colonialism's legacy of fragmentation and attempts to construct a poly-ethnic national narrative which defines Honduran identity and sets it against growing U.S. cultural intrusion" (Craft, "Ethnicity, Oral Tradition, and the Processed Word: Construction of a National Identity in Honduras" 6). By opting to look to "the nation" for strength and unity, Escoto is ultimately making an appeal for self-determination in spite of extreme hegemonic pressures from abroad. That explains the fact that identity negotiations are not necessarily encouraged up through the present beyond the country's national boundaries, at least not with an overwhelmingly hegemonic United States.

The danger of setting up an "us" against "them" dynamic is that, by definition, someone is always excluded in the construction of a collective subject. While this process of delineation can be a concerted measure of tactical resistance leveraged against a more powerful force, such as the cultural influences of the United States, it becomes problematic when it overlooks *internal* exclusions of disenfranchised sectors of society—especially if their abjection constitutes the basis for a proposed national unity. By looking to the nation as an imagined community that is meant to provide a measure of resistance to perceived threats from abroad, there is an underlying risk that nationalism and the ritualized devotion to patriotic symbols will forget internal conflicts for the overall purpose of protecting the nation. The nation itself then becomes a site of evasion. Escoto will thus have to walk a fine line between setting up the nation as site of resistance while not also evoking a national construct that becomes a potential site for erasure of internal differences.

The Quichua author, Armando Muyolema, writes about this dynamic with regard to twentieth century "Latin Americanism" (*latinoamericanismo*) and theories of *mestizaje*, with a particular focus on Ecuador, in his article "De la 'cuestión indígena' a lo 'indígena' como cuestionamiento. Hacia una crítica del latinoamericanismo, el indigenismo y el mestiz(o)aje":

> A simple vista América Latina se descubre enredada desde sus orígenes en una trama ideológica de naturaleza colonial; deja de ser una convención nominal neutra y pierde su inocencia política y cultural. América Latina es más que una idea; representa un conjunto de ideales, acciones y representaciones del mundo que, relacionadas entre sí, encarnan un proyecto cultural de largo aliento formulado en términos de una lucha que se libra en dos frentes: en la confrontación con la expansión cultural anglosajona y, casa adentro, como continuidad del proyecto "civilizador" heredado de la colonia frente a los pueblos originarios. Esta representa un deseo, un proyecto utópico que ha buscado fundir la diferencia para fundar la unidad. Es a esta construcción ideológica de matrices coloniales que gustan llamarse latinoamericanos, que llamaré latinoamericanismo.
>
> (Muyolema 329)

[It is easy to see that Latin America has found itself embroiled since its origins in an ideological plot of a colonial nature; it stops being a nominal or neutral convention and loses its political and cultural innocence. Latin America is more than an idea; it represents a group of ideals, actions and representations of the world which, related to each other, embody a long-standing cultural project that has been formulated as a battle fought on two fronts: in the confrontation against the Anglo-Saxon cultural expansion and, internally, as a continuation of the "civilizing" project inherited from the colony against native societies. This represents a desire, a utopian project that has sought to fuse difference in order to found unity. It is this ideological construction with colonial roots that some call Latin American, that I will call Latin Americanism.]

Muyolema highlights the costs paid by indigenous communities when national projects call for assimilation in the name of unity. In *Madrugada*, Escoto will have to find a way to use national distinctiveness as a strategy to interrupt cultural expansion from the United States and still allow for cultural differences to persist within Honduras so as not to perpetuate the Latin Americanist "civilizing" project as outlined by Muyolema. To this end, as mentioned above, Escoto has focused on the long, complicated process of tensions and confrontations between diverse ethnic components of Honduran society over time, and he has attempted to convey history from multiple points of enunciation through his fictional characters. It remains to be seen if it is enough to portray an inclusive account of multiple ethnic components of society throughout history to counteract the burden demanded from subaltern groups when espousing a project of national unity, or if it becomes necessary to establish an obvious critical distance from a tradition of assimilationist demands within the discourses of miscegenation and nationhood to break away from the hegemonic implications that have historically defined them.

The emphasis in the novel on the long process of identity negotiations is foregrounded in the short, interwoven chapters. Honduran literary critic Helen Umaña recognizes in Escoto's focus on the historical continuity of multicultural interactions a strategy of resistance against the looming threat of imperial power: "*Rey del Albor, Madrugada* [...] realiza una propuesta de continuidad (de no ruptura con las raíces históricas de la nacionalidad) y de integración multirracial y multicultural como única forma de vencer a los imperios" (Umaña 189) ["*Rey del Albor, Madrugada* ... carries out a proposal of continuity (of not rupturing the historical roots of nationality) and of multiracial and multicultural integration as the only way to defeat empires"]. Historical continuity, no matter how complex and painful, becomes a resource to counteract the assimilation conspiracy orchestrated from the United States, according to plan Madrugada.

A detailed example of transitioning relations and identity negotiations between ethnic groups that eventually come together on Honduran soil can be found in the historical chapter entitled "Mateu Casanga (1621)." The chapter follows a slave from Africa to the mines of Tegucigalpa. In his journey he initially expresses extreme dislike and distrust of the native indigenous community. Yet upon realizing the horrific labor conditions to which both the black slaves and the Amerindians are subjected, members of these subjugated groups eventually collaborate and work together to escape. The chapter captures the fear and discomfort that all newcomers to the land feel upon arriving, including recently arrived families from Spain. The new surroundings and new kinds of interactions constantly force Mateu Casanga to ask himself, "what are we?," "*¿qué cosa somos?*," a poignant question he will have to reassess throughout the chapter.

In the community of escaped Indians and slaves—the *palenque* to which he eventually escapes—his conversation with an old wise man, Juan Decidor, helps him try to make sense out of his hardships and understand the dynamic between masters and slaves. Decidor explains:

> [...] llega un momento en que al esclavo le gusta ser esclavo, ¿sabe usted? [...] los dotes del imperio son tan hábiles, Casanga, que la esclavitud no es sólo del cuerpo y la materia. Nos amansan primero quitándonos la lengua africana, después nos borran los dioses y nos lavan la memoria de nuestras historias y costumbres para que tomemos las suyas como buenas. (389)

> [... there comes a time when the slave likes to be a slave, you know? ... the leadership skills of the empire are so capable, Casanga, that slavery is not only of the body and of matter. They tame us first by taking away our African tongue, after they erase our gods and they erase all memory of our histories and customs so that we take on theirs as what is considered good.]

This insight and warning about the dangerous effects of losing one's language, religion, and history, clearly correlates to the process of cultural assimilation to the United States described in the chapters that take place in 1989 as part of plan Madrugada. Juan Decidor finds solace in the anticipated mixture between the races that will continue to take place during colonial times. He sees in the process of local *mestizaje* a form of resistance to imperial, cultural domination from abroad:

> Ya no somos lo que fuimos, Casanga, y aún no somos lo que seremos. [...] Yo pienso que vamos a parir una nueva raza [...] tenemos que esperar que los que hoy nos dominan mezclen su sangre con la nuestra, haciéndonos más fuertes [...] o nos desaparezcan para siempre. Pero esa es la lección que debemos aprender [...] de los antepasados que dejamos en el África y de la buena condición de estas tierras está naciendo un nuevo árbol, juntura de todas las savias, unión de todo, congregación de todo, simiente de todos ... Va a cambiar nuestro color y nuestra lengua, mudaremos dioses quizás [...] y entre más combinaciones se den y más número haya menos poder tendrán los amos, por lo menos los amos que vemos hoy. (390)

> [We are no longer what we once were, Casanga, and we still aren't what we will be ... I think we are going to engender a new race ... we have to wait for those who dominate us today to mix their blood with ours, making us stronger ... or disappearing us forever. But that's the lesson we must learn ... from the ancestors that we left in Africa and

from the good condition of these lands a new tree is being born, the joining of all of the sap, the union of everything, the congregation of everything, the seed of all ... Our color and our language will change, we will perhaps change gods ... and the more combinations that result and the more of us there are the less power the masters will have, at least the masters that we see today.]

With language that resonates with Vasconcelos's *Raza cósmica*, Escoto situates the desire for ethnic combination in the consciousness of an escaped slave. Moreover, through this expressed desire, Decidor perpetuates the assumption that combining biologically with European descendants will provide strength to future generations. According to the words of Juan Decidor, the articulation of ethnicities that will eventually result in a blended, multicultural Honduran national subject is set against Spanish imperial designs as a grass roots mechanism of syncretic cultural resistance and continual recombination.[23]

And yet, the beneficial nature of hybrid, cultural combinations is apparently not meant to carry over to the present. What appears problematic is the inherent contradiction of proposing *mestizaje*, the mixing of cultures and ethnicities, as a way to dilute imperial domination in colonial times when it does not logically correlate to the novel's contemporary strategy of preserving the Honduran national identity in the face of conspiratorial sociocultural influences from the "United States as empire." Why wouldn't the same formula—cultural mixture and articulation lead to dilution of imperial control—apply in the present situation? Perhaps because the conspiracy mindset in the novel attributes such foresight and control to the United States' Machiavellian plan that there is no room for adopting elements of the Anglo culture without feeding into the assimilationist intents of the superpower's all-encompassing master plan. Ominously, it would seem that any choice to turn away from long-standing national tradition toward pervasive North American influences would bring Madrugada closer to fruition. Perhaps also, the process of historical *mestizaje* is being perceived in an overly optimistic light, especially when the supposed desire for strength through future ethnic combinations is voiced by an escaped slave who is still in the process of lamenting the loss of his African language, religion, and history.

In her article "Ethnicity, Oral Tradition, and the Processed Word: Construction of a National Identity in Honduras," Linda Craft describes nationalism in Escoto's novel as a strategy of resistance and makes a case that the key to Honduran national identity in the text is inclusiveness and unity against foreign adversity, not necessarily a mixture of cultures and ethnicities.[24] Craft's article presents a study of three Honduran texts, including Escoto's *Madrugada*, Víctor Virgilio López García's *La Bahía del Puerto del Sol y la masacre de los Garífunas de San Juan* (1994), and *Loubavagu: el otro lado lejano* (1980) by Rafael Murilloselva Rendón:

> [...] while acknowledging the time-honored ideal of *mestizaje* in Latin America, the writers do not pretend that such a harmonious fusion has been achieved, nor that one biological "raza cósmica" is even desirable. *Mestizaje* represents an acceptable dynamic but not a universal goal [...] For Escoto, López García, and Murilloselva Rendón, subjectivity or agency involves staking one's claim to equal participation within the nation and to the full benefits of citizenship. They envision a post-modern, democratic, multi-cultural society of blacks, Indians, mestizos, and whites who unite spiritually under the blessings of nationhood. While ethnicity marks difference, the nation transcends these differences and promotes unity.
>
> (Craft 2)

The nation is then meant to provide the parameters (the ideological and literal grounds) for unity and self-determination toward the future—a dynamic that is to be inclusive of all cultural components from within the national territory while set against hegemonic forces imposed from abroad.[25]

However, in a disturbing scene that brings to the fore the costs that are sometimes paid and often downplayed in the pursuit of eventual national "unity" through miscegenation, a young indigenous girl is raped. Included in the chapter entitled "Como en los tiempos de Guerra (1542)," the scene follows Don Antonio Guzmán, a despotic and ruthless *encomendero* in the sixteenth century, entering his infant child's room, where a young Indian servant girl is sleeping on the floor, and he fantasizes about "possessing" her. He then proceeds to violate her and the narrative captures the young girl's thoughts as if she had expected this to happen to her, and she is not overly concerned:

> [...] la joven [...] comprendió inmediatamente que había comenzado el día más temido *y más deseado* [...] No le importó la urgencia del varón por explorar a palmo su piel morena ni su evidente agitación por conocer *el relieve de sus formas fragantes a tierra y mujer*, en cuyos movimientos lo seguía e imitaba, pero no podía comprender aquel gran vacío de ansiedad que la desarmaba al escuchar la angustia de niño, la profunda soledad con que el hombre gemía y suspiraba buscando algo que ella dudaba poseer [...] Luego la invadió una lava ardiente que

la cruzaba de lado a lado *y rezó en silencio a la bondad maligna de sus dioses que le habían hecho entregar al padre lo que ella guardaba secretamente para el hijo.* (424, emphasis mine)

[... the young girl ... understood immediately that the day she had most feared and had most desired had arrived ... She didn't mind the male's urgency to explore with his palms her dark skin nor his evident agitation to get to know the relief of her fragrant forms of earth and woman, whose movements she followed and imitated, but she could not comprehend the great void of anxiety that disarmed her when she heard the anguish of a child, the profound loneliness with which the man moaned and sighed searching for something which she doubted she possessed ... She was then invaded by a burning lava that ran across her from one side to the other and she prayed in silence to the evil goodness of her gods that had made her give to the father what she secretly had saved for the son.]

Having lost her virginity to the father of the house, she only laments not having lost it to the younger son [!]. Evoking parallels between the land and her womanly body, both anxiously await being "known" by the white man of European descent. Toward the end of the chapter the reader learns that this young girl becomes pregnant after this encounter and is expecting a *mestizo* child.[26]

My original (mis)reading of this scene was that it must have been written with ironic intent. Yet in a personal e-mail communication with Julio Escoto, the author clarified to me that the episode was not meant to be taken ironically.[27] Regardless of the original intent, however, I still find it much too convenient that the thoughts of a young Indian girl are portrayed, in the precarious situation of being a servant, as desiring to have her body violated by either the *criollo* son or the father of the house for the sake of embarking on a process of *mestizaje*. This approach to tracing a "desired" *mestizo* national subject, while putting the burden of desire on a powerless woman who is physically violated, rings to me like García Canclini's warning against using the nation as a site of evasion. In fact, to dilute the violence of the situation and focus on her presumed desire to be violated is akin to Dr. Jones's project in the main plotline of toning down the history of Honduras into a text that forgets any anger or resentment Hondurans might have against the hegemonic excesses of the United States.

From the vantage point of my misreading, the rape episode reads more like a strategy to lay bare and take to the limit some of the underlying assumptions inherent within discourses of domination. Preposterous generalizations such as "natives are prone to be lascivious" (included in many of the European chronicles of the time represented in the chapter, the 1500s) degenerate further to the assumption that "she really wanted to be raped." To wit, the supposed notion of lascivious Amerindians and women of African descent is recognizably prevalent in written discourses dating from the initial chronicles of the Spanish and Portuguese colony up through the so-called foundational fictions of the nineteenth century, when the genre of the romantic novel often relied on the desire of a woman marked with ethnic "otherness" to be seduced by a white man, proclaiming the harmonious future of newly independent republics through their love and their mixed-heritage offspring.[28]

When read in this light, Escoto's rape scene demands complicity with the reader's recognition of this discursive strategy by exaggerating it (through what I had perceived as irony) and taking it to an uncomfortable limit, thus laying it bare as a strategy, not as a facile and all-too-convenient truth. In the spirit of everything being a coded message in *Madrugada*, with everything meaning something deeper than what it appears to be on the surface, I initially took such perceived exaggerations as a critical commentary by the author, not meant as a realist text to be taken at face value, even though it is presented in a matter-of-fact tone. However, as the imagined thoughts of the young girl are not meant as a critical exaggeration, we shall ponder the implications of a literal reading of the scene.

Perhaps more in line with Escoto's actual intent, Umaña has read this episode as an indication of nuance and complexity, given that the young woman expresses desire toward her perpetrator. She perceives the servant girl's thoughts as a cross between love and hatred for the master of the house. "Who defeated who?" Umaña asks. In my opinion this question is less ambiguous, especially when the servant girl is gruffly and unceremoniously discarded from the room after being raped. With respect to the broader significance of the rape scene, Umaña writes:

Desde el inicio de la conquista, el ibero, sin detenerse por la barrera cultural o racial, sembró su simiente. Y muchas veces hubo violación, pero también hubo consentimiento. La india fue violentamente atraída a la fuerza gravitacional del blanco [...] En una escena de la violación de una india por un encomendero, leemos [... citation from the same scene presented above]. Ambigua es la relación sexual. Es cruce de amor y odio. ¿Quién venció a quién? (Umaña 191–92)

[From the beginning of the conquest, the Iberian man, undaunted by cultural or racial barriers, planted his seed. And on many occasions there was rape, but there was also consent. The Indian woman was violently attracted to the gravitational force of the white man ... In a rape scene of an Indian girl by an *encomendero*, we read [... citation from the same scene presented above]. The sexual relationship is ambiguous. It is the intersection between love and hate. Who defeated whom?]

Both Umaña and Escoto situate an ambiguous desire for union with the powerful Spanish white man within the imagined consciousness of the indigenous character. As with Juan Decidor, who expresses a desire for his descendants to fuse with Spanish blood to access a stronger position of local power in the future, in the case of the female indigenous character, this desire becomes eroticized. With a masculine gaze, Escoto imagines that the young woman might have desired and even enjoyed a physical union with her white masters even though she was taken by force. Words such as "el día más temido y más deseado," "su evidente agitación," "la invadió una lava ardiente" ["the day she had most feared and had most desired," "his evident agitation," "she was then invaded by a burning lava,"], belie the eroticism of a "successful" seduction that will eventually result in the desired *mestizo* offspring who will constitute the national subject of a future Honduras. If one reads this rape scene literally, without a critical distance, then the episode becomes complicit in a long tradition of texts that eroticize native women through a paternalistic, masculine gaze that is not concerned with the consequences of its own inherent violence. This becomes even more problematic when one reads the text as an allegorical commentary on the process of national foundations, identity construction, and *mestizaje*.

In fact, Muyolema writes specifically about the prevalence of images of desire and seduction in the discourse of *mestizaje:*

Al operar en la interioridad del imaginario colonizado, la cultura europea se convirtió en una seducción en tanto daba acceso al poder. Represión y seducción funcionan como dos estrategias de poder y de control del imaginario. La ideología del mestizaje ha sucumbido ante tal seducción y ha convertido a la cultura europea y a sus sistemas de representación del mundo, en una aspiración, operando por otro lado, como horizonte cultural que debe ser deseado por quienes no proclaman ser mestizos.   (Muyolema 343)

[By operating within the colonized imaginary, European culture became a seduction inasmuch as it gave access to power. Repression and seduction function as two strategies of power and control of the imaginary. The ideology of *mestizaje* has succumbed to such a seduction and has turned European culture and its systems for representing the world into an aspiration, operating on the other hand, as a cultural horizon that should be desired by those who do not proclaim to be *mestizos*.]

According to Muyolema, the ideology of *mestizaje* thus imagines that those whose self-identification is not with *mestizos* must certainly desire access to power through approximating Western forms of visualizing and representing the world. This ideological dynamic is often transposed to a *physical* seduction in many texts that are concerned with relations between men and women. The assumption that subaltern, disenfranchised women desire the seduction of Western men to gain access to power through their mixed-race offspring is central to many discursive representations of interethnic relations between the sexes.

One of the primary reasons for my initial misreading of the sixteenth-century rape scene in Escoto's novel is that there is another chapter, portraying the eighteenth century, in which the theme of interethnic sexual relations *is* treated with humor. In direct contrast to the rape scene discussed above, irony does become an organizing rhetorical factor in the plotline of the chapter entitled "Aurelina (1785–1786)." Therefore, I had originally considered that the rape scene should most likely be read within the overall context of the rest of the novel, in relation to the previous chapters that had led up to it.[29] In fact, "Aurelina" in particular can be read as an example of how Escoto sometimes plays with the narrative conventions of texts published roughly during the period portrayed, taking to extremes many of their rhetorical mechanisms and exposing some of their underlying assumptions through humor.

In the case of "Aurelina," the genre emulated is the traditional nineteenth-century romance as foundational fiction.[30] Such romantic texts were less self-critical participants in the crafting of national consciousness at the dawn of a new political independence in the hemisphere. While Escoto engages in dialogue with nineteenth-century foundational texts when he draws from the concept of the nation as the source for unity and identity formation, he does so by tracing a long, problematic historical process, and—filtered through the irony of this chapter—he sometimes lays bare the very devices he resorts to through playful exaggerations.

Through its thematic content of a young *criolla* girl that is kidnapped by Miskito warriors, "Aurelina (1785-1786)" starts out with a wink toward Argentinean Esteban Echeverría's well-known romantic poem *La cautiva* (1837). As the chapter unfolds, however, the story of Aurelina takes a drastically different direction. For one, the honor and virtue of Escoto's Aurelina—mirroring Echeverría's heroine, María—are set against the unbridled desires of Aurelina's companion in captivity, the *mestiza* washerwoman named Ana. Comparable to the young Indian girl raped in the chapter that takes place in the 1500s, Ana, as a non-White woman, is also portrayed as lustful. Highly titillated by her predicament, Ana attempts to facilitate being "taken advantage of sexually" by her indigenous captors, thus inverting conventional expectations fostered through traditional literature about female captivity in nineteenth-century Latin America:

> [...] lo primero que vio Aurelina fue las piernas entreabiertas, como un mudo compás de carne, que Ana exhibía desvergonzadamente ante el grupo de guerreros misquitos que había invadido la choza [...] Ana continuó allí, *expuesta la flor de su más instintiva sabiduría* a la vista huraña y macilenta de los guerreros misquitos embadurnados de carbón, hasta que el más viejo de ellos olfateó ralamente entre el aire de sus escasas barbas blancas, arrugó el ceño, barajó dos, tres palabras arrugadas. Los otros hombres retrocedieron aterrorizados y apartaron los ojos de la mórbida atracción del sexo expuesto como si asechara a sus espaldas el tigre o los rondara la presencia de una maldición. (258, emphasis mine)

> [... the first thing that Aurelina saw were the open legs, like a silent compass of flesh, that Ana exposed without shame to the group of Miskito warriors who had invaded the hut ... Ana remained there, the flower of her most instinctive wisdom exposed to the unsociable and unenthusiastic gaze of the Miskito warriors all smeared with carbon, until the eldest of them softly smelled between the air of his sparse white beard, furrowed his brow, shuffled two, three wrinkled words. The other men stepped back terrified and averted their gaze from the morbid attraction of the exposed genitals as if a tiger loomed at their backs or the presence of an evil curse haunted them.]

Despite her willing collaboration, the warriors are frightened by Ana's aggressiveness and are put off by the fact that she is menstruating. Even Aurelina's virtue is ridiculed when, on the one hand, she proves to be completely ignorant about the subject of sex, and on the other, she is offended because the warriors also "reject" her for being too thin: "Desde su rincón de viscosidad humosa Ana la volvió a ver alarmada, sorprendida por la violencia desarmada con que Aurelina reclamaba su derecho a que la violaran" (259) ["From her corner of smoky sliminess Ana turned to her alarmed, surprised by the disarmed violence with which Aurelina claimed her right to be raped"]. The absurdity of the situation becomes darkly comical, especially in relation to the set of expectations that carry over from nineteenth-century texts such as *La cautiva*.[31] A mockery is made out of assumptions that the indigenous captors will even want to take advantage of their defenseless women prisoners. Moreover, in extreme contrast to the ruthless and "savage" warriors of Echeverría's poem, the Miskitos of Escoto's chapter, only go to war out of dire necessity and hunger (260).

Hoping, in part, to find a solution to the severe poverty of his people and secure a better future, the Miskito leader Don Robinson[32] proposes a deal to his prisoner Aurelina. Like the foundational romances that rely on the marriage of people of different heritages to provide the model for a peaceful union upon national soil, Robinson asks for her hand in marriage:

> Serían los esponsales de dos grandes mundos [...] con nosotros se uniría la España civilizada y gentil con la más sedienta pasta humana del nuevo continente, ansiosa de aprender y conocer, huraña y dócil a la vez, que reclama al universo su derecho a constituirse como nación. Seríamos los progenitores de la moderna estirpe americana [...] el matrimonio que siembra el futuro, que da vida a los descendientes de la más hermosa generación que poblará esta inmensa, esta infinita tierra con amor, con una regalada paz. (294)

> [It would be the betrothal of two great worlds ... with us civilized and genteel Spain would be united with the most thirsty human mass of the new continent, anxious to learn and to know, gruff and docile at the same time, demanding the universe for its right to constitute itself as a nation. We would be the parents of the modern American lineage ... the wedding that plants the future, which gives life to the descendants of the most beautiful generation that is to populate this immense, this limitless land with love, with the gift of peace.]

With complete self-awareness, Robinson is blunt about wanting to provide the foundation for a new nation and a new race: "¡Un pueblo, todo un pueblo, imagine, una raza que se iría despertando con la enseñanza prodigiosa que haríamos los dos!" (294) ["A people, an entire people, imagine, a race that would awake with the prodigious teachings of us both!"]. Moreover, what they would be accomplishing through their union, would be akin to the project of nineteenth-century historical fictions themselves—they would, literally, be making history: "No le estoy solicitando que sea mi concubina, *le estoy pidiendo que hagamos la historia*" (295, emphasis mine) ["I'm not asking you to be my concubine, I'm asking you to make history with me"].

In the scene building up to his proposal, Robinson considers his people's position as a pawn between European powers and explains that to answer the question, who are we? (the same question posed by Mateu Casanga elsewhere) his people need to master how to speak with a full knowledge of whence they come and where they are headed (281). He articulates his goal in marrying her as giving his people access to "civilization,"[33] which he associates partly with the ability to read (a skill that he does not yet possess). Much like the underlying premise of traditional national romances, the civilizing process will be facilitated through marital love and the written word. Paradoxically, while acknowledging the importance of literacy as a marker of recognition from Europe, Robinson quotes, in English, the wisdom he has received from printed books by quoting Martin Luther (by memory) in a critique of the fallibility of reason: "human reason is like a drunken man on horseback; set it up on one side, and it tumbles over on the other" (289). The Miskito leader problematizes the recourse to "reason" alone in conceptualizing a future nation and proposes instead a mixture between Aurelina's heritage and his own. While she rejects his offer several times, the chapter ends with her posing no resistance to him holding her hand. It appears as though, upon the condition of his conversion to Catholicism, the project of a new *mestizo* nation has been set in place.

María Cristina Pons proposes, in *Memorias del olvido: La novela histórica de fines del siglo XX,* that the numerous historical novels that were written in Latin America in the last few decades of the twentieth century have engaged in a critical dialogue with both traditional historiographic discourses as well as the traditional model of the nineteenth-century historical novel.[34] This dialogue, filtered through an ironic distance, has allowed many late twentieth-century authors to critique early nationalistic discourses. Arguably, such critical distancing from the basic hegemonic assumptions inherent in the original texts of national foundation would also allow authors like Escoto to construct their own alternative projects in defense of national identity, albeit in a more self-aware fashion that acknowledges through ironic humor the problematic factors still present in looking to the nation for a coherent sense of collective identity.

As writers in a postmodern era, the authors studied by Pons tend to focus on language itself as a central component of the project of constructing national identities. The process of bringing language to the forefront as a mediating resource between events and their representation is categorized in Hayden White's *Metahistory* as the "ironic mode" of historical consciousness—one of the four ways of conceptualizing history that correspond, in turn, to the four tropes of poetic language:

> Irony represents a stage of consciousness in which the problematical nature of language itself has become recognized [...] The trope of Irony, then, provides a linguistic paradigm of a mode of thought which is radically self-critical with respect not only to a given characterization of the world experience but also to the very effort to capture adequately the truth of things in language. (37)

With this in mind, it becomes pertinent to ask, is it possible for Escoto to propose *the nation* as a site of resistance against powerful cultural forces from abroad without having the very same "nation-as-imagined community" become a site of evasion from internal power struggles? If he does not consistently use self-critical irony to separate himself from the problematic assumptions inherent in nineteenth- and twentieth-century discourses of national unity and *mestizaje,* does his project actually continue to propagate those very same assumptions?

On the one hand, intertextual chapters like "Aurelina" exaggerate recognizable conventions of nineteenth-century genres that were meant to consolidate a particular version of national consciousness. This allows Escoto to highlight the conventional language and rhetorical strategies of foundational texts while attempting to sidestep postmodern critiques that discredit the master narratives of modernity by acknowledging them as constructs.[35] Through appropriating, subverting, and deconstructing the language of traditional texts of foundation, Escoto could ostensibly try to rescue a sense of national consciousness as a unifying force against neighboring superpowers in current times. But to separate himself completely from the colonizing discourses of the past he would have to critique these rhetorical strategies in a way that does not ignore that national identities are often built upon denying possibilities for difference, and find a way to signify an understanding that this is profoundly problematic.

Yet the rape scene takes us back to the disturbing realization that the desire for a mixed union with the Spanish heritage, even if it is achieved through violence, is placed in the perceived thoughts of a powerless indigenous character. If this episode is to be taken literally, then it undoubtedly credits and continues to promote a key fallacy in the ideology of *mestizaje*—namely, the convenient misconception that situates the desire for assimilation in the colonized imaginary of subaltern subjects. Along with the nameless servant girl who is raped, the burden of desire for ethnic mixing is located as well in the figure of the escaped African slave, Juan Decidor; specifically, in his dreams for a stronger group of descendants through miscegenation. By not providing a critical commentary, but rather by continuing to locate the desire for *mestizaje* squarely in the thoughts and aspirations of those at the bottom of the power hierarchy, Escoto fails to keep these episodes from propagating a flawed set of assumptions that has long been used to construct images of the *mestizo* Latin American nation.[36] Escoto thus oscillates between the use of ironic humor and rhetorical exaggerations, on the one hand (presumably to distance himself from adhering blindly to an essentializing, monological sense of romantic nationalism), and the literal incorporation of some of the very same assumptions that helped sustain the historical discourses that are being critiqued elsewhere in the novel.

Taking into consideration the words of Don Robinson, in "Aurelina," that people need to know where they come from and where they are headed to define their identity and answer the central question of the novel—who are we?—we turn back to the central question with which we opened this chapter: why resort to a totalizing discourse when writing from the margins? From its position of resistance voiced from the peripheries of hemispheric power, *Madrugada*—while structured as a narrative of totality—participates in a strategy of national aware-ness and local pride as a means of standing up to the ominous forces of globalization. In the episodes that are filtered through humor, the author creates a dialogue with previous, hegemonic systems of representation by emulating totalizing perspectives and taking them to an extreme. His own fictionalized version of a totalizing narra-tive allows him to highlight top-down constraints to progress and social improvements, as well as the continuous, repetitive processes of resistance efforts against unmatched institutions of domination. Continuity and repetition set the background in which the theories of elaborate conspiracies become feasible.

What is more, a sense of a controlling "power behind the scenes," pulling the strings of history regardless of the will of the people, resonates with the eerie truth of the Iran-Contra affair. Many of the elements that Escoto presents in a matter-of-fact, realistic tone are indeed recognizable aspects of Honduran society in the late 1980s: the presence of U.S. Contras on its national soil, the proliferation of U.S. missionaries hoping to convert people to their religious beliefs, the economic influence that the United States still wields on the local economy, et cetera. But Escoto moves one step beyond, neatly tying these recognizable aspects all together into a centralized, intentional plot of total domination and indoctrination into "the American way of life." In this sense, *Madrugada* provides a disturbing, aesthetic commentary on U.S. hegemony in the country. Rather than justify a position of power, the novel's totalizing rhetoric reveals unease about the United States' overarching reach through recourse to both eerie recognition and defamiliarizing exaggeration.

By aesthetically simplifying the problem as a North American "master plan," the "solution" is boiled down to knowledge of the supposed intentions of the United States (so that Hondurans and the world at large can presumably respond to the superpower's secret plan to sustain its global power, instead of actually playing into it as unknowing pawns), as well as an awareness of local history and tradition that can draw together all components of Honduran society and be set against the forces of foreign assimilation. Accordingly, many of the characters in the novel express a profound need to know from where they come. In this way, primarily through its historical chapters, *Madrugada* itself is meant to become part of the solution, while at the same time, the main plotline's history-as-a-detective-mystery approach becomes reassuringly "resolvable" through generic expectations.

Since nationalism and *mestizaje* are arguably totalizing master narratives themselves, the question still remains: does it make a difference if a story of unproblematized totality is told from a place of power or a place of disadvantage? I would argue that it does. As the totalizing story of *Madrugada* is directed outward, to describe the supposed homogenizing intentions of the United States' plan for cultural domination, the application of a totalizing narrative is structured to delimit a space from which to maintain the possibility for difference—it intends to create a platform from which to resist assimilation by rallying around the Honduran nation. When the totalizing narrative of nationalism is turned back inward, however, it risks the danger of *erasing* difference and *limiting* the options for participation in internal power dynamics and identity negotiations. If it becomes necessary to imagine that those who are disenfranchised and abjected need to desire access to centrality within the nation through ethnic and cultural assimilation, then the process of attaining national "unity" becomes highly problematic. Perhaps the only way to separate from the long-standing hegemonic mindset is through humor. The critical distance that can be traced through irony indicates to the reader that at the same time that a male *mestizo* author in Latin America is appealing to the image of the nation as a site of resistance to powerful forces from abroad, he is also aware of the problematic assumptions and exigencies inherent in a totalizing narrative when it is turned within, especially when expressed from a vantage point of local power.

PART IV

THE OTHER
NEGOTIATING SPACES FOR
CULTURAL DIFFERENCE

CHAPTER 6

DEFINING A SPACE OF SHARED
CULTURAL IDENTITY: THE PAN-MAYA
CULTURAL MOVEMENT IN GUATEMALA

The possibility of voicing concerns around specifically "cultural" issues in Guatemala became increasingly viable during the period leading up to the signing of the peace accords in December 1996, when several foreign and domestic pressures called attention to the need to consider the perspectives of the indigenous majority on issues that concerned primarily indigenous affairs.[1] Taking advantage of the unprecedented platform that emerged from these pressures, institutions such as the government-sponsored Academy for Maya Languages of Guatemala (ALMG) have fostered programs of language revitalization and literacy training in Maya languages, organizing around notions of cultural matters rather than the primarily class-based issues that had dominated the discourse of popular activism in the past.[2]

Among the primary goals of the heterogeneous groups comprising the pan-Maya cultural movement is a push toward self-determination, collective self-knowledge, a demand for respect, and a sense of dignity implicit in the Spanish terms *concientización* and *reivindicación* often used to describe the diverse endeavors of current activism. A tactical coalition has been formed to include the twenty-two different indigenous ethnic groups in Guatemala under the name "Maya," uniting traditionally fragmented communities that had previously self-identified in terms of their diverse linguistic affiliations. "Maya" is the term under which indigenous groups have chosen to unite, resisting assimilationist policies of national development while collaborating to negotiate a space of cultural and political awareness, and working together in support of indigenous affairs.[3] Notably, this move to join together under the broader cultural term has been extremely controversial for some non-Maya or Ladino members of Guatemalan society who are concerned about the consequences of identity politics or feel excluded from the new *mayista* discourse.

Nonetheless, the movement has pushed forward by fomenting new opportunities for learning, cultural preservation, and revitalization in institutions such as the linguistic center ALMG mentioned above. Its efforts range from attempts to systematize the grammar and spelling of many Maya languages, to insisting on access to bilingual education, or access to translators in legal trials for people whose first language is not Spanish. The movement's activities also include other educational endeavors, such as workshops with archaeologists to learn how to interpret ancient Maya glyphs and seminars to discuss readings of colonial and precolonial texts like the *Chilam Balam* or the *Popol Vuj*. A collective turn toward the distant "archaeological" past, and at times the more controversial recent past, has served the purpose of defining a space of shared cultural identity from which to demand indigenous rights with a common voice.

The Maya cultural movement has thus resorted to looking back toward both a precolonial past and to the recent violence of the twentieth century to find common ground and define the parameters of the identity construct espoused by the term "Maya."[4] In the process of rereading the past, imagining new histories that are more representative of their experiences, and articulating a new identity discourse, many highly polemical questions emerge: How are "timeless" figures such as the iconic *mujer maya* located in a modern definition of indigenous identity? What does it mean to be "Maya" today? Who gets to decide?

Much educational and research activity has taken place in an attempt to address these central questions. Maya studies have been ongoing among groups with diverse interests ranging from linguistic, to religious, to political, to anthropological issues. Such initiatives have resulted in numerous academic workshops and publications deeply engaged with negotiating a space from which to claim Maya rights, while at the same time demanding accountability from intellectuals dedicated to studying their cultural heritage.[5] Writing in public newspapers or participation in academic forums have been practices frequently used by Maya scholars in the past few decades, not as evidence of assimilation into Western epistemology, but as active tools for articulating a position of difference. Writing and academia have been appropriated as sites of negotiation—as tools for learning, self-awareness, and visibility, while challenging previously held assumptions to further specific political and cultural needs. By self-identifying as "Maya" and insisting on their position of cultural difference, Maya intellectuals have maintained a defiant stance of resistance to assimilation.

At the same time, by positing the category of "Maya" as a marker of "authenticity" in voicing the movement's concerns, the *mayista* discourse has forced Ladinos and foreign intellectuals to adjust and reconsider their own positions of engagement with the Maya community. A counterintuitive inversion has surfaced in recent years, whereby postmodern discourses of "hybridity" have been appropriated by critics of the Maya movement. Some critics have, in fact, accused Maya intellectuals of outright racism and fundamentalism, and have attempted to discredit the movement's mobilization around what they perceive as problematic binary or "essential" categories.[6] In this way, pan-Maya endeavors to find new spaces and forms of organizing after a protracted period of violence and displacement—specifically, under the banner of cultural revitalization—have incited accusations of divisiveness and even racism from some of the movement's most virulent detractors.

In carving out a space for self-representation within the state, Maya scholars have argued for an essentialized subject position and a particular "way of knowing" that has sparked enormous controversy. Kay Warren describes the strategic nature of the movement's essentialist stance:

> Mayanists assert there is a culturally specific indigenous way of know-ing: a subject position no one else can occupy and political interests no one else has to defend. The essentialism is tactical and situational: they advance this position to claim unique authority as social critics. Their goal is clear: to undermine the authoritativeness of non-Maya, or *kax-lan*, accounts—be they Guatemalan Ladinos or foreigners—which, until the recent indigenous activism and resistance surfaced, monopolized the representation of Maya culture and national history. (*Indigenous Movements and Their Critics: Pan-Maya Activism in Guatemala* 37)

This position clearly asserts the need for intellectuals who are not Maya to redefine their own strategies of engagement with issues of ethnic and cultural concerns in Guatemala. The new discourse being formulated from areas of pan-Maya activism thus demands that the parameters defining interethnic and intercultural relations in the country be reconsidered.

The first part of this chapter addresses two texts written by non-Maya scholars provoked by such an incitement: *La articulación de las diferencias o el síndrome de Maximón: Los discursos literarios y políticos del debate interétnico en Guatemala* (1998) by Mario Roberto Morales and *A Finger in the Wound: Body Politics in Quincentennial Guatemala* (1999) by Diane Nelson. Both authors offer their distinct perspectives regarding the ways in which the discourse of the *movimiento maya* has been articulated, and reflect (explicitly or implicitly) on their own position as non-Maya scholars of intercultural dynamics. Each text is in itself illustrative of diverse responses to the discourse generated by Maya scholars and, even though both authors take on a self-proclaimed antiessentialist stance in their interpretation, their analyses of the movement take them in extremely different directions. Morales writes from the position of a Guatemalan author, academic, and journalist who was involved with the Left and the armed conflict in the 1960s, '70s and '80s,[7] and Nelson writes from the position of a North American intellectual, who has pursued her anthropological investigations in Guatemala since the mid-1980s.

In turn, the second part of this chapter returns to our central question: what kinds of stories are told through fiction when speaking about the past? This section provides a reading of several Maya texts regarding memories of the past, represented in different discursive forms: a novel, a series of oral tales recorded in an ethnographic report, poetry, and popular songs. While these texts tend to draw from a common cultural past (focusing on shared experiences of survival and resistance to craft a unified voice for a fragmented community during and beyond the civil war), in effect, their turn to the past is not generally meant to be a way to authenticate a static identity, but can be understood, instead, as a means to revitalize continually what is signified by "Maya" culture as a source of strength and pride.[8] As such, these stories often circulate as a strategy for cultural survival or as a recourse for personal reflection and healing under circumstances of extreme adversity.

Part of the strength that is derived from self-identifying collectively as "Maya" comes from demanding to be treated with respect and insisting that those who study Maya culture be held accountable for the way in which they conduct their investigations and provide access to their findings to the communities that make their research possible. Victor Montejo's novel *Las aventuras de Mister Puttison entre los mayas* (1998) addresses many of these issues in a satirical account of a North American anthropologist's travels to a remote highland town of Guatemala during the 1930s. The satirical figure of Mr. Puttison becomes exemplary of a stereotype of duplicitous foreigners that is to be mocked and avoided in future dynamics between scholars and indigenous subjects of study.

In both *Indigenous Movements and Their Critics: Pan-Maya Activism in Guatemala* (1998) and *The Violence Within: Cultural and Political Opposition in Divided Nations* (1993), anthropologist Kay Warren provides an analysis of the proliferation of traditional stories, in the region of San Andrés Semetabaj, about magical beings that can transform their human shape. These stories bring fears of duplicity and distrust of others within the bounds of the community. According to Warren's interpretation of their significance in postwar Guatemala, this turn to traditional stories may be seen as a mechanism to counter a legacy of silence and address the extreme feelings of distrust and betrayal experienced during the period of counterinsurgency, when many neighbors were forced to spy on each other as members of the so-called civil defense patrols. Traditional references then provide the vocabulary to give form to anxieties about duplicity and unstable selves, while it remains too dangerous and difficult to speak directly of the atrocities many were forced to witness during the violence of the late 1970s and early 1980s.

For those who were forced to leave their villages during this period, poetry and popular songs became a way of remembering particular historical events that led to exile and to the search for the common heritage of a fragmented, displaced community. Authors both within Guatemala and in exile—such as Kaqchikel poet Calixta Gabriel Xiquín, K'iché poet Humberto Ak'abal, and the Jakaltek and Q'anjob'al songwriters and poets interviewed by Montejo in Mexican refugee camps—have provided an important voice to counter the silence left in the wake of national conflict. Through their poems and songs these authors are able to begin a process of healing historical wounds, both on a personal, individual basis—by reconstituting the author's subjectivity from the fragments of memories left after the violence of war and by evoking and recreating each poet's particular way of experiencing the world—and, in a wider scope—by documenting common experiences and celebrating a continued process of resistance and survival that can draw a severely wounded community together through their cultural pride.

The Center at the Margin: Rethinking the Role of the Non-Maya Intellectual

Under what new parameters are Guatemalans interacting with each other since the signing of the peace accords in December 1996?

Given the end of the armed conflict and the much-touted collapse of master narratives globally, what spaces have opened up to negotiate and reformulate the terms that define the processes of identity formation and representation of the subjects who make up this multiethnic nation? How are the differences among the multiple ethnic groups in Guatemala articulated to find a functional balance between recognizing differences and cooperating under the structure of a shared national state? In what ways do tradition and modernity coexist as the country becomes integrated into the global market? How do national and foreign intellectuals figure in these negotiations?

These are some of the central questions explored in the texts written by Mario Roberto Morales and Diane Nelson, *La articulación de las diferencias o el síndrome de Maximón* and *A Finger in the Wound*, respectively. While there have been several texts published recently describing the pan-Maya movement, I have chosen to focus on these two in particular because of the fact that both authors approach the subject from intentionally "antiessentialist" vantage points that nonetheless lead them each to extremely different strategies of engagement with the movement as non-Maya scholars.[9] Their particular conclusions can be read as emblematic of the different attitudes that have been espoused by observers of cultural activism in Guatemala. Both authors reject old binary notions that divide the "Ladinos" and the "Mayas" of Guatemala as solid and stable categories and focus instead on the processes of articulation between multiple identity constructs.[10] In the process of searching for new spaces of interethnic articulation, Morales and Nelson are both forced to assess their own position as scholars of a movement that situates them necessarily as outsiders looking in.

Nelson opens her book by explaining that the title, "a finger in the wound," refers to a frequent comment that came up during her investigations: it was said that asking probing questions about Maya activism regarding cultural rights or ethnic differences was like putting a finger in the wound of a country that visualizes itself as a wounded body after decades of civil war. Focusing on the open sores of this wounded body may, however, be a first step in understanding how to begin to heal them. Visualizing the Guatemalan situation in terms of a wounded body helps Nelson maintain *the body*—tangible and vulnerable—always present in her discussions, both on the level of the "body politic" and on that of the individuals that constitute it. In her analysis she makes an effort to anticipate the concrete physical implications of her observations by taking into account how they could affect the people involved with regard to specific gender issues, the extremely violent context, and other such considerations.

The metaphor of the wounded body can easily be extended to the role of the socially engaged Leftist intellectual who has witnessed the dismantling of the narratives that defined his/her sense of solidarity. How can one suture these fissures in order to recreate a position of solidarity? Is solidarity possible in light of a new discourse that leaves the Western intellectual at the margins of its referential center? What are the demands that are generated by a relationship of solidarity? What other forms can empathic, ideological, or personal alliances take on? In large part, both of these texts can be read as a reformulation and questioning of the role of the intellectual—the negotiation of a new space to participate in the web of interactions that are being redefined since the peace accords in Guatemala.

For his part, Morales uses the concepts of "hybridity" of Néstor García Canclini, Antonio Cornejo Polar's idea of "heterogeneity," and Martín Lienhardt's notion of "diglosia" to construct an argument that posits a process of *mestizaje cultural* in opposition to binary essentialism, while still claiming to respect cultural differences. Despite referring to theoretical concepts defined by Latin American scholars from other countries, Morales insists on observing local particularities and resists the indiscriminate application of theories of identity politics formulated in the United States to the case of Guatemala. He opposes the divisive nature of identity politics and is particularly opposed to the collaboration between foreign intellectuals with intellectuals of the *movimiento maya* in the construction of the "Maya" entity that he considers exclusive, essentialist, and ideologically determined: "'Maya,' entonces, es no sólo una palabra que designa una realidad social, económica, política y cultural del pasado, una realidad arqueológica; es también una palabra que designa una construcción identitaria del presente realizada con fines políticos contrahegemónicos" (Morales 65) ["'Maya,' then, is not only a word that designates a social, economic, political and cultural reality from the past, an archaeological reality; it is also a word that designates an identity construct of the present with counter-hegemonic ends"]. He is not opposed to the use of the term "Maya" *per se*, but rather insists that its fundamentally political intentions be admitted. He is also not against the recognition and persistence of cultural differences or the rights of the Guatemalan indigenous community to organize around the defense of rights that he considers just.

His primary concern seems to be *the way* in which the *mayista* discourse is elaborated and its implications, for he argues that it is based on essentialist notions and that the effect is divisive. He also questions how representative the discourse elaborated by the Maya cultural movement's leadership is, as it pertains to the various indigenous groups and their diverse interests. He favors, instead, hybridizations and identity negotiations that take place spontaneously within the globalized market, beyond the parameters defined by the discourse of the *movimiento maya*—negotiations that do not constitute a threat that could destabilize the current hegemonic balance.[11] Richard Adams characterizes his prohegemonic intentions when he writes: "Morales's concern is to forge a Guatemalan nationalism that accepts all ethnic components democratically, but does not shift the balance of hegemony" (Adams cited in Morales 422).

In his article entitled "What Happens When the Subaltern Speaks: Rigoberta Menchú, Multiculturalism, and the Presumption of Equal Worth"—which appears in the edited compilation *The Rigoberta Menchú Controversy* (2001)—John Beverley insinuates a comparison between the attitude of the anthropologist David Stoll,[12] who criticizes the fact that Rigoberta Menchú has a political agenda when narrating her own story,[13] and the anxiety that Morales reveals when he questions the way in which the Mayanist discourse is being elaborated by the leadership of the Maya cultural movement. In the introduction to Morales's text, Beverley offers a possible explanation for such an anxiety:

> [...] sospecho que detrás de la apelación a la hibridez, la transculturación y el 'mestizaje cultural' perdura una ansiedad de clase (burguesa o pequeño burguesa) y de estamento (ladino-letrado) de ser desplazado por un sujeto popular-subalterno multiforme–ansiedad que se traduce en un deseo de contener el protagonismo y la posibilidad desbordante de ese sujeto dentro de un marco aceptable *para nosotros*, por decirlo así. (19, author's emphasis)

Beverley reiterates this point in English in his article "What Happens When the Subaltern Speaks: Rigoberta Menchú, Multiculturalism, and the Presumption of Equal Worth":

> But one also suspects in Morales's activation of these concepts against the force of Mayan identity politics the persistence of a form of class (bourgeois or petty bourgeois) and ethnic (ladino-letrado) *anxiety* about being displaced at the center of the national culture by a multiform popular subject (akin to what Jean-Francois Lyotard means by "the pagan"), an anxiety that works itself out in the desire to contain the protagonism of that subject within the limits that are familiar and acceptable *for us*. (233)

Suddenly, the Ladino intellectual (in general), and Morales in particular, is confronted with a discursive framework that not only has he *not* elaborated himself, but also excludes him, leaving him in the margins.

The question posed by Gayatri Spivak—can the subaltern speak?—always implies a second question: are we willing to listen to each other under different "inappropriate"/"inappropriable" terms?[14] As new spaces of expression are opened up around cultural awareness (*concientización*), the intellectual of former vanguards might become uncomfortable with the new direction the conversation with the "Other" is taking ("otherness" of both ethnicity and gender). Being willing to listen to others on their own terms—be they exclusive, inappropriate, et cetera—is a challenge that provokes further awareness and openness to the possible consequences of recognizing in others their dignity and their capacity of generating their own agenda, both political and personal.[15] In his attempt to outline a plan of hybridity and democratic coexistence (*convivencia democrática*), Morales resists accepting the formulation of *mayista* discourse because he does not see a way out of the divisions on which it is based. Instead, he seeks an interethnic coexistence that takes place under the conditions that he deems appropriate (and perhaps appropriable?).[16]

Morales takes his concern to an extreme by assuming an alarmist and exaggerated position when he warns against the possible consequences of a discourse that he qualifies as fundamentalist:

> La ladinidad necesita rechazar todo supuesto fundamentalista por parte de los mayistas, pero también necesita reconocer que los indígenas han sido tradicionalmente marginados, explotados y oprimidos, y que sus reivindicaciones concretas son justas, mas no sus puntos de vista religioso-fundamentalistas ni filosófico-esencialistas, *porque esas premisas justifican una política de dominación "maya" y de exterminio ladino.*
>
> (Morales 413–14, emphasis mine)

> [Ladinos need to reject all fundamentalist suppositions on the part of the *mayistas*, but they also need to recognize that the indigenous people have been traditionally marginalized, exploited and oppressed, and that their concrete claims are just, but not their religious-fundamentalist nor their essentialist-philosophical points of view, because these premises justify a policy of Maya domination and Ladino extermination.]

While speaking of anxieties of "Maya domination" and "Ladino extermination," the author ironically strengthens the premises of a binary vision that he has proposed to discredit by fanning the flames of latent Ladino fears of indigenous uprising in a country with a long history of extreme inequalities. He also inherently suggests that "fundamentalist" and "essentialist" points of view are capable of fostering a solid and stable collective Maya identity—the unified, angry, and vindictive Maya people—who will emerge together as dominant and will be capable of attaining the total exclusion of the Ladino.[17] But it is precisely this type of solid and rigid identity position that he is trying to discredit in his antiessentialist stance.

The chapter that he dedicates to his critique of Maya essentialism is the most virulent of the text. Morales insists that the Maya entity is a political construct, and by presenting itself as "pure," "anterior," or "superior" compared to the rest of the Guatemalans, it maintains a binary dichotomy between *ladinos/indígenas* that situates the Ladino in absolutely negative terms. In his analysis of the "Maya" identity construct, he points to various boundary crossings that prove the already inherent hybridity in the indigenous subject. For example, he points to the fact that many Maya intellectuals have been educated abroad; he argues that the indigenous people and their culture have been profoundly affected by "transculturating" encounters since the conquest; he also points to class differences that separate the Maya amongst themselves; and he proceeds to demonstrate the hybrid influences of current Maya poetry.

By attacking the legitimacy of the "essence" or the notion of Maya "purity," it could be argued that the author ironically provokes a defensive response that remains very much within the binary parameters that he is trying to avoid. The crucial question is not whether the Maya cultural movement is based on an identity that is *truly* "pure," "anterior," or "superior," or even whether it has an ideological intention, but rather, what turns can the conversation take to open more productive channels of sociopolitical engagement while recognizing and respecting the parameters that have been traced by the Maya intellectual leadership in defining a cultural space from which activism has become possible? What are the assumptions and consequences of resisting the strategic discourse elaborated by the movement from outside, especially when the cultural parameters that define the movement's activism are in large part an appeal to basic dignity that has often been denied the indigenous community in the past? Or even, what is ultimately the cost of demanding proof of such claims of essential legitimacy? What merits more analysis is not whether the Maya identity is a construct—for declaring oneself antiessentialist is equivalent to admitting that all identities are constructed up to a certain point.

If, as Kay Warren proposes, the movement's essentialism is "tactical and situational," then, what are the conditions that lead to the desire and perceived tactical need to create an exclusive cultural space from which to formulate a collective agenda? If the assumption is that there is a necessity "to undermine the authoritativeness of non-Maya accounts" so as not to be marginalized in the expression and enactment of their goals, then it seems counterproductive for non-Maya critics to respond to the essentialism of their discourse by claiming that it is *inappropriate* in the way it is formulated. Rather than foster the possibility of a democratic interethnic coexistence that is Morales's stated goal, his attack on the way in which the movement has chosen to express its exclusivist position provokes a detrimental positive feedback loop. Morales's negation of the parameters of their own Maya self-definition ironically seems to emphasize the need for a place from which to articulate the movement's own goals of self-determination, without the need for authorization from a non-Maya perspective.

How, then, can we avoid binary oppositions and the notions of solid and rigid identities to recognize the overflowing pluralities of the subjects that are being constituted amidst multiple articulations in a multiethnic Guatemala today? In part because of her concern for having "the body" always present in her discussions, Diane Nelson's text emerges as a promising alternative model—promising for keeping in mind the possible consequences or physical implications of the social dynamics that she analyzes and for always delving into the subtleties that distinguish these implications in terms of gender differences. Within this framework, she would perhaps observe that by posing his criticism of the essentialist pretensions of the *movimiento maya* in a way that provokes a defensive response, the price of such proof of "legitimacy" is paid primarily by the Maya woman, for in the national imagination the preservation of traditional customs ultimately is her responsibility as the archetype of a "pure," untainted marker of ethnicity. As such, the *mujer maya*, as a social icon, is preserved as a timeless, unchangeable essence, and is then excluded from the metaphorical table of identity negotiations in the framework of democratic coexistence proposed by Morales.

More than anyone, it is thus the Maya woman who pays the price for maintaining a traditional image intact, for it is expected of her, among other things, to dress in the *traje* of her town and to stay at home as tangible evidence of the preservation of her customs. Therefore, her possibilities of accessing other spaces of action, such as learning to read, or political organizing around the defense of human rights, are ostensibly limited. In a compelling section of

her book, Nelson argues very convincingly that the stability of the
identity of all other Guatemalan social sectors depends on the preservation of an unaltered image of the traditional Maya woman: the
mujer maya. It is important to note, however, that this idealized
notion of the *mujer maya* functions, according to Nelson, as an
artificial prosthetic for the rest of Guatemalan society (271). There
is a marked discrepancy between the *mujer maya* as an icon and
the Maya woman as a social individual. The author demonstrates
how in reality there are many strong Maya women who have been
able to negotiate tricky border crossings, whereby both traditional
and other spaces are valued without necessarily excluding each
other completely. What is more, the dynamic that Nelson proposes
between tradition and modernity is not one of exclusion, but rather
of mutual interdependence.

However, the anxieties that are generated by these border crossings
of Maya women in other social sectors—or even among some indigenous men—are palpable. According to Nelson, such transgressions
destabilize the symbolism that marks the differences defining the
diverse identities in Guatemala. Despite a manifested desire to generate national unity since the signing of the peace accords, this unifying
tendency is replete with contradictions that generate great uncertainties.
As Nelson puts it, "stable" identities need difference to constitute
themselves in the same way in which modernity needs tradition as a
defining counterpoint:

> [...] this ethnic "Other," far from being a straitjacket that limits national
> identity formation, is instead necessary for its very constitution–the
> loom on which it is woven [...] Despite a desire for the same (manifest,
> for example, in integrationist state policies and calls for mestizaje con-
> sciousness), there is a national need for difference, just as modernity
> needs tradition.   (Nelson 180–81)

Hence, at the same time that unifying intentions are expressed by the
state, Ladino anxieties generated by the crossing of fixed and easily
recognizable borders persist.

The most emblematic figure of such transgressions of categories
is the winner of the 1992 Nobel Peace Prize, Rigoberta Menchú.
In her chapter entitled "Gendering the Ethnic-National Question:
Rigoberta Menchú Jokes and the Out-Skirts of Fashioning Identity,"
Nelson includes a Lacanian reading of many jokes that have circulated
about Menchú in an attempt to identify the sources of such collective
anxieties. The jokes are centered above all around the sexuality of

the Nobel Prize winner and on her transgression of the conventional implications of the act of wearing the typical indigenous *traje*. Nelson proposes that the jokes present Menchú as a conceptual cross-dresser who hides something mysterious, menacing, and disturbing underneath her *traje*—be it a hidden "masculinity," a titillating promiscuity, or even the disconcerting capacity of articulation—of clear and able speech. She thus breaks away from the connotations associated with the visible factors of the *mujer maya* / artificial prosthetic that define and stabilize Guatemalan national identities.

One of the jokes that Nelson analyzes most frequently is the following: "¿Por qué verdaderamente ganó Rigoberta el premio Nobel (o en otra versión, ¿por qué ya no se pone un cinturón/faja con su corte la Rigoberta)? Porque ya es una indita muy desenvuelta" ["Why did Rigoberta really win the Nobel Prize (or, why doesn't she wear a belt with her skirt?) Because she's a little Indian who is very articulate/unwrapped"] (Nelson 373). Nelson explains the polysemous nature of the word *desenvuelta* that implies, on the one hand, the nakedness of Menchú—by unwrapping her from her traditional *traje*—maliciously insinuating that perhaps she accessed the prestigious prize through her sexuality. Or, on the other hand, to be *desenvuelta* implies her great capability of expressing her perspective and of communicating her cause clearly before the world. The traditional *traje* identity marker of the *mujer maya*—associated in the national imagination with her characteristic lack of a capacity to speak—has been completely transgressed. If the sexuality of the iconic *mujer maya* is perceived as utilitarian, for the procreation of children, or is even appallingly "accepted" at times as the object of sexual violations, then where does the notion of an indigenous woman who wears her traditional attire fit when—at the time of the publication of her *testimonio* and during her time in exile—Menchú is neither married nor has children as a matter of personal choice?[18] Nelson suggests that the jokes that "unwrap" the skirt (*corte*) of the Nobel Prize winner do so to reclaim control of her "errant" sexuality, which operates outside of the expected standards. The jokes demonstrate a desire to redirect it into recognizable and controllable forms. The desire is that underneath the *traje* will be the security of finding the stable figure that functions as a prosthetic for other Guatemalans.

Identifying in Rigoberta Menchú a *desenvuelta* person implies primarily recognizing her tremendous capacity to express her own political or personal ends, a fact that proves to be disturbing to many. This is the transgression that generates the greatest unease, and it has echoes in the anxieties of Morales with respect to the control that *mayista* leaders have over the discourse of the cultural movement and in the anxieties of David Stoll regarding the control that Rigoberta Menchú has over her own political agenda.

Despite the concerns generated by multiple transgressions of categories, Nelson repeatedly reveals that no person fits into simply one category or another—the idea of not being "either, or" but always "both, and." In a series of illustrative anecdotes, she reveals instances in which stable categories of identity are put in question for her as well, complicating the dynamic between victims of violence and foreign intellectuals, in some cases in a way that points to the vulnerability of foreign scholars and others, recognizing the multifaceted aspects of a subject who has suffered in the civil war, a subjectivity that extends beyond the notion of being merely a victim. Taking this into account, how can the dynamics between the intellectual and the subject of her research be rethought in a way that insists on recognizing the subjective complexities that necessarily go beyond the bounds of the specific role of a "body" of analysis? How can one keep in mind the assumptions and particular motivations that generate interest or solidarity on the part of the intellectual? Where does the overflow that does not fit exactly into the fixed and explicit notions of a project of solidarity get accounted for?

With the concept of *fluidarity* taken from James Clifford, Nelson explores a new kind of relationship between the intellectual and the subject s/he analyzes that hopes to take into account this overflow of identity potentialities.[19] Instead of a position of "solidarity" that is based on notions of solid and rigid identities, Nelson looks at the fluidity of relations that constantly cross boundaries of identification. Through her practice of *fluidarity*, Nelson emphasizes the spaces of contact and the relational dynamics themselves, instead of searching for fixed identity positions. In this way, she is able to sidestep the old binary parameters and signal a new way of thinking about Guatemalan identity negotiations.

A *fluidarity* stance depends largely on the intellectual's self-awareness, on insistently reflecting upon the position from which s/he speaks and the desires and assumptions that shape her research. Nelson reveals the importance of her positionality by insisting that her own version is *partial*: both in the sense of having a particular slant and in the fact that it is necessarily incomplete. She tries to counterbalance the conscious partiality of her text by including an analysis of the logic of perspectives that conflict with her own. Also, she attempts to understand how the subjects of her anthropological studies perceive her in her role as foreign intellectual, and how their perception differs from her own.

A particular incident helps her frame her discussion of the topic. Upon arriving at the remote village of Nebaj in 1985 and introducing herself as "Diana," the children of the community began calling her *la reina de las lagartijas*, the Lizard Queen. Nelson discovered that this designation referred to a science fiction program on television whose character, Diana, was in fact "the Lizard Queen." The author describes the plot of the U.S. program—called "V"—remarking that it is about the arrival on Earth of a group of extraterrestrials, who on the surface, appeared to have benevolent intentions, but secretly were lizards disguised as humans. They planned to "rape and pillage" the Earth's natural resources and steal human organs to eat them upon returning to their planet of origin (Nelson 247). Facing the suggestive designation of "Lizard Queen" upon the start of her investigations in the remote Guatemalan village provides a powerful metaphor for her as anthropologist and forces her to examine critically the way in which she should carry out her role as the "observer" of the community:

> Being designated Diana, Queen of the Lizards, forces me to consider the sorts of fantasy spaces that I inhabit for those I am "studying" and how my fantasies and romances inflect how I study them. This consideration is increasingly important to address because Mayan organizing calls into question the representational work of anthropologists and asks how much of our fieldwork makes it back to the fields we harvest it from.
>
> (Nelson 251)

Even though it might seem strange or far-fetched to take a science fiction figure as a metaphor for the role of the foreign intellectual in this remote town, the notion of a foreigner who steals human organs is very much a part of the Guatemalan collective imagination. As apprehensions about organs being sold for transplant markets elsewhere, or children being abducted to be sold in international adoption networks circulate locally, based on a combination of facts and rumors, Nelson must confront the understanding that the presence of foreigners such as her could potentially elicit distrust and hostility. This, in turn, forces her to reconsider the complexity of her role in Guatemala, despite her intentions of solidarity.

Thus assuming an antiessentialist position of *fluidarity* implies the loss of easy and comfortable identifications. The practice of *fluidarity* demands a self-awareness in terms of the partiality of any point of view and also implies the recognition that as new spaces of organizing and cultural expression open up within the framework of the state, dissonant voices will be heard—voices that will be antagonistic and exclusive and, for some, "inappropriate/ inappropriable." Nonetheless, the emphasis placed on the spaces of articulation—pointed to by both Nelson and Morales—and on the crossing of what have been perceived as rigid borders, opens up a full range of possible identity associations on multiple sites of confrontation or negotiation:

> So, even though Quincentennial Guatemala may demand that we give up last instances and final guarantees, I think it is also about new forms of antagonism, because it opens up every place as a site of struggle, including the terrain of the state. It is a moment bright with promise and peril of unintended consequences.   (Nelson 72–73)

By refusing to characterize the Guatemalan people as simple victims, she also recognizes the complex multiplicity of so-called "nodes" of power or agency: "[…] *fluidarity* refuses to see the people of Guatemala as only victims or dupes but suggests that nodes of power (both resistive and destructive) are scattered throughout Guatemala's wounded body politic" (Nelson 73). As indicated by Nelson, the current juncture in which the country finds itself suggests great possibilities of negotiation and collaboration, yet it is a road that will demand mutual respect, the recognition of dissonant discourses, and a carefully critical self-awareness at each step—so as not to unleash the furor and the violence of unintended consequences.

BORDER CROSSINGS, NARRATIVES OF DUPLICITY, AND UNSTABLE SELVES

Potentially constructive border crossings—such as direct access to the resources of academic discourse and the public media, or awareness of diverse forms of knowledge creation through higher education in urban centers or abroad, along with access to the means to circulate different perspectives on a global scale—open up new sites of struggle, visibility, and negotiation. As Nelson argues, these new sites of struggle for the revitalization of Maya culture are replete with possibilities and promise. The proliferation of publications written by Maya scholars and creative writers has the potential to appeal to a broad public readership. When focusing on the many narratives in circulation about the close and distant past, it is noteworthy to ask: What kinds of stories are being told from the stance of diverse indigenous perspectives? What kinds of interactions are taking place through these stories and their reception as they circulate on both small and large scales? On either a public or private level, how is language and narration helping to make sense of the violence of war and to get beyond the painful past? Do histories told on their own terms, and their respectful reception, help set the tone for healing wounds or effecting constructive changes? Does framing the past in a particular way help obstruct state projects of assimilation?

One notable storyteller is the prolific Maya intellectual Victor Montejo. He is a Jakaltek Maya who has gone through many "border crossings," from the time he was a young primary schoolteacher in the countryside of Guatemala to his exile in Chiapas, Mexico, during the extreme violence of the early 1980s, his subsequent education as an anthropologist in the United States, and his position as a professor in the Department of Native American Studies at the University of California, Davis.[20] Montejo is the author of multiple publications, including the documentation of Maya oral stories and fables, his own personal poetry, autobiographical accounts of state repression and exile, an anthropological study of Guatemalan exiles in Mexico, and a historical novel. His perspective is multifaceted, for he manages the subtleties of navigating from the Popb'al Ti' and Q'anjob'al Maya languages to English and Spanish, as he straddles the discourse of Western academia and his personal access to memories and current accounts of a rich, indigenous oral tradition.[21]

Montejo's satirical novel *Las aventuras de Mister Puttison entre los mayas* (1998) addresses, with poignant humor, many of the issues brought forth in current debates regarding the role of the foreign intellectual and the ethics of his or her relationship with his subjects of study.[22] Montejo's story is told from the perspective of a local Maya community in the western highlands of Guatemala that is visited in the 1930s by a fictional character, Mr. Dudley Puttison. Puttison is a North American anthropologist who identifies himself as an "investigator," "tourist," and "adventurer" in search of places that display the greatness of the Mayas of Mesoamerica (17). His very name, satirically evoking the Spanish word for prostitute, connotes the sacrifice of something of both abstract (moral?) and physical value for monetary gain, and announces the narrative's position with regard to this foreign interloper from the start. The protagonist's name also sets a humorous tone that is present through most of the text.

With a light-hearted tone and a focus on everyday conversations in the town of Yulwitz during Puttison's stay, Montejo addresses

many of the more profound issues that continue to reverberate
in Guatemala today, including the negotiation of the differences
between communal traditions and a capitalist system, and problematic attitudes between those perceived as "subjects of investigation"
and the investigators themselves. The rhythm and conversational
structure of much of the text recalls the primary source of inspiration
for Montejo's novel, which he describes as the weaving together of
many stories he had been told in his community about life in early
twentieth-century Guatemala:

> En esta obra he procurado ofrecer una visión del mundo Maya a través
> de la tradición oral durante los años más difíciles de la dominación
> indígena por los dictadores que gobernaron el país con mano dura [...]
> Esta novela es ficticia al igual que los nombres y personajes que pro-
> tagonizan la obra. Sin embargo, en su contenido literario, los eventos
> son históricos y se han tejido con los cuentos tradicionales que aún se
> mantienen en la tradición oral de los Mayas jakaltecos, y que se relacio-
> nan con esos eventos históricos de principio de siglo.
>
> ("Prefacio del autor")[23]

> [In this text I offer a vision of the Maya world through the oral tradi-
> tion of the hardest years of indigenous domination by the dictators
> who governed the country with an iron fist ... This novel is fictitious,
> as are the names and characters featured in the text. However, within
> its literary content, the events are historical and have been woven into
> traditional stories that are still kept alive in the oral tradition of the
> Jakaltek Mayas, and which are related to historical events of the begin-
> ning of the century.][24]

The contextual backdrop of the novel refers to the effects of the
vagrancy laws of the 1930s,[25] the push toward modernization under
the liberal dictatorships at the end of the nineteenth and the beginning of the twentieth century, along with a new interest in tourism
and state promotion of indigenous folklore as a potential source of
revenue.[26]

A tourist and adventurer himself, Puttison is one of the few foreigners to approach the remote rural town of Yulwitz other than the
occasional visit from a Catholic priest or missionary. This unusual
encounter with an outsider allows for particular attention to be paid
to initial feelings of curiosity, awkward interactions, distrust on behalf
of both Puttison and the members of the community, and the apparent
overcoming of these obstacles through friendship. Sometimes comical,
at other times uncomfortable and seemingly irreconcilable, cultural

clashes range from mispronunciations of words, different tastes in food, or customary etiquette, to the fact that many of the local practices revolve around tradition and collective pragmatism and not around individual profit: the town healer works to cure illness rather than to make money, the local musicians play the marimba to lift the spirits of the town without expectations of remuneration, and much emphasis is placed on the fact that both labor and land ownership are thought of in terms of benefiting the community as a collective entity.

Even though he initially promises not to disrupt local land ownership traditions, in a town meeting that allows him to remain for an unprecedented extended stay as an outsider, Puttison eventually asks for a bit of land to plant his vegetables, fences it off to keep out the stray animals, and takes on a tone of authority when instructing the people of Yulwitz how they should better organize their animals and clean the area to avoid illnesses. Insulted by his arrogant, condescending tone, many neighbors of Yulwitz react with anger and hostility. Montejo's account, from the town's perspective, is keenly sensitive to the offensive arrogance of the outsider's sense of entitlement to instruct the community in what is best for them. Nonetheless, while Puttison's antics disturb the normal rhythm of town activity, when he apologizes and backs down from his demands, he is able to remain undisturbed for a while longer.

However, normal town activities become much more strained by the sudden arrival of representatives of the state who inform the men of the area of the government's requirement that they carry out compulsory, unpaid labor on railways or roads in the south of the country for a period of thirty days: "El Supremo Gobierno ordena que todos los indios vagos como ustedes sean obligados a trabajar sin pago alguno en la construcción de los caminos del ferrocarril y la carretera allá en la costa sur" (141) ["The Supreme Government has ordered all indolent Indians like you to work without pay in the construction of railroads and highways on the southern coast (132)"]. The short notice of the order and the difficulty of travel logistics become highly disruptive for the families. The already intensive work distribution for basic subsistence farming and household chores becomes unfeasible and falls into disarray.

When read alongside Miguel Ángel Asturias's recollections in *El Señor Presidente* of the effects of authoritarianism and the push toward modernization on urban life (discussed at length in Chapter 3), Montejo's account of the profound disruption of rural communities problematizes Asturias's binary distinction between the oppressive capital city and an escape into a seemingly undisturbed, idyllic countryside.

In fact, Montejo's novel reminds us that much of the labor that went into paving the way toward "progress," literally, the building of the necessary infrastructure, was carried out by rural, largely indigenous communities. In his novel, the representatives of the government use the discourse of patriotic duty to help the nation achieve "progress" and "development":

> Todos los indios deben tener esta tarjeta para llevar el control de los días de trabajo que ustedes deben aportar para el adelanto de la patria. Con el trabajo de todos ustedes nuestra nación podrá desarrollarse y tener nuevas carreteras y ferrocarriles que tanto necesita Guatemala para progresar. (142)

> [All Indians must have this card so that an accounting can be made of the days of work you contribute to the advancement of the Fatherland. With your labor, our nation will be able to develop and have new highways and railways that Guatemala so sorely needs in order to progress. (132–33)]

Montejo highlights the large indigenous component of the labor force that built the roads and railways under development plans of dictators such as Manuel Estrada Cabrera and Jorge Ubico: "Por todo lo que hemos sufrido, podemos asegurar que la construcción de esos caminos es como un castigo que pesa sobre todos los pueblos indígenas del país" (174) ["Because of all we had to go through, we are sure road building must be a punishment inflicted upon all the indigenous people of the country (164)"]. In this way, his text interrupts any romantic notions of an undisturbed, precapitalist way of life in the countryside that can serve as an isolated, utopian escape from the excesses of the city.

Moreover, *Las aventuras de Mister Puttison* brings to the forefront individual accounts—which have been passed on from generation to generation through the oral tradition—of the effects of the labor laws that sustained the country's development. In fact, Montejo dedicates his text to his parents and to the Maya elders who lived through the period he documents:

> [...] a mis padres, por contarme las historias que vivieron sus abuelos cuando fueron obligados a servir en la construcción de las carreteras en el sur del país. A todos los ancianos Mayas de Guatemala, quienes vivieron los días de opresión durante las dictaduras del pasado. Doy gracias a ellos por su firmeza y resistencia al pasar la antorcha cultural a las nuevas generaciones que ahora están revitalizando la cultura Maya.
> (Montejo, *Las aventuras: dedicatoria*)

[... to my parents, for telling me the stories about what their grandparents lived through when they were forced to serve in the construction of the roads in the south of the country. To all of the elder Mayas of Guatemala who lived under the oppression of the dictatorships of the past. I am grateful for their resolution and their resistance by passing on the cultural torch to the new generations who are now revitalizing the Maya culture.][27]

His novel makes visible the part of the story that gets obscured by binary perceptions and dichotomies that clearly separate the city from the countryside or the modern from the traditional as essential opposites. Modernity relies on the labor of the rural indigenous community, and this rural life gets significantly taxed by the imposed exigencies of the state's push for development. Montejo's text is a reminder that no sector of society can be bracketed out of current events no matter how remote the town or how logistically difficult it is to reach. At the same time, the text is also a testament to the resilience of community practices, for as personal memories of the disruption caused by forced labor are incorporated into the oral histories of the town, local traditions nonetheless persevere.

This local way of life is of particular interest to the protagonist of Montejo's novel. In time, the North American traveler develops a friendship with a few townspeople, including Xhuxh Antil, the auxiliary mayor; Koxkoreto, the catechist; and two of the town elders, Lamun and Lopin. On several social occasions, Puttison is privy to traditional stories and legends told by the village elders over drinks and laughter. He becomes fascinated with the different versions of the tales he is told—particularly with details that might indicate remaining material objects that could be pilfered—and asks permission to record some of their conversations.

When Puttison brings out his tape recorder and camera, the reaction is not one of the complete awe depicted through clichés that often appear in accounts of first encounters between native communities and Western travelers. Instead, his indigenous friends are familiar with, but suspicious of, his objects of modern technology based on previous experiences with Catholic priests. The elders of Yulwitz had expressed their discomfort with the consequences of photography to the priest who had first brought cameras to the town:

Nada nos ha dolido, pero nos ha quitado algo. Ya no nos sentimos íntegros cuando nuestra cara o imagen pasa a ser pertenencia de otro. Sentimos como que perdemos control de nuestro mismo ser. La seguridad que tenemos de nosotros mismos y nuestra integridad, es lo que perdemos. (42)

[You haven't hurt us, but you have taken something from us. We no longer feel whole when our image becomes the property of someone else. We feel as if we have lost control over our very being. Our personal security and our integrity, that's what we lose.   (39)]

The elders' concern over relinquishing control of their image and voice—fearing the dangers of manipulation of their words and faces in unfamiliar contexts—is expressed to Puttison as well when he pulls out his tape recorder for the first time:

Uno nunca sabe lo que los extranjeros pueden hacer con lo que se llevan. Además, dejarse robar la voz, es perder el control de uno mismo [...] Lo que se dice es llevado afuera de la comunidad y pasa a ser propiedad de otros, y hasta le pueden cambiar el mismo sentido a los relatos. Así es pues, que hay que saber lo que se dice, cuándo y cómo se dice, insistió Lamun.   (45)

[You never know what foreigners are going to do with what they take. Besides, letting your voice be stolen is the same as losing control of yourself ... What is said is taken outside the community and becomes the property of others, and they could even change the meaning of what we tell them. And so, you have to watch what you say, when and how you say it, insisted Lamun.   (42–43)]

Even though Puttison's new friends soon let their guard down and their curiosity leads them to experiment playfully with his camera and recorder, Lamun's words resonate with some of the central aspects of the current pan-Maya movement: a desire to control the use of one's own voice, the importance of keeping a particular context in mind, and a demand for accountability and greater reciprocity on the part of scholars who engage in studying Maya communities.[28]

The powerful and, sadly, recurrent, metaphors of "blood-sucking," "organ stealing," "parasitic," duplicitous, "vampire-like" researchers/outsiders circulate in Guatemala's indigenous consciousness as a cautionary tale to warn against potentially colonizing tendencies of intellectual investigations. As mentioned above, Diane Nelson describes her own fortuitous identification by the children of Nebaj as a "Lizard Queen," referring to the name she shares with Queen Diana, from a science fiction television program. Diana, the "Lizard Queen" from television is a member of a group of extraterrestrials that secretly plans to take the Earth's natural resources and steal human organs to consume them on their own planet. Nelson appropriates the image as a useful reminder of long-standing skepticism and local perceptions of outside observers in Guatemalan towns. The metaphor serves Nelson as a motivation to work deliberately against the failures that generated such negative associations with scholars of indigenous communities.

It is telling that the figure of "the vampire" appears in Montejo's novel as well precisely within the context of Puttison's first ethnographic encounter with the town elders. Upon asking Lamun and Lopin to tell him about the origins of the town, the old men begin to recount different versions of their ancestors' foundation story. One of the versions speaks of a curse put on the previous location of their people's town by a Catholic priest. At a time when the priest was converting many from the town to Christianity, baptizing them and teaching them his version of the word of God, a young indigenous man asked his girlfriend to bring him one of the blessed holy wafers from the Catholic mass for him to study it. When she brings it to him, he spits it out and throws it into the river saying: "Tiraré al río a tu Dios" (29) ["I'm going to throw your God into the river (27)"]. The priest then puts a curse on the couple's town and sends a plague of vampires to devastate the community:

Pues, algún tiempo después vino la desgracia sobre el pueblo cuando la maldición del padre se cumplió. Una plaga de murciélagos o vampiros, a los que nosotros llamamos *sotz'*, atacaron a las gentes durante las noches, desangrando a todo ser viviente que encontraban [...] varias noches hicieron destrozos en la comunidad, causando gran cantidad de muertos al resultar contaminados de extrañas enfermedades. De esta forma los habitantes abandonaron aquella comunidad maldita, cuyo templo quedó convertido en refugio de los vampiros [...] la comunidad de Peb'al de que estamos hablando, fue destruida por los *sotz'*; y por eso desde entonces se llamó Tzotz'iles a los habitantes de esos lugares a causa de la destrucción de esos pueblos por los murciélagos o vampiros, *sotz'*. (32–33)

[Well, a short time later a calamity befell the community when the priest's curse was fulfilled. A plague of vampire bats, the ones we call *sotz'*, attacked people at night, tearing to pieces every single living creature they could find ... for several nights they wreaked destruction in the community, causing a large number of deaths due to infections from strange diseases. So the inhabitants abandoned that condemned community, whose church became a place of refuge for the vampires ... the community of Peb'al that we're talking about was destroyed by the *sotz'*. So, ever since, the inhabitants of those places have been called Tzotz'iles on account of the destruction of those villages by the vampire bats, or *sotz'*. (30–31)]

This version of the foundational tale points to the deadly results that plagued their ancestors after their interaction with the Christian priest—an outsider attempting to change their traditions. According to this legend, the very name of the people from these parts, the Tzotz'iles, is derived from the traumatic memory of an attack from "blood-sucking" creatures. Even the temple remains a refuge for the vampires and is subsequently off-limits to the previous dwellers of the town.

On one level, the story can be read as an allegory of the disruptive repercussions that the process of religious conversion has on the community's traditions. It is an account of how the imposition of Christian notions of "sin" and "sacrilege" ultimately forced their ancestors to abandon their familiar temple and home. It is a story of violent disruption and anxieties about the inability to "go back home" because of what is taken from them by blood-sucking beasts—creatures who come to embody the violent process of dramatic loss itself. Yulwitz's tale of origin is one of previous disruption and displacement that signifies caution when engaging with powerful outsiders, such as the angry priest.

There is also a hint in this episode (early in the text) that the vampire metaphor will extend to Puttison as an "outsider who is suspect" when he interrupts the elders' story with revealing questions. Koxkoreto, the town catechist, adds to the story his own internalized definition of "sacrilege" when referring to the young man's actions: "¡Un sacrilegio!, dijo Koxkoreto, el catequista. Cuando se profanan las cosas sagradas se comete sacrilegio. Así dice el catecismo y así decía el último cura que recogió los cálices de oro y de plata que se guardaban antiguamente en el templo" (30) ["A sacrilege!" exclaimed Koxkoreto, the catechist. "When sacred things are profaned, a sacrilege is committed. That's what the catechism says, and that's what the priest said, the one who took the gold and silver chalices from the church (29)"].

Puttison then intervenes by inquiring where one could find the golden chalices these days—thus revealing his personal greed as an underlying interest in the elders' stories. Puttison's peaked curiosity about the golden chalices is reminiscent of earlier "ethnographic" encounters between native communities and many of the conquistadors and colonizers from Spain, whose obsession with finding gold in the New World remains documented in their written accounts of their own conversations with local informants.

Therefore, in the short conversation between Puttison and his new friends, the vampire metaphor alludes, however tenuously, to multiple types of outsiders (the evangelizing priest, the conquistador with hunger for material gain, the intellectual researcher) who can often take away more than they contribute, despite their proclaimed intentions. By the end of the novel, the foreign adventurer indeed betrays the trust of the community when he steals the valuable contents of a sacred burial he "discovers" through conversations with his local contacts. Puttison fulfills the assumptions that his name connotes by sacrificing the ethical responsibilities he has to the people with whom he has fostered a relationship during his stay in Yulwitz and by desecrating the physical integrity of the town's ancestral treasure for material profit.

Puttison's predictable behavior at the end of the novel conjures up many underlying questions: What is the ultimate purpose of Montejo's tale of recognizable betrayal by a duplicitous outsider, especially when told from his position as anthropologist and ethnographer? Who is meant to be the ideal reader of the novel? Are there any lessons to be learned? On the one hand, the text warns against the townspeople being overly hasty in granting their trust to others and advises against collaboration with outside observers without demanding accountability for their research and respect for the way they conduct their work. In this sense, the author seems to encourage Maya communities to pose critical questions and to hold researchers accountable for their investigations to the extent that this is possible.

However, on the other hand, the novel seems to be directed to "the academic scholar of Maya communities" as an ideal reader. By providing a satirical representation of local skepticism about outsiders through the figure of a researcher who proves to be a disrespectful, duplicitous thief, the novel demonstrates a blatant example of a stereotype to avoid. As an anthropologist and ethnographer himself, the text can be read as an invitation to other scholars to be mindful of engaging in more positive, reciprocal interactions with the communities that make their projects possible. Much like Diane Nelson's metaphor of herself as "Lizard Queen," Puttison serves as a marker of collective past failures that researchers should be aware of and attempt to amend in the spirit of improved interethnic/intercultural dynamics.

Montejo shares this concern with other current scholars, including Kay Warren, who has worked in the highland town of San Andrés Semetabaj, Sololá, since the early 1970s. Warren writes of her own adaptations to her methodology in response to changing expectations voiced by Maya scholars. Some of these practices include sharing early drafts of her publications with Maya colleagues, publishing in translation, participating in local Guatemalan workshops and conferences, engaging in rigorous question and answer sessions, and giving her original cassettes of rituals from San Andrés to local scholars interested in revitalization.

In her fieldwork in the Guatemalan highlands in 1989, Warren encountered multiple tales of "duplicity" and "transforming selves" that pointed to local uncertainties and situated the parameters of distrust very much *within* the bounds of the community. Distrust and paranoia are only a few of the destructive, long-term legacies of the most repressive period of the state's counterinsurgency campaign (1978–1985), during which many people were forced to betray their neighbors and families when serving as members of civil defense patrols, established as a form of internal control and surveillance to denounce potential guerrilla sympathizers to the army. Since the army often insisted that civil patrols provide captives to prove their obedience, villagers were forced to denounce people whose only distinguishing factor might have been to be outsiders belonging to a different ethnic group or to be on the opposite side of a personal dispute (Montejo 1999). The violence of the counterinsurgency was thus brought within communities, eventually implicating everyone. This resulted in severe social fragmentation and a lingering need for self-censorship and caution for the purpose of self-preservation. Understandably, this heightened level of distrust has made people reticent to share their personal memories of the violence of the late 1970s and early 1980s: "for most, surviving counterinsurgency warfare involved embracing silence and living with chronic ambiguity and uncertainty" (Warren, *Indigenous Movements and Their Critics: Pan-Maya Activism in Guatemala* 90).

Warren writes of the strategically ambiguous language that is often used when survivors are asked to speak of this period:

> [...] there was great reluctance to discuss *la violencia* in any detail. 'It is best to avoid the subject,' one man explained, 'because there might be informers' (*orejas*, literally ears). So people usually responded to questions from anthropologists and others with generalizations [...] the language was often veiled or oblique, often condensed into fragmentary observations with unspecified agents [...] those unable to deal with strategic ambiguities were by definition strangers with whom it was not wise to share information.
>
> (Warren, *Indigenous Movements and Their Critics: Pan-Maya Activism in Guatemala* 93–94)

In this climate of cautious silence, evasiveness, and denial regarding personal memories of *la violencia* (a term broadly used to refer to the most violent period of Guatemala's national conflict in the late 1970s and early 1980s), Warren documents a notable turn by many Mayas in San Andrés to traditional tales of duplicitous beings capable of magical transformations.[29]

Even members of the community who had previously turned away from traditional Maya practices (*costumbre*) appeared to find a way to talk about anxieties of duplicity, distrust, uncertain alliances, betrayal, and the triumph of catching someone in a lie through traditional figures of magical transformation:

> Local leaders, who ironically had struggled to destroy the institutional bases of Maya *costumbre* in the 1960s and 1970s, began to revitalize elements of traditionalist culture—specifically, narratives about the capacity of certain people to transform themselves into supernatural beings. Renewed interest in these narratives stemmed from their resonance with the frightening existential dilemmas Maya families faced during the violence.
>
> (Warren, *Indigenous Movements and Their Critics:*
> *Pan-Maya Activism in Guatemala* 90)

These beings include figures that have long been referred to in Maya oral tradition in different variations such as the "masters of the night" (*rajaw a'q'a* in Kaqchikel Maya) who wander in the night, up to no good, and oscillate between human and animal figures. Their identity is generally unknown, so they tend to blend into the community unnoticed. In her chapter "Civil War: Enemies Without and Within" Warren describes several of the form-changing beings that appear in local stories of transformation:

> Other spiritual forms, called *rajaw kab'il*, go out at night with the specific purpose of bringing sickness to neighboring towns. Still other individuals gain their animal form when they are transformed by the *rajaw juyu*,—the master of the mountain—who lives in a plantation inferno inside the sacred mountain.
>
> (Warren, *Indigenous Movements and Their Critics:*
> *Pan-Maya Activism in Guatemala* 106–7)

The author proposes a link between the many stories of transformation she encountered in San Andrés during her fieldwork in 1989 with coping mechanisms to address the silences imposed by distrust of neighbors and even family. Recognizable figures from Maya oral

PRACTICING MEMORY

214

tradition have thus given aesthetic form to expressions of continuing anxieties too difficult or even dangerous to express mimetically.

In his satirical account of duplicity and betrayal by an outsider, in *Las aventuras de Mister Puttison*, Victor Montejo refers to the oral tradition of his own ancestors as a historical source that interrupts any versions of the past that downplay the effects of labor laws on rural, mostly indigenous individuals and their families during the push toward development in the early twentieth century. The oral stories that are interwoven in his written text also give form to the conversational, mostly jovial rhythm and tone of the novel. In addition to serving as a source of the historical content and the rhythm of speech present in Montejo's text, according to Kay Warren's analysis, traditional Maya stories and spiritual beliefs have also provided the rhetorical figures and recognizable narratives for some to speak indirectly about the legacies of recent terror (fear of betrayal, not knowing who one is dealing with despite outward appearances, and general distrust of others, even those within the community). In this way, traditional Maya tales have supplied the language and source of references to draw from to allow people to begin to face the silence and fragmentation that have devastated survivors of a long history of repression and violence.

HEALING AND REVITALIZATION THROUGH POETRY

For some survivors of Guatemala's civil war, poetry has also provided an aesthetic outlet to counter the silence and express the consequences of extreme violence and displacement. During the most violent period of national conflict, thousands of people were forced to leave their homes, either recruited into military service or as refugees. This displacement significantly contributed to the drastic fragmentation of communities and resulted in profound feelings of unsettlement. Warren quantifies the scope of population dispersal during the worst period of *la violencia*:

> Between 1978 and 1985, an estimated 50,000 to 70,000 people were killed; half a million people out of a national population of 8 million became internal refugees; 150,000 fled to Mexico as political and economic refugees; and 200,000 found their way to other countries such as the United States.
>
> (Warren, "Interpreting *La Violencia* in Guatemala: Shapes of Mayan Silence & Resistance" 25)

To convey the grief and longing stemming from the losses suffered, some have resorted to personal poetry as a way to remember and pay tribute to specific incidents of loss. In the 1980s and early 1990s, poetry and popular songs also gave collective voice to recognizable emotions shared with others in the refugee camps of Mexico. In *Voices from Exile*, Victor Montejo documents such poems and songs he encountered during his field research in some of the refugee camps along the Mexican-Guatemalan border region. References in songs and private poetry often manifested similar experiences and provided a common ground for the many displaced Guatemalans of different linguistic groups and communities to find solace in recognizing their similarities rather than their differences. Focusing on their commonalities, in turn, reminded refugees of their joint endurance in the face of tremendous odds and fueled the desire to work together to revitalize a common cultural heritage that had been so ruthlessly disrupted by the counterinsurgency campaigns.

Besides personal testaments of loss and joint commemorations of shared histories, lyrical poetry has served for others as a means to heal from the devastation of violence and displacement by piecing together personal memories and capturing specific perceptions of the world that help reconstitute the author's unique sense of self. Paradoxically, when such specific poetic perceptions are able to capture and convey identifiable essences of experience they simultaneously appeal to a more universal sense of humanity.

With a style that is historically topical, Calixta Gabriel Xiquín writes poetry that often refers to particular situations, people, or events. A Kaqchikel Maya, she is a poet and a social worker who lost three of her brothers during the war, when they were kidnapped and murdered. Her collection of poems *Tejiendo los sucesos en el tiempo / Weaving Events in Time* (2002) is a tribute to her brothers, a testament of her time in exile in the United States from 1981 to 1988, and a reflection regarding the political and social systems that have repeatedly excluded her Maya brethren with tremendous violence. Her poem "Comunismo, Capitalismo, Socialismo" cited below,[30] speaks of some of the "isms" that she criticizes for their failure to consider the integrity of indigenous cultural values with due respect.

"Comunismo, Capitalismo, Socialismo"

Nos acusan de ser comunistas
mientras apoyan a gobiernos genocidas
en nuestros países.

Comunismo, socialismo, capitalismo.
En Guatemala, se vive el capitalismo.
Es un gobierno militar.
Campesino que cruza la calle
es matado o ametrallado.
Capitalismo.
Ser indígena es pecado en mi país Guatemala.
En nuestra América, no es respetado ser indio.
Se nos niega la vida,
se nos explota,
se nos discrimina.
Los indios de América sabemos:
La idea del exterminio es la solución de países
"desarrollados",
y desconocen nuestra resistencia por muchos siglos.
A los indios de la América
no nos han "vencido como pueblos".
Nosotros hemos confrontado las balas,
hemos sobrevivido, guardando nuestros secretos.
Comunismo, socialismo, capitalismo.
No son la solución de los problemas.
No son la bandera de una nación
con sistema impuesto;
son los anti-valores de los pueblos, como en Guatemala.

(Gabriel Xiquín 34)

["Communism, Capitalism, Socialism"[31]

They accuse us of being communists
while they support genocidal governments
in our countries.
Communism, socialism, capitalism.
In Guatemala we live under capitalism.
It is a military government.
A peasant who tries to cross the street
is murdered or machine-gunned.
Capitalism.
To be Indian is a sin in my country, Guatemala.
In our Americas, being Indian is not respected.
They deny us life,
exploit us,
discriminate against us.
We Indians of the Americas know:
Extermination is the solution of "developed" countries,
and our resistance has been ignored for centuries.

The Indians of the Americas
have not been "defeated as a people."
We have confronted the bullets,
we have survived, and kept our secrets.
Communism, socialism, capitalism.
They are not the solution.

They are not the banner of a nation
with an imposed system.
They are enemies of the people.
They are the anti-values of the people of Guatemala.   (35)]

In this poem, Calixta Gabriel denounces the destructive violence and inherent hypocrisy of policies supporting states that carry out genocidal campaigns against their own citizens for fear of suspected "communism," or in the name of socioeconomic "development." The poet makes an ironic reference to José Martí's essay "Nuestra América" (1891), in which Martí argues for the need to learn about the particularities of the hemisphere's history, especially including the indigenous cultures that make each nation unique, to foster a rich self-knowledge that will propel the region toward its own distinct future—presumably distinguishable from received European models of government. Nonetheless, from Gabriel Xiquín's perspective, the inclusive spirit of Martí's vision for the hemisphere fails miserably in practice due to a lack of basic respect for indigenous communities: "en nuestra América, no es respetado ser indio" ["in our America, the Indian is not respected"]. There is an abysmal difference between Martí's optimistic theory for the future of the hemisphere—based on creative systems of government that would take into consideration an inclusive awareness of the autochthonous—and Gabriel Xiquín's experience of historical practices and interethnic strife in Guatemala's painful past. Her reference to Martí's "Nuestra América" marks the contrast between his original vision for thoughtful systems of government that correspond to regional and cultural particularities and the subsequent adherence to capitalist, socialist, or communist systems, without taking into account the distinct specificities of local cultural issues.

Not only does Gabriel Xiquín denounce the exploitation and discrimination suffered by the hemisphere's indigenous population, with Guatemala serving as a synecdoche for the broader region, but she also insists on speaking of history under different, unconventional terms. By focusing on survival and endurance, she does not accept the notion of the Amerindians as a "vanquished" people. Perhaps alluding to Miguel León Portilla's "Visión de los vencidos," Gabriel Xiquín writes defiantly: "A los indios de la América/no nos han 'vencido como pueblos'" ["The Indians of the Americas/ have not been 'defeated as a people'"]. This sentiment resonates with the *movimiento maya* and its emphasis on rereading the past with a focus on resistance, cultural perseverance, and continuity with a strong, precolonial society. She insists that imported systems do not provide solutions for Guatemala's problems and, moreover, through the violence of their exclusionary structures, she accuses them of being "anti-values," set against the tradition of the cultural values they ignore.

Her poem "Escribiendo" also echoes some of the ideas put forth by the current *mayista* movement. While describing the themes she addresses in her poetry, she criticizes those who have viewed Guatemala's indigenous communities as mere objects of interest, be they tourists or academic researchers. Through her writing she asserts her own subject position as a Maya woman and she reaffirms, with poetry, the cultural values of all indigenous communities:

"Escribiendo"

Con sangre voy a escribir la historia,
el sufrimiento del pueblo en la miseria.
Con poesía redacto la frialdad de la injusticia,
el hambre,
la miseria y
el dolor.

Hoy alzo mi canto al cielo,
canto que es la voz del pueblo.
Los turistas conocen
sólo la pantalla de los países.
Violan los valores culturales,
explotando nuestros trajes
y a veces pisando nuestra dignidad,
contribuyendo a la explotación y discriminación.

Los investigadores
usan al indígena para sus investigaciones;
estudian al ser humano como espécimen
reliquia de la historia.

Desconocen nuestra filosofía,
nuestra cultura e
ignoran nuestras tradiciones.

Hoy con poesía sello la vida
que todos somos seres humanos sobre la faz de la tierra.   (2)

["Writing"

In blood I will write the story,
the people's suffering in misery.
With poetry I record the chill of injustice,
hunger,
poverty and
pain.

Today I raise my song to heaven,
my song, the voice of my people.
Tourists see only
the surface of countries.
They offend our cultural values,
exploiting our native dress
and at times trampling our dignity,
contributing to
exploitation and discrimination.

Researchers
use the indigenous people for their studies,
examining human beings as specimens,
relics of history.

Ignorant of our philosophy
and our culture,
they do not understand our traditions.

Today with poetry I claim life.
We are all human beings upon the face of the earth.   (3)]

Speaking for those who have been mistreated, exploited by injustice and
discrimination, Gabriel Xiquín reminds her readers that the indigenous
people of Guatemala are not mere "relics" from a glorious past, but
active participants in history, whose unique philosophy, culture, and
tradition deserve to be treated with dignity. Her poetry focuses on the
human subjectivity and cultural values of those who might be lost in the
narratives of history, in the structural systems of government, in the discourse of academia, in the fetishes of travelers, or in the violence of war.
   In addition to voicing particular remembrances of people or
events, Gabriel Xiquín's poetry also aspires to rally Maya survivors

together, pointing to a historical legacy of continued endurance and defiant perseverance in response to shared experiences of loss:

"Arrancarán nuestras vidas"

Arrancarán nuestras vidas,
nos despojarán de nuestras casas,
violarán nuestros derechos,
pero no nos vencerán.

Las semillas brotadas,
el espíritu en nuestros pueblos no morirá.

Arrancarán nuestros corazones,
torturarán nuestros cuerpos,
pero no acabarán con las nuevas generaciones
y serán ellos el futuro del pueblo maya.

Muchos somos, muchos refugiados,
muchos quedamos huérfanos,
muchas quedamos viudas,
y muchos vivimos peregrinando con la esperanza,
llorando por el martirio.

Nuestros ideales siguen germinando,
buscando nuevos soles
hacia nuevos horizontes
que iluminarán nuestras vidas.

No podrán acabar con nosotros; somos muchos.
Somos un pueblo, estamos unidos para seguir adelante
unidos en la visión,
unidos en nuestras luchas.

La sangre derramada de nuestros hermanos,
nos alimenta, nos fortalece
nos compromete a seguir adelante,
confirma en nosotros el carácter de un pueblo en
comunidad.   (76)

["They Will Take Away Our Lives"

They will take away our lives,
they will rob us of our homes,

they will violate our rights,
but they will not defeat us.

Sprouted seeds,
the spirit of our people will not die.

They will tear out our hearts,
they will torture our bodies,
but they will not destroy the new generations
and these will be the future of the Maya people.

There are many of us, many refugees,
many of us were orphaned,
many of us were widowed,
and many of us are pilgrims wandering with hope,
weeping from the martyrdom.

Our ideals continue to germinate,
seeking new dawns,
toward new horizons
that will illuminate our lives.

They cannot finish us off; we are many.
We are one people, we are united moving forward,
united in vision,
united in our struggles.

The spilled blood of our brothers and sisters
nourishes us, strengthens us
impels us to go on
confirms our character as a people in community.   (77)

"Arrancarán nuestras vidas" exemplifies Gabriel Xiquín's hopeful
vision of a future in which a strong sense of union and shared community will enable the Maya people to continue drawing strength
from each other in the face of adversity. Following a pounding
sequence of verbs of aggression—*arrancarán, nos despojarán, violarán, torturarán* ["they will yank away," "they will rob us," "they
will violate," "they will torture"]—signaling the extent of suffering
an anonymous "they" might continue to inflict on the community,
the poet draws strength and hope from the seeds of solidarity sown
from her people's joint suffering. From these metaphorical seeds
will emerge a defiant spirit of unity, and a self-conscious commitment to turn to the Maya people in general for the fortitude of

a revitalized community in solidarity: "La sangre derramada de nuestros hermanos,/ nos alimenta, nos fortalice/ nos compromete a seguir adelante,/ confirma en nosotros el carácter de un pueblo en comunidad" ["The spilled blood of our brothers and sisters/ nourishes us, strengthens us/ impels us to go on/ confirms our character as a people in community"]. Despite the profound sense of loss and the unsettling disorientation of anguish and displacement, Gabriel Xiquín calls forth the fragmented groups of survivors (widows, homeless refugees, and orphans) and invites them to join together and persevere in unity as a tribute to their lost loved ones.

Similarly, in his ethnographic research at some of the refugee camps established along southern Mexico in the late 1970s through the 1990s, Victor Montejo encounters many popular songs and poems that highlight joint experiences of mourning and violent loss, also stressing the need to join together and find strength in a revitalized community. In *Voices from Exile*, Montejo transcribes some of the poems and songs written to capture the experiences of the Maya refugees in exile and their memories of their homeland. He underlines the particular importance of fostering a sense of belonging and joint cultural heritage for the displaced refugees in the camps, noting that many of the children born in exile only have access to memories of Guatemala through the stories and perspectives of the adults at camp. Montejo describes the heightened state of political awareness in the camps and the process of education and consciousness-raising (*concientización*) as mechanisms of cultural survival:

> The revitalization of Maya culture through songs and poetry is a form of cultural resistance in the refugee camps [...] the Mayas in the refugee camps succeeded in establishing a positive self image and redefining themselves as a group. Their lives were transformed in many ways, and because of their status as refugees, they learned new skills and techniques to survive. After more than a decade in exile the refugees understood better the sociocultural, political, and economic circumstances that motivated their exile, and they have resisted a destructive assimilation and the erosion of their cultural traditions.
>
> (Montejo, *Voices from Exile: Violence and Survival in Modern Maya History* 197)

Within the camps, several proactive cultural groups emerged precisely to tackle the goals of saving and promoting a sense of cultural pride and a joint sense of belonging in the midst of the anxiety of being displaced from their hometowns. Montejo cites a newsletter published by one such organization, the Ah Mayab', during his visit to the refugee camps in Comalapa and Comitán in 1992: "[...] we wish to reaffirm and revive our cultural identity, making it flourish amidst an atmosphere of extreme anxiety. And so we stand after five hundred years, a wise and dynamic people, intensely participating in the process of rewriting our own histories" (Ah Mayab' cited in translation by Montejo, *Voices from Exile: Violence and Survival in Modern Maya History* 199–200).

With these high stakes, musical groups like the Maya-Honh, interviewed by Montejo, became popular promoters of cultural and political expression within the refugee camps. Their songs often addressed issues of political commentary regarding the contemporary situation in Guatemala and provided reflections about the experience of being in exile. Musical groups in the camps also provided public entertainment that brought refugee communities of different ethnic backgrounds together. Some songs were meant to preserve and propagate the recent memory of specific traumatic events from the civil war. For instance, "The Sixteen Men" is a song written by a musical group at the Cocalito camp. The song refers to a massacre in El Limonar, Guatemala, on January 6, 1982, and stands as a reminder of the sixteen men who died, and the violent reasons why many of the refugees from that town were forced to disperse and leave their village. A few of the verses of the song try to make sense out of the event and ensure that the massacre will not be forgotten: "Let's understand what happened to them so we may see the truth, and from this we may realize that we should live in a better way. That is why that day January sixth none of us can ever forget; how we all became dispersed as we took different paths to save our lives" (cited in Montejo, *Voices from Exile: Violence and Survival in Modern Maya History* 210–11). Songs such as this one become a way to begin to confront the legacy of silence and distrust left by the traumas of war. They simultaneously address a need to record specific events that could not be spoken of freely in Guatemala for many years to come, a need to understand what happened, and a need to find common ground with other exiles that left their own towns under similar circumstances.

The songs and poetry documented by Montejo serve as a testament of endurance and survival. Part of the revitalization strategy by cultural groups in the camps has been a deliberate attempt to trace the resilience of the Maya people throughout history and to foster an awareness of a joint cultural heritage between diverse linguistic groups that goes back to precolonial times. Montejo notes that this notion is often conveyed through storytelling and songs: "both groups [the Maya-Honh and the Ah Mayab'] traveled to various refugee camps, singing, reading poetry, and telling stories and stressing that the refugees are Mayas because their roots come from the ancient Maya civilization" (Montejo, *Voices from Exile: Violence and Survival in Modern Maya History* 196). Many songs and poems address recent issues of displacement, violence, and foster the pride of common ancestry and continued resistance, in spite of tremendous adversity. By addressing such issues, they help to generate a voice with which to speak of history from a distinctly indigenous perspective.

Facing extreme historical circumstances (a dispersed, displaced society both within Guatemala and in exile, the inevitable distrust generated by forcing community members to spy on each other and denounce their neighbors as part of the state's counterinsurgency campaign, and the ensuing legacy of fear and silence), Maya cultural groups have deliberately looked to strengthen the notion of a common heritage to find a joint voice and a revitalized cultural pride that will help suture the wounds left by the violence. Being able to discuss historical processes of exclusion and resistance allows survivors of the more recent violence to understand their own circumstances. Articulating a strong voice from the vantage point of a cultural platform—amidst legacies of severe displacement and silence—is one of the ways the pan-Maya movement has attempted to heal the wounds of war. Being "Maya" and demanding respect for the cultural differences that this entails within the postwar Guatemalan state engenders a "place" from which to rebuild strength through pride and cultural awareness, especially after the devastation of protracted national violence wielded primarily against indigenous people.

Within this climate of heightened cultural identification another, more subtle, healing force in the cultural realm can be found in the work of poets such as Humberto Ak'abal, whose poems tend to be more lyrical and less historical in subject matter. Ak'abal writes about small and deceptively simple subjects that appeal to a universal sense of humanity. His poetry tends to evoke a profound engagement from his readers by simultaneously surprising them with his unique perceptions of the world, while also conveying familiar kernels of essential truths. In this way, even though his references are from the perspective of his K'iché upbringing, non-Maya readers can relate to the profound reality he is able to evoke in his short poems.

In the poem "Xul" Ak'abal captures a snippet of a memory from childhood:

"Xul"[32]

Un hoyito
en el pecho
y uno en la cola:
si lo soplás
canta.

Juguete de patojitos
pobres.

Tiene forma de pollo,
es de barro;
se llama Xul.

Yo tuve uno.

"Xul"

Jun jül
k'o pa uwëch uk'ux
xuquje' jun pa ri uje';
we kaxut'ij
koq'ik, kab'ixonik.

Ketz'ab'al ri ak'alab'
ri e meb'a.

Junam ruk' jun tux ëk'
b'anom che kach'ulew,
xul ri ub'i

In xk'oji'jun we.

(Ak'abal, *Guardián de la caída del agua* 15)[33]
(Ak'abal, *Ajkem Tzij Tejedor de palabras* 398)[34]

["Xul"

A small hole
on its chest
and one on its tail:
if you blow on it
it sings.

A toy of young boys,
poor ones.

It has the shape of a chicken,
it's made of clay;
it's called "Xul."

I had one.]

"Xul" reveals the poet's nostalgia for the toy he remembers from his childhood, conjuring up a distinct image of the clay whistle through his description. Like the toy he played with as a child, Ak'abal's poem sings with tenderness about the playfulness of childhood. However, the poet's fond memories of this specific object also situate him within a context of poverty: *"juguete de patojitos pobres"* ["a toy for little boys who are poor"]. Nonetheless, Ak'abal distinguishes as a positive memory the xul's ability to make a child sing, despite the characteristic austerity of poverty. Most readers can relate to such nostalgic remembrances associated with a specific object from childhood, but the author also evokes a sense of understated dignity by emphasizing a tender moment of innocent joy, despite his background of poverty.

In a short commentary that serves as an introduction to the compilation *Con los ojos después del mar* (2000), entitled "Ausencia recuperada," Ak'abal writes about the poverty of his childhood: "No tuve niñez por la pobreza de mis padres, y la guerra interna del país me robó la juventud. La necesidad de la existencia despertó en mí la responsabilidad del trabajo y aplastó mi temprana edad" (9) ["I did not have a childhood because of my parents' poverty, and the country's internal war robbed me of my youth. The basic needs of existence woke up in me the responsibility for work and crushed my early years"]. After writing about the atrocities that he witnessed in the trajectory between his town of Momostenango and Guatemala City as an adult during the violence of the early 1980s, Ak'abal adds: "Era difícil la vida en aquellos días. Mi rostro se tornó áspero por la sal de las lágrimas. Comencé a escribir algunos poemas en los que sentí la necesidad de volver a mi infancia. Recupero, o mejor dicho, intento recuperar en cada texto esa niñez que no tuve" (14) ["Life was hard in those days. My face became rough from the salt of the tears. I began to write some poems in which I felt the need to return to my childhood. I recover, or rather, I try to recover in each text that childhood that I never had"]. In this way, his poetry serves as a very personal source of comfort and healing, providing a contrast to the losses endured through poverty and war. However, for both Maya and non-Maya readers, his poetry also provokes a comforting sense of delight and identification. The reader connects to the text by recognizing the universal truths he evokes in the succinctness of his images and colloquial language—while also gaining access to Ak'abal's unique perspective of his surroundings, conjured up through particular references to his Maya heritage.

The systematizing and revitalization of Maya languages through educational programs and publications is a key component of the Maya cultural movement. According to Ak'abal—whose poetry has nevertheless been published in many languages including English, French, German, Italian, Japanese, Catalan, and Swedish—the K'iché language captures a unique vision of the world. In the short introduction to the bilingual (K'iché-Spanish) collection entitled *Aqajtzij Palabramiel*

(2001)—without including the source of the citation or the name of the poem—Carlos Illescas quotes Ak'abal's insightful verses on this matter: "Para quienes / no hablan nuestras lenguas / somos invisibles" (12) ["For those who / don't speak our languages / we are invisible"]. For those who do not speak any of the Maya languages many of the nuances of their world vision is lost; they become "invisible." Nonetheless, even in translation, Ak'abal's poetry evokes subtle traces of recognizable truths that transcend specific contexts and the nuances of language.

For some, the fact that Ak'abal is informed and influenced by his readings of Western and Far Eastern poetry is an issue of contention when characterizing him as an "authentic" Maya poet. Mario Roberto Morales includes his perspective on this issue in his chapter about Maya essentialism. He suggests a performative aspect to Ak'abal's traditional image and questions how representative the poet's aesthetic portrayal is of the essence of a "Maya voice" (whatever that may be):

> El poeta Humberto Ak'abal, por ejemplo, se autodenomina "maya" (Luis de Lión se autodenominaba indio), se viste con ropa llamada "típica" de la que se vende al turismo, se deja el pelo largo y luce chachales en el cuello, logrando así un *look* de "maya" posmoderno que hace honor a la estética del *pastiche*. Ak'abal escribe un tipo de poesía corta, estilo haikai y poema chino antiguo, contemplativa, descriptiva y colorida, como las artesanías hibridizadas que se encuentran en los mercados hoy día y que responden a la demanda turística, para lo cual sus artesanos han cambiado los iconos, los colores, los diseños y las formas (que ya eran híbridas). Ak'abal es considerado como indio o "maya" "auténtico" por el pater(mater)nalismo euronorteamericano y por la ladinidad "progre" local, y él ha aprendido a manejar muy bien su persona y su literatura en términos de mercado.
>
> (Morales 254–55)

> [The poet Humberto Ak'abal, for example, calls himself "Maya" (Luis de Lión called himself Indian), he dresses in clothes said to be "typical" of the type that is sold to tourists, he wears his hair long and sports *chachales* around his neck, putting together in this way a postmodern "Maya" look that does honor to the pastiche aesthetic. Ak'abal writes a type of short poetry, in the style of the haikai and the ancient Chinese poem, contemplative, descriptive and colorful, like the hybridized handicrafts found in the markets today that respond to the demands of tourism, for which the artisans have changed the icons, the colors, the designs and the shapes (which were already hybrid). Ak'abal is considered an "authentic" Indian or "Maya" by the Euro/North American pater(mater)nalism and by the local "progressive" ladinos, and he has learned to manage his persona and his literature very well in marketing terms.]

Morales's tone rings slightly accusatory, insinuating an intention of duplicity on behalf of the poet who, ostensibly, is trying to manipulate his readers through his personal appearance to draw them to "consume" his texts.[35] Morales criticizes progressive Guatemalans and Western readers of paternalism when searching for indigenous "authenticity" in Ak'abal's poems; and he insists that it is flawed to search for essential "purity" in a highly hybrid generic form, so clearly influenced by foreign literature. Moreover, Morales fervently resists notions of an "untainted" precolonial voice being passed from ancestors to contemporary indigenous writers—a link that, in my estimation, should not be taken quite so literally. The turn to precolonial history is meant to foster pride and a sense of community among a victimized society, not as a claim to ventriloquism.

Guatemalan author Mario Monteforte Toledo also finds a need to refer to Ak'abal's extensive reading of Western texts, although he concludes that this exposure to other literature is an inevitability that does not take away from his "legitimacy" as an indigenous voice: "Ak'abal tiene la capacidad de percibir y expresar esencias. Inevitablemente tiende a apropiarse del mecanismo de la expresión occidental. De sus vastas lecturas no puede salir inmune; pero siempre será un poeta indio"[36] ["Ak'abal has the capacity to perceive and to express essences. Inevitably he tends to appropriate the Western mechanism of expression. He could not have been left immune from his vast readings; but he will always be an Indian poet"]. What makes Ak'abal's poetry "Maya," regardless of Western influences, is his unique perspective that comes from growing up within the indigenous K'iché community and speaking from a position built upon the set of sensations and experiences that this entails. In his poetry, he is able to draw from all of his influences and rearticulate his perceptions from this distinct vantage point. His poem "El sabor" captures Ak'abal's keen awareness of the source of his perspective. The flavor with which he experiences and interprets his surroundings stems from his condition of poverty and his indigenous tradition:

"El sabor"[37]	"Ri uki'al"[38]
Aprendí el sabor de la vida como cualquier indio pobre	Xinwe'tamaj ri uki'al ri k'aslemal ruk' ri wachalal e meb'a
Los demás sabores	We k'o chi jun ki'al chik

me vienen sobrando.   man k'o ta we che.
(Ak'abal, *Guardián de la caída del agua* 128)
(Ak'abal, *Ajkem Tzij Tejedor de palabras* 530)

"The Flavor"

I learned the flavor of life
as does any poor Indian.

The rest of the flavors
are superfluous to me.

Much like Diane Nelson's analysis of what she terms "Maya hackers," or Maya men and women in contemporary Guatemala who understand how to use modern technology and the tools of modernity to advance their own causes for the indigenous community, Ak'abal's access to world literature serves as a resource for him to craft his own voice, shaped by references to his particular upbringing and tradition.

Like any talented poet, Ak'abal masterfully straddles the division between distinct particularity and universal truth. A concrete example in which Ak'abal's traditional points of reference help illustrate a broader concern is the poem "Nawal Ixim":

"Nawal Ixim"   "Nawal ixim"

Ronda en mí.   Kab'in chuwij.

Telén telén telén...   Telén telén telén...
Lo siento caminando   Kinna'o kab'in
en mi sangre.   pa ri nukik'el.

Talalán, talalán talalán...   Talalán, talalán talalán...
Baila cada vez que canto.   Kaxojow are chi'
                                       kinlalatik.

Nawál Ixim   Nawal ixim
habla en mi lengua.   katch'aw pa ri nuch'ab'al.

De vez en cuando   K'o k'u junjun mul
sale a mirar por mis ojos,   Kel uloq che ri ilem
y se pone triste[39]   pa ri nub'oqoch

rumal k'uri
kuchap b'isonem.
(Ak'abal, *Guardián de la caída del agua* 85)
(Ak'abal, *Ajkem Tzij Tejedor de palabras* 300)

"Nawal Ixim"

Within me it wanders.

Telén telén telén ...
I feel it walking in my blood.

Talalán, talalán talalán ...
It dances every time I sing.

Nawal Ixim
speaks in my tongue.

Every once in a while
it comes out to look through my eyes,
and it gets sad.

Like the stories of magical, transforming selves encountered by Kay Warren in San Andrés Semetabaj, "Nawal Ixim" features a traditional figure of a supernatural being living inside the speaker of the poem. When the *Nawal,* or protective spirit, peers through the speaker's human eyes, the sadness of the human world overtakes it.[41] In an inversion of the stories told to Warren, "the reality" that surrounds the human speaker of the poem shocks the spiritual being rather than the other way around. According to Warren's analysis of the stories circulating in the San Andrés area after the period of extreme violence, many of them have been a way of speaking of lingering anxieties from the war, without having to speak of them directly. The fear and indignation projected toward deceptive creatures of magical transformation thus provide an outlet for pent-up emotions that cannot yet find a mimetic expression for themselves. While horror and anger is cathartically garnered against the magical creature of the stories transcribed by Warren, Ak'abal's poem directly acknowledges the source of sadness: human reality. He writes more about this lamentable inversion in his essay "Ausencia recuperada":

Muchas noches no pude dormir. A veces me sentía más seguro cuando estaba nublado: le temía a mi propia sombra. Y no es que no supiera del miedo. Sabía de él en el sentido cultural. Soy de la cultura del espanto. De ese algo que sabemos que está ahí, invisible, que convive con uno. Ese algo cuya presencia nos eriza la piel o, que por su fuerza energética, nos hace palpitar el corazón. Pero frente a esa realidad que vivimos, el terror hizo palidecer a nuestros espantos.

(Ak'abal, *Con los ojos después del mar* 13–14)

[Often I could not sleep at night. I would sometimes feel safer when it was overcast: I was afraid of my own shadow. And it's not as if I didn't know about fear. I knew of it in a cultural sense. I am from the culture of fright. Of that something that we know is there, invisible; that lives with us. That something whose presence makes the hair on our skin stand on end or who, due to its energetic force, makes our heart beat faster. But in the face of that reality that we lived, the terror made our ghosts pale in comparison.]

Despite a cultural tradition filled with horror stories of the invisible and the supernatural, the despicable events of Guatemala's recent history makes the terror instilled by such stories pale by comparison. "Nawal Ixim" draws from the traditional belief in a *nawal,* or protective spirit associated with each person in the community, to convey the horror of *la violencia* without having to describe it outright.

The ultimate example of Ak'abal's ability to capture a complex thought in a short phrase is his poem "Hablo." In a sense, Ak'abal conveys the underlying sentiment of every text analyzed in this book through this particular poem, succinctly captured in the evocative notion of "covering the mouth of silence":

"Hablo"[42]   "Kinch'awik"[43]

Hablo   Kinch'awik
para taparle   che utz'apixik
la boca   ri uchi'
al silencio.   ri tz'inowik.
                    (Ak'abal, Guardián de la caída del agua 92)
                    (Ak'abal, Aqajtzij Palabramiel 147)

"I speak"

I speak
to cover
the mouth
of silence.

By countering official narratives of the past, all authors in this study provoke their readers to rethink received versions of national histories, and challenge their readers to reconsider critically their own participation in furthering these narratives. With the understanding that the way in which one speaks of the past helps provide a society with the categories that organize spaces of action—especially in light of imposed silences, and the frequent difficulty of commenting openly about counterhegemonic perceptions of history—Humberto Ak'abal's poem "Hablo" rings particularly profound. In his extremely succinct style, Ak'abal has captured the essence of the defiant objective of all of the authors included in this study: they all speak and write "to cover the mouth of silence."

CONCLUSION

In each of the four parts of this study we have considered "the isthmus," "the city," "the nation," or a "space for expressing cultural difference" as productive sites for rethinking assumptions that have long defined perceptions about Central America. Understood as a potential passageway to riches and well-being to be found elsewhere, as a place of confrontation between world ideologies vying for power, as the defining model of banana republics, as a viable route for drug-trafficking, as a site for reconsidering the ongoing relevance of the nation in a globalized landscape, or as a place in which multiple cultures interconnect in their daily existence, reconsiderations of perceptions of place are fundamental to our analysis of ongoing regional identity negotiations.

In *Dividing the Isthmus*, Ana Patricia Rodríguez has coined the term "transisthmus" in approximating the cultural production of Central America: "I offer the trope of the *transisthmus*—an imaginary yet material space—as a spatial periodizing term and as a 'cultural provision' for reading Central American literatures and cultures outside of categories that up to now have elided larger regional complexities" (2). Her use of this trope, which draws from both physical and symbolic referents, allows her to analyze the literature of the region by taking into account local responses to broader, global forces through an often shared, regional perspective evidenced in the texts that she examines. At the same time, this imagined spatiality helps Rodríguez navigate the polemical complexities that arise when defining what constitutes the Central American experience and what voices are better suited to represent this cultural vantage point.

Much like Rodríguez, my own turn to spatial metaphors, in both their concrete and symbolic connotations, resists any rigid definitions of what constitutes a Central American perspective. By focusing on various categories of place as sites of contention, I highlight instances of cultural expression and examples of regional voices through texts that should neither be taken in isolation nor be read as representative of a cohesive, all-encompassing whole. Rethinking the ways in which these spatial concepts are characterized within particular socio-historical contexts can shed light on the regional implications and ultimate consequences of such representations. The dynamic interplay between the symbolic and the material connotations of these spaces is illustrative of how cartographies of thought actively trace potential maps of action beyond the textual realm.

In Part I, I have examined "the isthmus" as a metaphor for deeply rooted historical conflicts in a narrow and constricted landscape where worlds have collided for 500 years. What Pablo Neruda termed the *dulce cintura* or "sweet waist" of the Americas is a landscape that historically has been treated as the shortest route for the achievement of Manifest Destiny (both North to South and East to West). As such, the isthmus has often been used as a stage for the enactment of strategies of hemispheric and global hegemony in microcosm. In my analysis, I have included only a few of the various consequences that this unique geographical formation has had upon the countries of the region.

In *El estrecho dudoso*, Ernesto Cardenal clearly demonstrates the source of the perception of the region as an obstructed, failed passageway to attain desired riches elsewhere (in a mythologized Orient) starting with the arrival of the Spaniards in the area, with their search for a link to the Pacific Ocean. When Cardenal contrasts the violence and self-centered ambition of European colonizers with an idealized Amerindian community, he sets up a parallel critique of all other greedy, materialistic, and power-hungry individuals during his present-day timeframe (that is, Nicaragua in the 1960s under the Somoza dictatorship). Within this setting, the idea of the isthmus as a disappointment—as an obstruction rather than a viable connection to well-being—is extremely suggestive; especially since along the "dubious strait," toward personal ambition and power, many get left out, resulting in a system of sociopolitical relations that is a notable failure for the interests of the majority. The dubious element of the sought-after strait thus acquires an ethical dimension. The metaphor conjures up a place that privileges a system geared toward the selfish amassment of wealth and power for some, over one that is more equitable and inclusive.

This same dynamic of unequal power and wealth resonates with the metaphorical and physical "wound" carved into the land of the isthmus in repeated cases of foreign intervention in the nineteenth and early twentieth centuries, when foreign enterprises set up passageways for interoceanic transport via railways and eventually through the Panama Canal. The establishment of U.S. control on terrain along the canal and the setting up of the infamous School of the Americas in the Panama Canal Zone, where much of Latin America's military leadership received U.S. training for the preservation of the status quo under the guise of internal security concerns, signal the painful extremes to which this inherent dynamic was taken. The isthmus as a concept that has accumulated significance over time thus circulates in the imaginary of Central Americans as a potent symbol that triggers the memory of many sociopolitical failings and painful enactments of the imbalance of power throughout the region's history.

Another frequent association with the figure of the isthmus that I include in my analysis is the clash of world ideologies in the region (capitalism versus communism) during the twentieth century. The isthmus became an important site of confrontation between Cold War ideologies, as the place where the East and the West came to blows without much consideration for the particularities of local complexities. Miguel Angel Asturias, in *Weekend en Guatemala,* and Arturo Arias, in *Después de las bombas,* both demonstrate, through their fictional representations of events in Guatemala after 1954, the disconnect between fears of communist infiltration in the country and the incongruently violent reactions to such fears from within the country and also from the United States. Both authors also underline the incongruous discrepancy between the terminology imposed on particular situations (that is, accusations of being communist, or signaling who is a dangerous enemy to the state) and the actual social dynamics that need to be considered within a complex history of local interactions. This theme resonates strongly with other writers from the region and is repeated in Calixta Gabriel's poem "Comunismo, Capitalismo, Socialismo."

Much like the isthmus, the metaphor of "the city" is also marked historically and has acquired particular symbolic baggage in the region, as noted in Part II. In the representation of urban spaces, it becomes evident that aspirations of "progress" and "modernity" (defined as the regional integration into capitalist world-systems and access to advances in technology) are implemented under the control of a violent, authoritarian state. Asturias's *El Señor Presidente* is a perfect reflection of how such models of progress and modernization imagined elsewhere come to Guatemala at the cost of paternalistic authoritarianism. The portrayal of the city in this novel is a testament to how fear permeates both public and private spaces in the early twentieth-century push toward technological and economic progress, at the expense of many. However, the distinct opposition that Asturias sets up in his novel between a corrupted, violent city and a bucolic countryside gets problematized in Victor Montejo's account, in *Las aventuras de Mister Puttison entre los mayas,* of how indigenous, rural labor provides the foundation for the advancement of Guatemala's modern infrastructure.

The painful trajectory toward modernization marks the city at other stages of the process as well. Manlio Argueta's *Caperucita en la zona roja* captures a fictional rendering of San Salvador from the hidden "underground," where a group of dissatisfied, young Salvadoreans have opted to join the opposition movement and publish clandestine information against the political regime. Their dissatisfaction with the failures of capitalism and of the political system in place leads to the marking of the city's public and hidden spaces with their activism. Eventually, the young protagonists of Argueta's novel decide to join the armed resistance and move to the countryside to pursue a heightened battle against the inequitable system in place in El Salvador in the 1960s and 1970s. With a similar concern for the social disparities heightened by capitalism and personal greed, Carmen Naranjo's critique of a fictional city that is much like Costa Rica's capital, San José, in the 1960s (in *Diario de una multitud*), makes a case for needed social reform voiced from within the bourgeois, capitalist system set in place in Costa Rica. Through her mediocre, self-satisfied characters, she demonstrates the importance of creativity and critical thought within the monotonous complacency of a capitalist society. In both novels, urban spaces are replete with instances in which capitalism and the myths of progress have fallen short of becoming a recourse that benefits the majority.

In Part III, I have addressed "the nation" as a polemical and problematic site for assuming a homogenous sense of collective identity, based on national mythologies, and as a tool for resisting external forces for cultural change within a post–Cold War, global framework. Julio Escoto's *Rey del Albor, Madrugada* demonstrates a persistent return to the parameters of the nation as a place from which to insist on cultural particularity. This strategic turn to the nation is especially understandable for the countries in Central America in proximity to the United States. Situated in the United States' "backyard," they are geographically susceptible to the strong cultural, political, and economic influences of their neighbor to the North. In my analysis, nonetheless, I point out the persistence of problematic assumptions when the author resorts to the mythologies of the nation as a primary referent for the definition of collective identities.

As a counter to how all-encompassing concepts like "the nation" (as rhetorical and sociopolitical constructs) inflict systemic violence on the internal diversities and histories within (and between) the geographic boundaries of modern nation-states, I have addressed the conceptual category of "the other" in Part IV. I ask why a marginalized group would resort to essentialized notions of identity when such "essences" have been traditionally used against groups of people to exclude them from privileged positions based on their ethnicity or gender. In my analysis, I find that the use of essentialist categories of identity are strategic and are meant to provide a safe place from which to speak of collective needs after the trauma of state-implemented genocide that targeted indigenous communities of Guatemala in the late 1970s and early 1980s.

Whereas these core spatial metaphors have helped me organize my thoughts thematically, and provide an important frame of reference to think about the assumptions that configure them in Central America's regional context, I consistently turn back to the representation of history in fiction as the central focus of this project. In his reflections about Rabindranath Tagore's concept of historicality, the subaltern studies scholar Ranajit Guha captures perfectly the approach to the past that is taken by many of the authors included in this book. By viewing history through the specific experiences of the individual in his or her everyday life, we are able to listen to the "sighs and whispers" that traditional historiography tends to exclude from its accounts (Guha 73). Historicality differs significantly from historiography in that, as Tagore suggests, the past "renews itself creatively in literature" (Guha 5). Accordingly, I propose that when fiction is used as a way to revisit historical memories, creativity becomes a tool for subverting official ways of understanding the past and, in the process, literature renovates the language of history, breaking open a multiplicity of silenced perspectives and tracing new forms of acting within the confines described.

My approach in this book is innovative in that, while rooted in political realities, I look at literary form according to the interplay between space and chronology. I insist on the need to take into consideration specific geographical and historical contexts to fully understand the implications of particular representations of sociopolitical events. Within the diverse political contexts that have made it difficult to write about historical issues throughout Central America, the authors that I engage in this study have all chosen to counter the silences and blank pages of official accounts through literature. The particular aesthetic form with which each author has crafted his or her text, in itself, reveals to the reader the effect the text is meant to produce beyond documenting a distinct interpretation of the events represented; as such, we read them as textual cartographies. The form in which the text is crafted can disclose the author's underlying intent, such as the interruption of a totalizing sociopolitical movement's ideology through fragmented discourse; the ironic, self-aware distancing from official interpretations of events through exaggeration, satire, and humor; the desire for a coherent, linear narrative as a palliative for the unpredictability of an unstable world through tales of totalities that incorporate the insinuated "happy endings" of detective stories or epic poetry; or the circulation of oral accounts that borrow rhetorical figures from traditional indigenous tales of transformation to speak indirectly of the unspeakable memories of violence in Guatemala.

Through their accounts of history in the realm of fiction, these stories about the past supplement official histories while conveying each author's individual stance with regard to the events represented and triggering critical reflections on the part of the reader. As the shape of each textual account interrupts, provides a desired coherence, draws a roadmap for eventual paths of "liberation," or supplies the vocabulary to speak of unfathomable truths, et cetera, it becomes evident that the position or place from which one speaks, the vocabulary chosen to tell stories of the past, and the focus on margins, fragments, peripheries, centers, totalities, essences, antiessential hybridities, or metaphorical doubles, all come together to trace the textual cartographies that ultimately outline the parameters for the ways a society can imagine possibilities for action at a given point in time.

Through the stories that circulate about recognizable events, a society defines the categories and vocabulary that help its members make sense of their surroundings, their history, and their own identity in a way that ultimately shapes "spaces" that can be conceptualized for engaging with one another—spaces from which one can position oneself and interact with others. To speak of oneself as "Maya," for example, and demand to be treated with dignity and respect as a member of that collective identity construct significantly alters the scope of progressive activism and the possibilities of sociopolitical engagement of the indigenous population in Guatemala. To paraphrase Victor Montejo, the process of naming carries with it the power of defining the choices others will have to make when they interact with a revitalized Maya community. This active claim to shape creatively the language of sociopolitical engagement with the world beyond the text underlines the importance of circulating nonhegemonic versions of history, such as the ones analyzed in this study.

NOTES

INTRODUCTION

1. This is the Spanish version of the poem.
2. This is the K'iché version of the poem.
3. Cited with kind permission from the author. The English translation is mine. Unless otherwise indicated, translations into English in all the chapters in this book are mine.
4. A good, concrete example of this dynamic is the insistence on the use of the term "Maya" on the part of the current indigenous cultural movement in Guatemala today. The shift from linguistic divisions as primary identity markers to this more inclusive term, and certainly the move away from the negative historical baggage of the word "Indian" has allowed for new ways to imagine sociopolitical and cultural mobilization around shared Mayan concerns.
5. Refer, for example, to my article about the Panamanian novelist Rosa María Britton, in which very similar issues are addressed: "Laberintos de apariencias y reiteraciones: reconstruyendo la integridad psíquica/ nacional en *Laberintos de orgullo* de Rosa María Britton," *Rosa María Britton ante la crítica*, ed. Humberto López Cruz (Madrid: Editorial Verbum, 2007).
6. Refer to Aínsa's "La reescritura de la historia en la nueva narrativa latinoamericana" (1991), Menton's *Latin America's New Historical Novel* (1993), Pons's *Memorias del olvido: La novela histórica de fines del siglo XX* (1996), and Perkowska's *Historias híbridas: La nueva novela histórica latinoamericana (1985–2000) ante las teorías posmodernas de la historia* (2008), among others, about the emergence and characteristics of Latin America's "new historical novel."
7. Nineteenth-century historical novels in Latin America responded to the need for coming to terms with great historical changes brought about by the hemisphere's new independence from Spain and the national plans that were in the process of being formulated. Through rewriting the past, a plan of national foundation was being forged and legitimated. In the words of María Cristina Pons, "las novelas históricas latinoamericanas del XIX se constituyen [...] en discursos de legitimación de la ideología liberal, de ratificación del poder y de una búsqueda para confirmar la identidad de las nacientes repúblicas frente a esa otredad que era el pasado colonial. La novela histórica

latinoamericana del XIX no sólo tenía que colaborar a construir el futuro de estas nacientes repúblicas, sino que también tenía que participar en la construcción del pasado" (88) ["Latin American historical novels of the nineteenth century constitute ... legitimizing discourses of the Liberal ideology, of the ratification of power, and of a search to confirm an identity for the newly born republics before that otherness that was the colonial past. Latin America's historical novel of the nineteenth century not only had to collaborate in the building of the future of these new republics, but also had to participate in the construction of the past"].

8. See Magdalena Perkowska's introduction and the first chapter of *Historias híbridas* for a thorough discussion of the engagement with history in an era of postmodernism (which has declared the theoretical "end of history") in recent Latin American historical fiction.

9. For a complete list of the characteristics of Latin America's new historical novel identified by Fernando Aínsa, refer to his article "La reescritura de la historia en la nueva narrativa latinoamericana."

10. In her historical novel *Asalto al paraíso*, first published in 1992, Tatiana Lobo provides an alternative reading to the whitewashed, official memory of Costa Rica's past by resurrecting stories of violence regarding indigenous and slave communities on national soil. In the caption on the back of the novel, Joaquín Gutiérrez underlines the novel's function in collective identity production: "La novela nos da, no la visión externa y objetiva de los historiadores, sino nuestra historia interior. Aparte del gran deleite con que se lee, es una inapreciable ayuda para conocernos mejor a nosotros mismos" ["The novel provides us with, not the external and objective vision of the historians, but our own internal history. Besides the great pleasure with which it is read, it is an inestimable help for us to get to know ourselves better"].

11. See Noé Jitrik's *Historia e imaginación literaria: Las posibilidades de un género* (1995).

CHAPTER 1

1. [... in Central America, the Banana Republics, a passage way, a bridge between two oceans, the backyard for continental security ...].

2. Refer to Carl Sauer's *The Early Spanish Main* for an account of Columbus's initial encounter with the isthmus and Vasco Nuñez de Balboa's journey to the South Sea (the Pacific Ocean) in Chapter VI, "Veragua, Last Venture of Columbus (1502–1504)," and Chapter XI, "Entry to Darién and the South Sea (1511–1514)."

3. This simultaneous movement toward both the past and the future, the dual concern for record and prophecy, is traced by Derrida in *Archive Fever*, where the author links the archive with a promise and responsibility for the future: "[...] the question of the archive

is not, we repeat, a question of the past [...] It is a question of the future, the question of the future itself, the question of a response, of a promise and of a responsibility for tomorrow [...] A spectral messianicity is at work in the concept of the archive and ties it, like religion, like history, like science itself, to a very singular experience of the promise" (36).

4. Fragments of *El estrecho dudoso* are cited with kind permission from the author Ernesto Cardenal. Reprinted selections of the English translation have been authorized by Indiana University Press. [He found the Strait in Veragua: / Veragua, in the province of Mango, / which borders on Cathay ... / But it was a Strait of land / it was not of water. (5)] I have used John Lyons's translation of Cardenal's text throughout this chapter, unless otherwise noted.

5. [The Most Magnificent Pedrarias Dávila/ *Furor Domini!!!* / was the first "promoter of progress" in Nicaragua / and the first Dictator (57)].

6. By representing the place where aspirations of material and spiritual well-being were to come true, "the Orient" became the embodiment of hope in the imagination of the West in the sixteenth century. Beyond concrete colonial dreams of finding the Spice Islands or the coveted Asian provinces of *Cipango* (Japan) or *Cathay* (China), a turn toward the East was an expression of hope for something better. More pragmatically, those who could gain control of an interoceanic strait would be able to amass a fortune charging others for the transit toward their dreams.

7. All the primary texts included span from the approximate time period of the events narrated in the poem and range from diaries, letters, and chronicles to transcripts of legal proceedings, etc., thus creating a pastiche of various styles and voices. The *Chilam Balam* does, however, include entries that extend beyond the sixteenth century.

8. Even though Cardenal did not call them "cantos" *per se*, in the interest of clarity we shall refer to the individual poetic sections as "cantos."

9. In both *Vida perdida* (Cardenal 222) and in a frequently cited interview with Mario Benedetti from 1970, Cardenal has stated that his primary poetic influence is Ezra Pound.

10. The translation of Oviedo is from Ephraim George Squier's book *Nicaragua* (1852), in which he cites the same section of Oviedo's text.

11. In Oviedo's words: "Y ése mismo debía ella ser, y si éste decía verdad, no se puede negar su comunicación de los indios y el diablo" (27) ["In short, he described her as like the devil, which she must have been. If this cazique told the truth, it cannot be a matter of doubt that the Indians were in connection with him"].

12. "Statistical data, fragments of letters, editorials from a newspaper, historical chronicles, documents, jokes, and anecdotes (things that used to be considered elements of prose and not poetry) all fit in a poem," notes Cardenal in his interview with Benedetti when speaking of the impact of Pound's work on his own (Benedetti 176).

13. In his chapter entitled "Ernesto Cardenal and North American Literature: The Formulation of an Ethical Identity," Steven F. White insists that Ezra Pound's influence on Cardenal's poetry goes beyond merely technical and stylistic aspects. More important is what he identifies as the "underlying moral urge to manipulate history" found in the work of both poets (170). At issue for White is the question: "How does one utilize the past in a contemporary manner in order to create a moral platform for the prophetic?" (159). He underlines the fact that "both poets, [Pound and Cardenal] although from opposite ends of the ideological spectrum, are engaged in an intense dialogue with the past, and hope to manipulate history in order to create a more ethically sound future" (178).

14. Refer to Tamara Williams's article "Ernesto Cardenal's *El estrecho dudoso*: Reading/Re-Writing of History" for an in-depth discussion of the correspondence between Cardenal's historiographical perspective and some of the basic tenets of Liberation Theology. Greg Dawes's chapter entitled "Poetry and 'Spiritual Materialism': Ernesto Cardenal" also provides a useful background to connections between Cardenal's poetic work and his adherence to Liberation Theology.

15. This is not to imply that the original colonial texts purported to be disinterested versions of events, but to remind current readers to keep such interests in mind when searching for "truths" in primary documents.

16. Michel de Certeau proposes that all historical discourse is marked by traces of the repressed information that has been omitted; that there is an "uncannily familiar" kernel of truth that can be found within the text itself despite the original intentions of the historian (*The Writing of History* 340–41).

17. As his *Cartas de Relación* were intended, in a sense, as positive "propaganda" to defend his endeavors in the region before the monarchy, even if his men would have been driven to the desperate extremes of cannibalism, it would not have served Cortés to report such facts in his chronicles. Other Spanish accounts such as Álvar Núñez Cabeza de Vaca's *Naufragios*—in which Cabeza de Vaca intends to portray a picture of the hardships he witnessed and endured after being shipwrecked and stranded—do include instances of cannibalism by the Spaniards.

18. Tamara Williams stresses the heroic stature that both Catholic bishops assume in the poem: "Within the context of the struggle, Bartolomé de las Casas and Antonio de Valdivieso, both Catholic bishops recognized for their commitment to Indian rights and justice in the New World, emerge as heroes [...] The poem's heroes, las Casas and Valdivieso, are portrayed as characters worthy of moral praise and historical reminiscence in their life-threatening struggle to secure integrity, dignity and survival of a community facing possible annihilation. Their heroic stature is enhanced by the continuous support they appear

to receive from a divine source whose anger consistently humiliates those who perpetrate sin, violence and oppression" ("Ernesto Cardenal and the New Latin American Epic" 639).

19. In his description of the epic in *The Dialogic Imagination*, Bakhtin writes: "The world of the epic is the national heroic past: it is a world of 'beginnings' and 'peak times' in the national history, a world of fathers and of founders of families, a world of 'firsts' and 'bests'" (13).

20. Ernesto Cardenal is a Catholic priest who has practiced and preached according to the ideals of Liberation Theology. Refer to his text *El evangelio en Solentiname* (1978) for excerpts of community discussions interpreting the gospel among members of his parish in the Nicaraguan islands of Solentiname in Lake Nicaragua.

21. Williams cites Gustavo Gutiérrez, *The Power of the Poor in History* (New York: Orbis, 1984).

22. The contrast with the materialistic and despotic rule of the Spanish conquistadores is particularly remarkable when set against the initial descriptions of the Amerindians in canto ii: "No tienen jefes ni capitanes de guerra / sino que andan sin orden, cada uno libremente. / Esta gente vive en libertad, no obedece a nadie / ni tiene ley ni señor. No riñen entre sí [...] desprecian el oro y las piedras preciosas" (Cardenal 6) ["They have no chiefs or war leaders / moving about uncommanded, each one freely. / These people live in freedom, obey no one / and know neither law nor master. They do not quarrel among themselves [...] they show no interest in gold or precious stones" (7)]. This peaceful, nonhierarchical indigenous community is set against the tyrannical rule of Pedrarias, who rules by silencing his opponents through fear: "Después Pedrarias se hizo residencia él mismo. / Publicó por pregón que el que tuviera quejas /las fuera a presentar ... (Ejemplo de democracia)" (Cardenal 22) ["Then Pedrarias instigated his own impeachment. / He broadcast through the crier that whoever had complaints / should go and present them ... (model of democracy)" (23)].

23. There is ultimately no contradiction in proposing that Cardenal engages history as an *open-ended* process and situates this struggle within an overarching *closed* system of justice. While the resolution of justice lies in the future, the author has faith that it will arrive someday.

24. Clearly, I am oversimplifying the binary nature of "good" versus "evil," and it is precisely this type of binarism that got problematized during the course of the Nicaraguan revolution itself (1979). However, in 1966, when the poem was published, much effort was focused on rallying support against the Somocista dictatorship and condemning its excesses despite the vigilant censorship imposed by his regime. In the process, all groups that opposed Somoza coalesced under a broad alliance. Moreover, the binary world vision of the time was undeniably shaped by the backdrop of the Cold War.

25. Williams cites Bakhtin in *The Dialogic Imagination* to describe the concept of double-voiced dialogues: "It serves two different intentions: the direct intention of the character who is speaking, and the refracted intention of the author ... A potential dialogue is embedded in them, one as yet unfolded, a concentrated dialogue of two voices, two world views, two languages" (Bakhtin, cited in Williams, "Narrative Strategies and Counter-History in *El Estrecho Dudoso*" 56).

26. The allusion here is clearly to Anastasio Somoza García's two sons Luis Somoza Debayle and Anastasio Somoza Debayle, who had their turn in the leadership of Nicaragua. Upon his assassination in 1956 by Rigoberto López Pérez, Somoza García left the rule of Nicaragua to his two sons, Luis and Anastasio.

27. William Walker (1824–1860). A commemorative plaque placed on his house in Nashville, Tennessee, summarizes his life as follows: "William Walker 'Grey-eyed Man of Destiny.' Born May 8, 1824, Walker moved to this site from 6th Ave. N. in 1840. In early life he was doctor, lawyer and journalist. He invaded Mexico in 1853 with forty-six men and proclaimed himself Pres., Republic of Lower Calif. Led force into Nicaragua in 1855; was elected its Pres. in 1856. In attempt to wage war on Honduras was captured and executed Sept. 12, 1860" (Rosengarten 12).

28. Cornelius Vanderbilt (1794–1877) was a New York businessman who created the Accessory Transit Company in 1850 to open immediate access and passenger service across Nicaragua in the wake of the discovery of gold in California in 1848, given the resulting urgency for easy transit between the East and West coasts of the United States. When William Walker, as the president of Nicaragua in 1856, took over Vanderbilt's transit company, the Commodore suspended his other company "The Nicaragua Line" from providing a rapid steamship service bringing passengers from New York to Greytown and then from San Juan del Sur or Corinto to San Francisco. This, in turn, isolated Walker and assisted Costa Rica in ousting him from office (Woodward 138–145, Rosengarten 93–109).

29. Anastasio Somoza García was the president of Nicaragua from 1937 to 1947 and again from 1951 to 1956. His son Luis Somoza Debayle was the president of the Nicaraguan congress from 1951 to 1956, and he took over the presidency of the republic from 1957 until 1963. Subsequently, Somoza García's other son, Anastasio Somoza Debayle ("Tachito"), took over control of the presidency from 1967 to 1972 and from 1974 until he was ousted by the revolution in 1979.

30. In fact, it was Walker's associate in San Francisco, Byron Cole, who was offered "a large land grant in Nicaragua in return for help in ousting the Conservatives. Cole persuaded Walker [...] to support the Liberal cause in return for additional land grants. By this time both Cole and Walker were thoroughly imbued with the mentality of 'Manifest Destiny,' and they looked upon Nicaragua as a field

for expansion of democratic ideals as well as land development" (Woodward 139).

31. Nonetheless, as Ralph Lee Woodward, Jr., reminds us, Walker did have some local support within the ranks of the region's Liberal party. Once again, one can trace back to this time a connection between despotic, authoritarian figures that interrupt a chaotic environment under the pretenses of order, reform, and development at the costly expense of extreme violence and the suspension of basic individual rights: "Although the Liberals were, generally, out of power throughout Central America, they praised and defended Walker's intervention; Walker's efforts to bring the Jacksonian Revolution to the isthmus coincided with their own political ideologies of reform and development. They agreed with him that Central America needed a renaissance of republican and democratic values, destruction of the aristocratic party, development of public education, and increased production and trade" (Woodward 141).

32. Ernesto Cardenal wrote another collection of historical poems specifically about William Walker entitled *With Walker in Nicaragua and Other Early Poems, 1949–1954.*

33. Translation by Lewis Bertrand in *Selected Writings of Bolívar.*

34. According to Laurence Greene, Spanish efforts to bridge the two seas were stopped during colonial times as a matter of strategic protection against the British maritime forces: "Scarcely fifty years after Columbus visited the eastern coast, a Portuguese, Antonio Galvao, proposed that the river and lake [in Nicaragua] be used as an interoceanic waterway; and from that day on, all classes of men interested themselves in the project. King Philip of Spain saw the danger of connecting two oceans through the very center of his colonies, with a nautical Great Britain as his arch-enemy, and he prohibited any efforts to build a canal" (Greene 56).

35. For an in-depth account of the events surrounding the construction of the canal in Panama, refer to David McCullough's *The Path Between the Seas: The Creation of the Panama Canal 1870–1914.* For a more recent and nuanced description of current scholarship regarding Panama and the canal, refer to Peter Szok's article "Beyond the Canal: Recent Scholarship on Panama," published in the *Latin American Research Review.*

CHAPTER 2

1. Cited in Ranajit Guha's *History at the Limit of World-History* (2002). Tagore's citation is taken from a transcription of his comments during a conversation with Bengali writer Buddhadev Basu in May 1941. The transcription was published in a compilation of Tagore's works and is entitled "Historicality in Literature." Guha includes his own translation of the text into English as an appendix to his book.

2. The irony is not lost on me that immediately after discussing Guha's insights into the value of turning away from historiography that privileges state and public affairs my own text resorts to a section of historical context that is grounded in these very terms. The framing of historicality in fiction within a broader understanding of "big picture" events in history can only enrich the dialogue between both approaches to engaging with the past.

3. According to Schlesinger and Kinzer, President Eisenhower's secretary of state, John Foster Dulles, had been a senior partner in a New York law firm that provided legal assistance to the Schroder Bank, the institution that was the key financial advisor to the International Railways of Central America (IRCA), which was subsequently controlled by the UFCO. His brother, Allen Dulles, the director of the CIA, also did some work for the same law firm and served on the board of directors of the Schroder Bank. "Schroder, meantime, maintained a share of stock in IRCA; indeed, as late as 1954, the president of Schroder was himself on the board of the railroad company, even while it was controlled by United Fruit. The Schroder bank, was, coincidentally or not, a depository of secret CIA funds for covert operations" (Schlesinger and Kinzer 106). In addition, the assistant secretary of state for inter-American affairs, John Moors Cabot, had family members who owned stock in United Fruit. His brother Thomas served as the president of the company in 1948, and United Nations Ambassador Henry Cabot Lodge was a stockholder too (106–7). Even President Eisenhower's personal secretary, Anne Whitman, happened to have connections to the United Fruit, as her husband, Edmund Whitman, was the UFCO's public relations director.

4. Ironically, the U.S. Department of Justice was conducting an investigation regarding UFCO's operations and "reached the conclusion that its monopoly on banana exports from countries like Guatemala was a violation of American antitrust laws" (Schlesinger and Kinzer 220). The Department of Justice sued the UFCO only five days after Arbenz resigned. The lawsuit lasted for several years and had a significant effect in breaking up the company's banana business in Guatemala (Schlesinger and Kinzer 221).

5. Regarding his take on the communist influence, Gleijeses writes: "In no country of Latin America had the communists ever been as influential as they were in Guatemala. And no president had ever been as close to the communists as was Arbenz. It required no manipulations by UFCO minions for U.S. officials to appreciate these truths" (362). But he then clarifies that: "U.S. officials were alarmed by the rising influence of communism in Guatemala. And yet they knew that the communists were not in control of Guatemala. Neither the CIA nor embassy officials nor the military attachés ever claimed that the Guatemalan army was infiltrated by communists—and the army, they noted, was Guatemala's key institution" (365).

6. Schlesinger and Kinzer cite a revealing quote from Bernays in a 1928 text entitled *Propaganda*: "The conscious and intelligent manipulation of the organized habits and opinions of the masses is an important element in democratic society. Those who manipulate this unseen mechanism of society constitute an invisible government which is the true ruling power of our country ... it is the intelligent minorities which need to make use of propaganda continuously and systematically" (80).

7. "Castillo Armas's 'rather ramshackle army' of *liberacionistas* consisted of about 250 men: approximately 150 rebels crossed the border on June 17 and headed in the direction of Zacapa; the others attacked Puerto Barrios, to the north, a few days later" (Gleijeses 320).

8. The conclusions of the United Nations Commission for Historical Clarification (CEH) outline the causes for armed confrontation in Guatemala, which include the closing of political spaces after 1954 as well as other "parallel phenomena" such as "structural injustice, racism, the increasing exclusionary and anti-democratic nature of institutions, as well as the reluctance to promote substantive reforms that could have reduced structural conflicts" (http://hrdata.aaas. org/ceh/report/english/concl.html).

9. Asturias is very clear about implicating the media in the process of emptying the discourse of current events of any credible content. In the story "Los agrarios" partially about North American professor Carey (recently back from having to testify before the Committee of Un-American Activities for an article he wrote on Guatemala for *The Economist*), the predominance of compelling signs over substantive ideas becomes evident: "El hallazgo del término 'comunismo' aplicado a este pequeño país no hubiera trascendido, no hubiera pasado de un mal chiste, si la publicidad masiva no lo vacía de su contenido ideológico aplicado a la realidad y la convierte en un signo de peligro ... nadie al ver el signo de la muerte en un frasco de veneno, averigua si el contenido es en verdad mortal [...] y esto fue lo que nuestra publicidad hizo con la palabra 'comunismo' aplicada a un país de tres millones de habitantes que en manera alguna podían ser un peligro para nosotros ... se creó el peligro por el signo, por la palabra repetida, martillada, multiplicada, por nuestra basta utilería ... por eso sostengo que la escritura publicitaria es ideográfica y que el publicista debe pensar en signos, no en ideas" (Asturias 232) ["The use of the term 'Communism' as applied to this small country would not have had much significance, would not have been more than a bad joke, if the mass publicity had not emptied it of its ideological content as it applies to reality and converted it into a sign for danger ... upon seeing the sign for death on a bottle of poison no one tries to find out if its content is truly mortal ... and this is what our publicity did with the word 'Communism' applied to a country of three million inhabitants that could not possibly be a danger to us ... danger was created

by means of the sign, of the repeated word, hammered, multiplied, by our vast arsenal of resources ... that is why I maintain that publicity writing is ideographic and that the publicist should think about signs, not about ideas"].

10. Evidently, a contemporary magazine that reported events unfolding in Guatemala at the time was named *Visión*. By using the plural of an actual title, Asturias creates the effect of multiple levels of meaning. The author's allusion to real publications gives immediacy to his description of media outlets putting forth a very particular version of events. Schlesinger and Kinzer mention *Visión* when describing the activities of Crede H. Calhoun, a journalist sent to Guatemala to cover UFCO's troubles in the region: "Calhoun dutifully wrote a series of alarming reports about 'Reds' in the country. Bernays later called Calhoun's articles 'masterpieces of objective reporting.' They sparked the interest of *Time, Newsweek, U.S. News & World Report, The Atlantic Monthly* and the Latin magazine *Visión*, among others, all of whom dispatched journalists to Guatemala to document what was said to be the advance of Marxism there" (Schlesinger and Kinzer 86–87).

11. Similarly, in *Después de las bombas* it is also up to the women of the family to tell the story of Máximo's predecessors' political involvement against the previous dictatorships of Manuel Estrada Cabrera and Jorge Ubico. See *Después de las bombas* (126–29) and also Linda Craft's discussion of the subject (*Novels of Testimony and Resistance from Central America* 139).

12. While Asturias's story may seem like a far-fetched exaggeration, a similar account is described by Schlesinger and Kinzer in *Bitter Fruit*: "Thomas McCann of the Fruit Company's press office circulated photographs of mutilated human bodies about to be buried in a mass grave as examples of the atrocities committed by the Arbenz regime uncovered by Castillo Armas. McCann later admitted that the bodies in the pictures could have been almost anything from earthquake victims to executed foes of Castillo Armas himself" (187).

13. In her article "America and Guatemala in the Anti-Yankee Novels of Miguel Ángel Asturias: A Love-Hate Relationship," María Salgado ties together all four novels by stating that: "Implicit in these four works is the accusation that Guatemala has become a *de facto* colony of the United States thanks to the shameless cooperation of the many Guatemalans who have sold out to the Yankee dollar" (79).

14. Later on, his son, Rodrigo Asturias, would heed his father's implicit call to revolution by joining the guerrilla forces. He assumed a leadership position in the Unidad Revolucionaria Nacional Guatemalteca (URNG) under the pseudonym of Commander Gaspar Ilom, the mythical character of his father's novel *Hombres de Maíz*.

15. The citation is from Bakhtin's essay "Forms of Time and Chronotope in the Novel" in *The Dialogic Imagination*, 236.

16. The novel is cited with kind permission from the author, Arturo Arias. The English translation is by Asa Zatz, published by Curbstone Press.

17. This "other truth" of which Max speaks is reminiscent of Ranajit Guha's reflections on the telling of the Mahabharata and other ancient tales of India that fall outside the scope of a Westernized "World-history" that privileges "unmediated" *experience* as truth. By contrast, such tales would look instead to the process of *delivery* of the story in a way that would evoke wonder and thoughtfulness from its listeners and lead to a different, and profound, form of knowledge.

18. Once the anticommunist military gained access to the government, a massive campaign to destroy literally all potential centrist or reformist leaders resulted in a climate of extreme polarization and repression.

19. In "The Signification of the Phallus," published in *Ecrits*, Lacan writes that "[the phallus] is the signifier that is destined to designate meaning effects as a whole, insofar as the signifier conditions them by its presence as signifier" (690).

20. For Linda Craft, the nonproductive nature of masturbation is also linked to Max's initial clumsiness with words and even to the perceived sterility of literature as a genre: "The time finally comes for Max to act. For him action entails picking up a pen rather than a gun. He starts writing secretly at night. To her horror, his mother suspects he is masturbating, implying perhaps at a symbolic level the 'sterility' of literature in public opinion; his pen has become a substitute phallus" (*Novels of Testimony and Resistance from Central America* 142).

21. In *Inevitable Revolutions: The United States in Central America* (1984), Walter LaFeber describes how in the 1960s such military training was implemented for the preservation of the status quo under the guise of internal security concerns: "Military funds inundated small economies, transformed government budgets, and created a large military group trained by U.S. officers in such special schools as the Southern Command's School of the Americas in the Panama Canal Zone. Secretary of Defense Robert McNamara announced in 1963 that the newly trained military leaders' responsibility was not 'hemispheric defense,' but 'internal security'" (151).

22. See citation above regarding the Irreverentes 70.

23. Hayden White would surely add that a writer's perception of the past is itself already conditioned by the linguistic tropes that inevitably define our relationship with the world around us.

24. A "closure" that Cardenal's faith situates in the future.

25. This painstaking process of language acquisition is traced from the point of his awareness of the link between words and meaning, when he is four years old: "Todo tenía su nombre. Tenía que aprender los nombres de muchas cosas" (19) ["Everything had its own name. He had to learn the names of a lot of things" (17)]. And yet, the reader follows this learning process with the additional knowledge that words

can convey multiple meanings at the same time. Shortly after the citation above, Máximo reflects further as he walks along the city streets: "Podía seguir cualquier dirección. Caminar por cualquier calle. Eso se llamaba libertad. Claro, a menos que la calle estuviera bloqueada por muros caídos o montañas de cadáveres" (20) ["He could go in any direction. Walk on any street. That's what's called freedom. Sure, unless the street was blocked by fallen walls or piles of corpses" (18)]. With the satirical caveat that poses dead bodies as a potential obstacle to the new concept he has learned (*libertad*), one quickly sees that Máximo's sense of liberty will be severely restricted. The word "liberty" cast in this horrific context, with a knowing wink to the savvy reader, comes to mean both freedom and its negation in actual practice.

26. In his essay, "Discourse in the Novel," Bakhtin emphasizes the importance of the process of turning a discourse one is struggling against into an image of language, thus exposing its limitations within the novel as a genre: "This process—experimenting by turning persuasive discourse into speaking persons—becomes especially important in those cases where a struggle against such images has already begun, where someone is striving to liberate himself from the influence of such an image and its discourse by means of objectification, or is striving to expose the limitations of both image and discourse. The importance of struggling with another's discourse, its influence in the history of an individual's coming to ideological consciousness, is enormous" (Bakhtin 348).

CHAPTER 3

1. Robert Armstrong and Janet Shenk note the direct relation between the *matanza* of 1932 and the turn away from traditional indigenous culture as markers of difference: "In the Indian communities of the western coffee areas—the scene of the uprising—the traditional ways were abandoned; the traditional garb discarded and Nahuatl no longer spoken in public" (30).

2. The idea of a *forward* motion is commonly linked to a perception of future improvement in a linear fashion. However, among the lessons of history is the fact that if such improvements only affect a select few then, as time passes, the tensions that are created by an exclusionary system lead to a more complex and volatile dynamic. Ironically, the most extreme inequities are often created in the course of the push "forward."

3. Even in publications of the time, one can find a self-awareness of the enormous price being paid for Liberal reforms through the implementation of terror. In Mariano Zeceña's 1898 text, *La revolución de 1871 y sus caudillos*, the author remarks: "Hubo necesidad de la tiranía para no perder lo conquistado; y he aquí por qué la Reforma social se

impuso por medio del terror en nuestra patria, por qué se vertió tanta
sangre, por qué nos cuestan tan caros esos progresos" (96) ["There
was a need for tyranny so as not to lose what had been attained;
and this is why social reform was imposed by means of terror in our
country, why so much blood was shed, why the costs of progress are
so expensive for us"].

4. ["... my administration will be of a short and provisional nature, but
just because of that, History will not cease to demand from me a strict
accounting of the acts that I carry out in its duration ..."].

5. Taken from a speech given by Estrada Cabrera on February 11, 1898,
cited by Raúl Agüero (*Guatemala, la Revolución Liberal de 1871 y
las administraciones del Benemérito Licenciado don Manuel Estrada
Cabrera* 40).

6. [Instead of the alphabet, the Protector of the Studious Youth's
"Great Luminous Minerva" brought us the United Fruit Co., to
which she gave the initial incredible concessions that we endure ...
"She, the cosmic maid," in her temple of Corinthian columns, in our
indigenous country of a forgotten culture of its own, would feel very
odd indeed with the imaginary transplant.]

7. Asturias and his family were personally affected by the Estrada
Cabrera regime. When the author was only five years old, his father
fell out of the president's favor and was forced to move to Salamá,
in the countryside, for several years. Once Asturias returned to the
capital, he was exposed to the atmosphere of repression that perme-
ated Guatemala City; and as a university student he became deeply
involved in the fight against Estrada Cabrera. Between February and
April 1920 he contributed several articles attacking the dictator and
the Liberal Party in the university publication *El Estudiante* (Taracena
680), and he was among the delegation that escorted the tyrant from
his residence to prison when Cabrera was overthrown on April 14,
1920.

8. This is particularly true of Minerva, the Roman goddess of wisdom,
who became Estrada Cabrera's preferred symbol to celebrate his
government's accomplishments. As such, temples dedicated to the
goddess were erected throughout the country and yearly celebrations, "*las Minervalias*," were observed in October in honor of the
"advances" achieved during his regime. Refer to William Clary's
article, "La máscara de la impostura: el retrato paródico de las Fiestas
de Minerva en *El Señor Presidente*," for a discussion of the role of
Minerva in the Estrada Cabrera period.

9. It is during his regime that many concessions are signed that established foreign monopolies in the country, especially in the transportation and infrastructure sectors.

10. All of the page citations for *El Señor Presidente* are from the 1984
Alianza Losada version, unless otherwise noted.

11. All translations of *El Señor Presidente* are taken from Frances Partridge's version in English published by Atheneum in 1969.

12. When President Reyna Barrios was assassinated in 1898, Estrada Cabrera was appointed provisional president, and within a few months was elected to a full six-year term, serving as constitutional president until 1905. Thereafter, despite article 66 in the Guatemalan constitution, which prohibited the reelection of the Executive leader, he was consecutively reelected for three more terms in 1905, 1911, and 1917.

13. Gail Martin notes the origins of the link between Estrada Cabrera and Minerva: "En 1899, en los primeros meses del régimen, el adulador Rafael Spínola, ya secretario de Estrada Cabrera cuando era ministro de Gobierno, concibió la idea de dedicar el sistema de educación pública a la diosa Minerva [...] cada octubre durante veinte años, sería celebrada una enorme fiesta de inspiración helénica consagrada no solamente a Minerva sino a su hijo predilecto, el licenciado Estrada Cabrera" (548) ["In 1899, during the first months of the regime, shameless flatterer Rafael Spínola, already Estrada Cabrera's secretary when he was Minister of Government, came up with the idea of dedicating the system of public education to the goddess Minerva ... for twenty years every October an enormous festivity of Hellenic inspiration was celebrated. It was dedicated not only to Minerva but also to her favorite son, Mr. Estrada Cabrera"].

14. Clary notes that among the "men of letters" who contributed to the so-called *Albumes de Minerva* are such *modernista* writers as José Santos Chocano, Enrique Gómez Carrillo, José Enrique Rodó, Manuel Ugarte, and Porfirio Barba Jacob (Clary 672).

15. Rather than give a detailed physical description of the president as a tangible character within the novel's plot, the author usually presents him as a vague, yet all-pervasive entity directly affecting the life of every individual through the fear of falling into disfavor. This quality of being simultaneously everywhere and nowhere transforms the dictator into a mythological presence hanging over every Guatemalan's conscience.

16. "Discerniósele el dictado de educador del pueblo y maestro del espíritu; y durante su administración subió el número de analfabetos del noventa y dos al noventa y siete por ciento" (Arévalo Martínez 313–14) ["He was given the dictate of educator of the people and teacher of the spirit; and during his administration the number of illiterate people increased from ninety-two to ninety-seven per cent"].

17. In *Miguel Angel Asturias's Archaeology of Return*, René Prieto suggestively calls attention to Asturias's profound identification with his mother and its possible effect on his writings: "The truth is that Asturias's involvement with his mother cannot be overstated and yet, it has been mentioned only in passing by a handful of critics [...] The body of the mother, forbidden above all things, would explain

the *ausencia* that permeates his writings. I do not think it in any way farfetched to suggest that the unquenchable longing that Asturias expresses in all his writings is directly connected to the very ambiguous love that he reveals in the two 'Sonetos a María'" (116–17).

18. The depth of his sadness for his absent mother leads el Pelele to kill Colonel Parrales Sonriente, of the innermost circle of el Señor Presidente's paternalistic regime, by sinking his fingers into the Colonel's eyes. The murder that propels the actions of the novel clearly echoes, although skewed, the ill-fated patricidal murder committed by Oedipus: "El bulto se detuvo—la risa le entorchaba la cara—, acercándose al idiota de puntapié y, en son de broma, le gritó: —¡Madre! No dijo más. Arrancado del suelo por el grito, el Pelele se le fue encima y, sin darle tiempo a que hiciera uso de sus armas, le enterró los dedos en los ojos, le hizo pedazos la nariz a dentelladas y le golpeó las partes con las rodillas hasta dejarlo inerte" (Asturias 13) ["The new arrival stopped; his face lit up with a smile. Going up to the idiot on tiptoe he shouted jeeringly at him: 'Mother!' That was all. Torn from the ground by the cry, the Zany flung himself upon his tormentor, and, without giving him time to get at his weapons, thrust his fingers into his eyes, tore at his nose with his teeth and jabbed his private parts with his knees, till he fell to the ground motionless" (11)].

19. An example of the author's manipulation of time would be, for instance, that while the first and second parts of the text take place in three days each, the third part takes "weeks, months, years ..." to transpire. As time is stretched into infinity, the president appears to achieve immortality, and the immanence of his tyrannical abuses becomes a constant threat as a continual historical presence in Guatemala.

20. Krauel cites Asturias: page 284 in *El Señor Presidente* (1984).

21. Refer to de Certeau's chapter "Quotations of Voices," in *The Practice of Everyday Life*, for an analysis of the voices and cries of those excluded from the written and the modern scriptural economy: "the savage, the madman, the child, even woman" (156–58).

22. A similar notion of the maternal emerging as the voice of alterity in a paternal/patriarchal system can be found in the article "Approaching Abjection," where Julia Kristeva designates that which is not signifiable under the law of the father as *maternal:* "[...] it is in the work of Joyce that we will discover that it is the feminine body, the maternal body in its unsignifiable and unsymbolisable aspects which support, for the individual, the fantasm of this loss [a collapse of paternal laws] where he is engulfed or intoxicated through his inability to name an object of desire" (140).

23. It was not until the earthquakes of 1917 and 1918 that people found the courage to voice their opinion regarding Guatemala's situation, given the regime's relative vulnerability with respect to the natural disasters.

24. Refer to the critical edition of *El Señor Presidente*, edited by Gerald Martin, for a detailed mapping of corresponding references to actual locations in Guatemala City (344–45).

25. According to Héctor Gaitán, the actual Portal del Señor, destroyed in 1916, was located in the spot on which the National Palace currently stands. The name is apparently a reference to the Christ figure that was venerated there. In a letter to Gaitán from Rubén Ramírez Corzo, published in *La calle donde tú vives*, the legend of the Portal del Señor is told as follows: "Dicen las tradiciones que en ese Portal, al hacerle la capilla, en parte oculta fue colocada una placa que decía: 'Este Portal no ha de ser botado por la mano del hombre; y si algún día fuere destruido, o su SEÑOR fuere quitado de él, la ciudad de Guatemala será destruida'" (Gaitán 169–72) ["Tradition says that in that Portal, when the chapel was made, a plaque was placed in a hidden part which said: 'This Portal shall not be torn down by the hand of man; and if some day it should be destroyed, or if its Jesus figure were to be removed from it, the city of Guatemala will be destroyed'"].

CHAPTER 4

1. ["... it was my fault for thinking too much" (134).] Permission to include citations of *Caperucita* has been kindly granted by the author, Manlio Argueta.

2. Edward Waters Hood translates Argueta's title as *Little Red Riding Hood in the Red Light District* for the English version of the novel published by Curbstone Press. However, like much of the symbolism of the novel, the color red in the title operates on more than one level—a complexity that gets leveled out in the translation. In Spanish, the word red refers to the *caperucita roja* of the fairy tale; it also has the seedy sexual undertones that get privileged in the English translation as the red light district. But *la zona roja* (the red zone), in the midst of the cold war, in a novel that deals with the underground guerrilla movements of El Salvador, clearly points to the real and perceived "Communist" affiliations of the resistance groups described in the text.

3. All English translations of *Caperucita* are taken from Edward Waters Hood's version of *Little Red Riding Hood in the Red Light District*.

4. In the prologue to the 1999 edition published by UCA Editores (originally written in February, 1981), Ítalo López Vallecillos makes note of the distressing effect produced by this very persistence of different versions within the text: "Mas no se crea que la novela es en sí un discurso, un alegato de bien probado, una introducción a la buena o mala conciencia de los personajes. Entre el narrador y su amante, la Hormiga, hay toda una relación dialéctica, amor y destrucción en y por el amor, conflicto entre dos seres unidos fervorosamente en el anonimato de un transcurrir que, a ratos, llega al pánico, dado

NOTES255

que persisten visiones distintas sobre lo que acontece" (6) ["But do not think that the novel is in itself a discourse, a well-proven claim, an introduction to the good or bad conscience of the characters. Between the narrator and his lover, Hormiga, there is a dialectical relationship, love and destruction in and by love, a conflict between two beings fervently united in an anonymous passage of time which, at times, reaches the level of panic, given that different visions persist about what it is that happens"].

5. Among the literature currently available in the corpus of critical analysis about *Caperucita* are: Linda Craft's chapter about Manlio Argueta, in which she notes a particular interest in the development of female roles within the author's narrative (more evident in Argueta's later texts); Ineke Phaf briefly mentions *Caperucita*, and the passive role that women continue to play in this text, in her article "Cómo narrar la historia viajando en microbús por El Salvador," in Amelia Mondragón's edited volume entitled *Cambios estéticos y nuevos proyectos culturales en Centroamérica: Testimonios, entrevistas y ensayos*; upon the publication of Edward Waters Hood's English translation, Patrick Markee wrote a review for the *New York Times Book Review* that helps contextualize the novel for readers who might not be familiar with Argueta's work; Esther María Osses provides both an analytical essay and an interview with Manlio Argueta, conducted in 1979, that address the fragmentary structure of the novel in her text *La novela del imperialismo en Centroamérica*; and, in 1981 Ítalo López Vallecillos wrote a very useful synopsis of many of the underlying issues at stake in *Caperucita*, which is included as a prologue to the novel in subsequent publications, such as that of 1999.

6. Alegría is cited on the back cover of the English translation of the novel published by Curbstone Press.

7. In 1975, two years before the 1977 publication of *Caperucita*, Roque Dalton was put to death by opponents within the Revolutionary Army of the People (ERP). Dalton was accused and charged with treason for his critical thinking regarding the strategies of the guerrilla organization that he had joined.

8. Of course, she remains uncertain of her knowledge about his situation as it comes to her in dreams.

9. Unless indicated otherwise, the emphases in citations are in the original text.

10. I would translate this final section: "Mounted on a horse more beautiful than light, my pawing horse seemed like a mountain, a wave of blood."

11. Incorporating the language of the fairy tale that gives the novel its name, the phrase *para mirarte mejor* echoes the words of the wolf impersonating Little Red Riding Hood's grandmother to deceive the young girl in the story. The girl wants to know why her grandmother's eyes are so big. "So that I can see you better," lies the wolf in disguise.

The recognizable phrase conjures up the imminent danger lurking behind deceptive images, even in the most intimate, familiar settings.

12. Another notable instance of deceptive images seeping through the window is a photograph of a young Al in a café with a colonel who happens to be the infamous chief of security: "Al otro lado del vidrio estaba el Chele, el famoso coronel, tomando café con un estudiante, era el mismo estudiante de la fotografía que me estaba dando. ¿Lo conocés? Claro, es el poeta" (192) ["On the other side of the glass was Chele, the famous colonel, drinking coffee with a student, it was the same student in the photo he was giving me. Do you know him? Of course, he's the poet" (225)]. In a setup by the security forces, Manuel's brother, a police informant, is given this photograph so that Manuel and his colleagues will turn against Al. Yet the reader learns that the conversation between Al and the colonel is in fact a stern warning on the part of the security chief after he had been detained and released for his activities as a student dissident.

13. Astvaldsson describes *Cuzcatlán* as a continuation of some of the central themes that appear in *Caperucita*: "Argueta's second novel, *Caperucita en la zona roja*, can be said to constitute an homage to his friend, compatriot and fellow poet Roque Dalton, a revolutionary savagely executed by his own comrades, a group of hard-line guerrillas. *Cuzcatlán, donde bate la mar del sur* continues that theme by developing ideas of how to escape the impasse of misconstrued dogma that led to Dalton's murder and to find a way toward a new humanism inspired by the history and logic of the Salvadorean people" (Astvaldsson 614).

14. Ítalo López Vallecillos sees in the figure of the mother, projected in this poetic prayer, the representation of the wounded nation itself: "Si algún sentido tiene el concepto patria, hay que buscarlo en las madres de este país, deformado en sus valores y en sus instituciones. Ella es la masa y el hijo es el pueblo. Ella, sin duda, es la patria ofendida" (10) ["If there is any sense in the concept of the motherland, one has to look for it in the mothers of this country, deformed in its values and its institutions. She is the masses and the son is the people. She, without a doubt, is the offended motherland"].

15. Robert Armstrong and Janet Shenk describe a student demonstration in 1975 much like the one Argueta includes in *Caperucita*. The details are extremely similar, down to the bridge that is used by the students in their attempt to escape the armed forces and the coalition between dwellers of the shanty towns and the high school and university students: "The protest march would become a milestone in the history of the popular movement. It was El Salvador's Kent State" (Armstrong and Shenk 73–74).

16. ["The glance was not bad, the country progresses, we all progress and the fable of progress has a sad ending: that of the sinister absence."]

17. ["It's about breaking the prosaic with the very weapons of the prosaic."]

18. Based on an interview with Carmen Naranjo, Alicia Miranda Hevia documents the fact that *Diario de una multitud* was originally titled *En San José el desesperante*, first published in 1965. The name was changed when the text was submitted to a literary contest sponsored by the *Editorial Universitaria Centroamericana* (EDUCA). The first edition of *Diario* by EDUCA was launched in 1974 (Miranda Hevia 45).

19. In his chapter entitled "Carmen Naranjo y la ironía de la nada: voces furibundas martirizándonos con el relato" in *Gestos Ceremoniales*, Arturo Arias refers to Naranjo's narrative strategy in *Diario* as the stylization of ordinary discourse to create an ironic distance from the voices in the text (which, clearly, should not be taken at face value). This distance invites the reader to examine the novel critically and recognize the humor in some of the outrageously egotistical, materialistic, banal, apathetic ... attitudes transmitted by the voices "overheard" in the novel.

20. Among the other public positions held by Naranjo are: assistant administrative director of the Bureau of Social Security, ambassador to Israel, United Nations delegate for children's affairs in Mexico, UNICEF representative in Guatemala, director of EDUCA, and director of the Costa Rican Museum of Art (Nelson, "Carmen Naranjo and Costa Rican Culture" 186).

21. In an article entitled *"El significado de una renuncia"* (*Universidad*, May 19, 1976), Naranjo explains the circumstances that led to her resignation: "Se ha criticado al Ministerio que dirijo por los programas de cine, en que hemos expuesto al país ... lo que está pasando con ... la realidad nacional ... Se nos ha criticado por introducir la pobreza en los hogares acomodados, que no quieren saber de las poblaciones que no tienen basureros, de las familias que viven en tugurios, de las quemas inclementes para las limpias de cultivos, del alcoholismo alarmante y creciente en que se centra nuestra cultura. Es cierto que hemos incomodado hasta el cansancio con imágenes que todos tratamos de olvidar. Pero no es cierto que con ello estemos provocando subversión ... La subversión se abona cuando ocultamos verdades que están creciendo y reproduciéndose y reclaman con justicia pronta atención. La subversión se propicia cuando vamos cediendo la independencia de una cultura propia en aras de una cultura ajena, que nos ve y concibe en términos de mercado" (cited in Gibian 174) ["The Ministry that I direct has been criticized for film programs in which we have exposed the country ... what is occurring with ... the national reality ... They have criticized us for introducing poverty into well-to-do homes, that do not want to know of populations that don't have garbage dumps, of families that live in hovels, of inclement fires to clear off the land for crops, of alarming and growing rates of

alcoholism on which our culture is centered. It is true that we have made some uncomfortable to the point of exhaustion with images that we all try to forget. But it is not true that we are provoking subversion with all of it ... Subversion gains strength when we hide truths that are growing and reproducing themselves and demand with justice prompt attention. Subversion becomes propitious when we cede the independence of our own culture for the sake of a foreign culture that sees us and thinks of us in terms of the market."]

22. Naranjo develops this idea throughout the novel. She extends it to a national level when questioning the way in which her compatriots tend to look abroad for legitimizing models to be copied, particularly in Europe and the United States: "Si yo hubiera nacido en París, otro gallo me cantara ... Aquí sólo se da la imitación, la mala imitación por falta de modelos originales, recibimos copias de cuarta y quinta mano. Mientras allá se dice: a crear, aquí decimos a probar ... Pero, nací aquí, aquí, en un hueco, donde se mira con ansiedad lo que pasa en otras partes y a nadie le importa lo que pasa aquí, a nadie. Un destino de mirón y una idiosincrasia de conformidad" (183) ["If I would have been born in Paris, it would have been a different story ... Here only imitation takes place, bad imitations due to a lack of original models, we receive fourth and fifth-hand copies. While over there they say: let us create, here we say let's try ... But, I was born here, here, in a hole, where one looks with apprehension at what happens elsewhere and no one cares what happens here, no one. A destiny of an onlooker and an idiosyncrasy of conformity."]

CHAPTER 5

1. [The writer Rafael Heliodoro Valle stated that the history of Honduras could be written on a teardrop ...]. Permission for all citations from *Rey del Albor, Madrugada* was kindly granted by the author, Julio Escoto, on behalf of Centro Editorial S. R. L.

2. In her chapter regarding *Madrugada* in *Estudios de literatura hondureña*, Helen Umaña compares the episodic style of the novel with nineteenth-century romantic texts, or *folletines*: "los novelistas del siglo XIX eran hábiles en interrumpir el relato en el punto de mayor interés para retomarlo en la edición siguiente del periódico o revista" (Umaña 184) ["Nineteenth century novelists were adept at interrupting the tale at the point of greatest interest in order to continue the story in the next installment of the newspaper or magazine"]. Likewise, in the introduction to *Dimensions of Detective Fiction* (1976), the authors identify the episodic style as characteristic of the fictional detective genre itself (Landrum, Browne, and Browne 5). In both genres the episodic fragments are used to peak the reader's curiosity and ensure her continued interest in the eventual resolution of the mystery or romantic tension of the tale.

3. [What could be the supreme key, the master key that will open all secrets?]

4. The resistance rally ties into one of the overall projects of the novel, as described by Ramón Luis Acevedo in his article "La nueva novela histórica en Guatemala y Honduras." According to Acevedo, *Madrugada* is meant to counter erroneous notions of a complacent, "sold out" Honduran people who passively facilitate foreign interventions against their neighbors, highlighting instead multiple efforts of resistance and opposition throughout the country's history: "La imagen que se afirma del pueblo hondureño no es la de una colectividad complaciente, conformista, y acomodaticia, fácilmente manipulable y vendida a las grandes potencias, como se concibe con demasiada frecuencia; sino la de un pueblo enfrentado a fuerzas muy superiores a las suyas que, en ocasiones, ha sucumbido, pero siempre ha resistido con inteligencia, valentía y dignidad, padeciendo terribles consecuencias" (Acevedo, "La nueva novela histórica en Guatemala y Honduras" 14–15) ["The image that is reinforced of the Honduran people is not one of a complacent, conformist, and accommodating collectivity that is easily manipulated and sold to the major world powers, as it is too frequently conceived; but rather that of a people confronted with forces much superior to its own that, on occasion, has succumbed, but has always resisted with intelligence, courage and dignity, suffering terrible consequences."]

5. In the thoughts of the fictional president of Honduras, Jones's final publication should help transform the Honduran mentality to be more prone to tranquility and order, and steer people away from thoughts of rebellion.

6. In his book *Firewall: The Iran-Contra Conspiracy and Cover-Up* (1997), Lawrence E. Walsh, the Independent Counsel in the Iran-Contra Investigation, documents the series of events that became known through his team's investigation of the affair. In a complicated series of covert operations, President Ronald Reagan's regime resorted to selling arms to Iran to negotiate the release of Americans kidnapped by Hezbollah in Beirut in 1984. When the U.S. Congress officially cut U.S. funding for the Contras in the mid-1980s, Oliver North sold arms to Iran at three times the actual cost and sent the difference to the Contras based in Honduras and Costa Rica. By the summer of 1987, many involved in these covert operations were brought to testify before a congressional committee.

7. It turns out that the joke is only a humorous play on his preconceptions of the guerrilla potentially having deep-rooted Soviet affiliations. In reality, as his guerrilla contact and romantic decoy, Sheela, explains to him, the Honduran opposition groups are in the process of rethinking their strategic plans in the face of the fall of the Soviet Union and the new world order: "Es que allí es donde reside la raíz del problema: no creemos ya más ser comunistas [...] los cambios

que están pasando en el Este, las transformaciones de la perestroika de Gorbachev nos están moliendo la doctrina a todos y a decir verdad ya ni sabemos qué más esperar. Hemos comenzado por abandonar el lema de la dictadura del proletariado, uno de nuestros principios más queridos y ahora ninguno de nosotros se atreve siquiera a pronunciarlo en público" (Escoto 221) ["That is where the root of the problem lies: we no longer think of ourselves as communists ... the changes that are taking place in the East, Gorbachev's perestroika transformations are wearing out our doctrine and to tell you the truth we no longer know what to expect. We have started to abandon the slogan of a proletarian dictatorship, one of our most prized principles and now none of us dares to even mention it in public."]

8. In *A Forest of Kings: The Untold Story of the Ancient Maya*, Linda Schele and David Freidel describe the termination rituals in Copán that often make the past "unreadable" when attempting to unearth it: "Late Classic Copanec kings considered that their authority sprang from Yax-Kuk-Mo' and his charismatic performance as king. From his reign onward, Copán's dynastic history unfolded steadily until the system itself collapsed four hundred years later when the civilization of the Classic Maya as a whole failed ... even when we uncover a buried building or find a fragmentary stela, we rarely find names associated with it ... inscriptions are often unreadable, either because they were already old and worn when they were buried or because they were ritually 'terminated' when they were placed in their final resting places. Earlier monuments were torn down to make room for the newer ones, and older buildings were either buried or broken up to be recycled as building materials ... The Copanecs, like other Maya, probably defused the power of places and objects they wished to cover or dispose of through special termination rituals involving defacement and careful breakage. These rituals are the source of much of the damage to early inscriptions at Copán" (313).

9. When Jones is invited to meet with the guerrilla leadership, he is guided through the tunnels built underneath an urban apartment, through the remnants of the old colonial mines set up underneath modern-day Tegucigalpa. The architecture of the apartment and the city, where the political "underground" is literally *under the ground,* also functions as a metaphor for the novel's premise that there is always something else occurring beneath the visible surface, a secret underground city, as it were. The old mine tunnels are also a physical testament to the labor and strife of many generations of slaves and laborers who came before the opposition movement, in whose name a more accurate version of events is being pursued.

10. Population statistics tend to categorize 90 percent of Honduran citzens as *mestizos.*

11. Sheela equates the level of U.S. influence in Honduras in 1989 with an "occupied country" (Escoto 223).

12. Moreover, at a deeper level of espionage, the reader discovers the Israeli intelligence forces, the Mossad le Aliyah Beth, have also acquired a copy of the U.S. embassy's "Madrugada" file through Dr. Jones's Jewish assistant, Erika. The intrigue of a small Central American nation thus takes on a broader, more global significance.

13. [History does not travel in circles, it moves in a spiral. There is always a new layer to study, other circumstances for which one has to find in each its own depth.]

14. Shortly after, the isthmus proclaimed its annexation to Mexico, on January 5, 1822. Annexation meant joining the Mexican Empire under Iturbide's Plan de Iguala, securing a moderate constitutional monarchy that declared independence from Spain, while vowing to conserve the Catholic religion without tolerating any other. The polemical decision whether to declare independence as an autonomous Central American nation or in conjunction with Mexico thus resulted in favor of the moderate position of joining Iturbide's Plan de Iguala and his system of constitutional monarchy. Yet after Iturbide's abdication in 1823, Central America declared its absolute independence and became the United Provinces of Central America on July 1, 1823.

15. This citation refers to the text of the first article of Central America's Declaration of Independence from Spain, which reads in its entirety: "Que siendo la Independencia del Gobierno Español, la voluntad general del pueblo de Guatemala, y sin prejuicio de lo que determine sobre ella el Congreso que debe formarse, el señor Jefe Político la mande publicar para prevenir las consecuencias que serían temibles en el caso que la proclamase de hecho el mismo pueblo" (cited in Luján Muñoz 437) ["Being that the Independence from the Government of Spain is the general will of the people of Guatemala, and without prejudice of what the Congress that should be formed may determine about it, it should be published by the Political Chief to prevent the consequences that would be feared if the people themselves were to proclaim it"].

16. This is taken from article 10 of the Declaration of Independence, which states: "Que la religión católica que hemos profesado en los siglos anteriores y profesaremos en los siglos sucesivos, se conserve pura e inalterable, manteniendo vivo el espíritu de religiosidad que ha distinguido siempre a Guatemala, respetando a los ministros eclesiásticos seculares y regulares, y protegiéndoles en sus personas y propiedades" (cited in Pinto Soria 94) ["That the Catholic religion that we have professed in previous centuries and will profess in the centuries to come, be preserved pure and inalterable, keeping alive the spirit of religiosity that has always distinguished Guatemala, respecting the ecclesiastical ministers, both secular and regular, and protecting them in their persons and in their properties"].

17. Like most of the short historical chapters interspersed in the story line that takes place in 1989, this chapter is triggered by a subtle reference

to the historical events described in the contemporary chapter that precedes it. When Professor Jones discovers a bullet in his office, he wonders how it got there. He speculates whether it is a result of recent gunfire or whether it can trace back in time to other volatile periods in Tegucigalpa. This reminds him of a magazine article that describes a violent siege of the capital city in 1924. The subsequent historical chapter, "Diario de la guerra," is meant to be the original text that is reproduced in the magazine Jones uses to research this event.

18. One of the most obvious Cold War allegories can be found in the chapter titled "Aurelina (1785–1786)," in which the alliance between the Miskito Indians with the British is perceived as a threat by the Spanish settlers. A Miskito leader accuses the ladinos of parceling out the globe without genuine concern for the inhabitants of the land: "Los ingleses es lo único que les atormenta a ustedes los ladinos, lo único que ven y entienden de los misquitos. No les preocupa si perecemos o sobrevivimos, si nos hundimos o nos salvamos. Les importa solamente nuestra alianza con otro imperio [...] lo que les duele es que hagamos y tengamos amistad con el otro gran poder que les disputa Europa y estas tierras nuevas. La política ... política de los reyes ... ¿cuánto creen que nos importa la política si nos estamos muriendo de hambre?" (269–70) ["The only thing that torments you ladinos is the English, that's the only thing that you can see and understand of the Miskitos. You don't care if we survive or if we perish, if we sink or if we are saved. You only care about our alliance with another empire ... what bothers you is that we have a friendship with the other great power that challenges you for control in Europe and in these new lands. Politics ... the politics of kings ... How much do you think that we care about politics if we are dying of hunger?"]. Like in the Cold War, global politics is disputed among world powers (or "empires") without much concern for the ultimate well-being of local citizens or the particularities of their circumstances.

19. ["Nations and ethnicities continue to exist. For the majority of people, they are ceasing to be the principal producers of social cohesion. But the problem does not seem to be the risk that globalization will do away with them, but to understand how ethnic, regional, and national identities are reconstructed amidst globalized processes of segmentation and intercultural hybridization."]

20. In "'Rey del Albor, Madrugada,' de Julio Escoto: la última novela nacional y la primera novela cibernética," Seymour Menton remarks accordingly: "en cuanto al panorama histórico, *Madrugada* da más importancia a los temas del mestizaje y de la lucha por la libertad que al panteón de los héroes nacionales" (Menton, *Caminata por la narrativa latinoamericana* 282) ["as far as the historical outlook, *Madrugada* gives more importance to the themes of *mestizaje* and the fight for freedom than to the pantheon of national heroes"].

21. The language of the contemporary story participates in this process by aptly conveying the particular expressions and distinct mannerisms used in Honduras, capturing a recognizable local flavor.

22. García Canclini himself imagines a certain amount of "choice" in identity negotiations and the practice of global citizenship: "la globalización aparece como una necesidad que debe expresarse en un desempeño global de la ciudadanía, pero existen diversas formas de ser ciudadano global" (210) ["globalization seems like a necessity that must be expressed in a global performance of citizenship, but there are diverse ways of being a global citizen"]. With civil society defined less by national boundaries and more by trends as consumers of ideas and tastes, García Canclini foresees new spaces of collaboration and citizenship on a global basis: "la expansión de las comunicaciones y los consumos genera asociaciones de consumidores y luchas sociales, aun en los grupos marginales, mejor informadas de las condiciones nacionales e internacionales: las comunidades imaginarias son a veces 'escenas' de evasión y en otros casos circuitos donde se rehacen los vínculos sociales rotos por la diseminación urbana o deslegitimados por la pérdida de autoridad de los partidos y las iglesias" (212) ["the expansion of communications and consumerism generates associations of consumers and of social struggles, even in marginal groups, better informed about national and international conditions: imagined communities are sometimes scenes of evasion and in other cases they are circuits where social links, which have been severed due to urban dissemination or have been de-legitimized by the loss of authority of political parties and churches, are reestablished"].

23. The implication is that blending, rather than fostering a sum of discrete ethnic entities, will result in a stronger national subject that can come together to resist colonial designs from abroad. Muyolema would surely point out that the onus of such combinations would have to be carried by cultures outside of the framework of an imagined *mestizo* ideal.

24. This article can be found on the internet at http://utexas.edu/project/lasa95/craft.html.

25. Craft concludes her article by underlining the fact that ethnic discourse is used in the three texts she analyzes as a response to postmodern symptoms of anonymity, loss of identity and of autonomy, and even the loss of an anchor for meaning: "In these texts, then, ethnic discourse is a backlash against postmodern anonymity and eventual disappearance. Ethnicity gives meaning and individuality, where meaning has otherwise been stripped away. By going back to roots, the writers find inspiration to continue the struggle for survival. Going backwards also inspires them to press forward to a new beginning—'una madrugada'—a dawn of hope that it is possible to avert a monstrous cultural collapse and a complete loss of identity and autonomy" (10).

26. Umaña proposes optimistically that acceptance and a true synthesis between both cultures may come with the passage of time, through the children born of this type of violence: "Lo que sí es cierto es que, andando el tiempo, en la descendencia del hijo que la india lleva en las entrañas, quizá se dé la síntesis, la aceptación de los contrarios" (Umaña 192) ["What is certain is that, with the passage of time, in the descendants of the son that the Indian woman has in her womb, there will perhaps be a synthesis, an acceptance of opposites"].

27. E-mail communication dated September 28, 2003.

28. Refer to Doris Sommer's *Foundational Fictions: The National Romances of Latin America* (1991).

29. Note that the order of the interwoven historical chapters in the novel are placed in decreasing chronological order, so the chapter that takes place in the eighteenth century is read before the one situated in the sixteenth century.

30. While the events narrated are supposed to have taken place in the 1780s, the style emulated is that of the period of Romanticism, from several decades later, after the wars of Independence throughout Latin America.

31. In *Captive Women: Oblivion and Memory in Argentina*, Susana Rotker reads Echeverría's *La cautiva* as a gesture that demarcates clearly the separation between what was perceived as European civilization and indigenous barbarism. Thus the poem is meant to serve the overall national project of imagining a primarily white (rather than a *mestizo*) nation: "In the foundation or delineation of a style of national identity, bodies are used to trace clear frontiers, to demarcate spaces, and to leave well differentiated who is who [...]. Against the background of the body of the captive, the map of the abject and the discourse of progress are drawn; upon her (textual, pictorial) body the identity of what we are not and do not wish to be is constructed. [...] The captives who made it into the collective imaginary—since the captives of flesh and blood did not—were in reality an instrument, an excuse, another justification to brandish in the fight against barbarism and to legitimate a political project" (Rotker 97).

32. A name given to him by the British pirates he has engaged with in the contraband business. Previously, he had been baptized Catholic by the Spanish settlers of the region with the name Carlos Yarrinche Tercero. (273).

33. In the words of Don Robinson: "Lo que pido es solamente un poco de amor para mi buena raza, no para mí, un pedazo de vida civilizada [...]" (295) ["All I ask for is a bit of love for my good race, not for me, a slice of civilized life ..."].

34. Some of the texts included in Pons's analysis are: *Noticias del imperio. La trágica historia de Maximiliano y Carlota* (1987) by Fernando del Paso, *El general en su laberinto* (1989) by Gabriel García Márquez, and *El entenado* (1983) by Juan José Saer.

35. As we have repeatedly noted, another way in which Escoto tries to avoid providing a flat, oversimplified version of the process of *mestizaje* is to emphasize the long historical process and the complexity of changing relations between the diverse cultures that have come together on Honduran soil.

36. It is precisely these types of hegemonic assumptions within assimilationist ideologies that the pan-Maya cultural movement is currently organizing against in Guatemala, as we shall observe in depth in the following chapter of this study.

CHAPTER 6

1. Refer to Kay Warren (1998) and Diane Nelson (1999) for detailed accounts of the series of events that helped open the primarily class-based negotiations between the guerrillas and the state to considerations of cultural rights. Among the more notable international events giving visibility to indigenous affairs in the years leading up to the Guatemalan peace accords are the 1989 ratification of the United Nations International Labor Organization's *Convention 169 on the Rights of Indigenous and Tribal Peoples in Independent Countries* and the Nobel Peace Prize awarded to Rigoberta Menchú in 1992.

2. Coalitions based primarily on socioeconomic class considerations and polarized ideologies of the Left or the Right are still active today in the so-called *popular* movements operating alongside organizations that have emerged as a result of cultural demands.

3. In the words of the Maya anthropologist Victor Montejo: "To call ourselves 'Mayas' is a political act [...] modern Mayas view themselves as inheritors of the great Maya culture and are proud of calling themselves Maya. With this consciousness of being Maya and not just "Indians," modern Mayas will contribute to the awakening of the Maya nation, to ensure its life for the future. I believe that by renaming ourselves with historically established Maya names, we will begin to overcome domination and control imposed by those who insist on considering us inferior. Until now the power of naming has been in the hands of outsiders, and of course, the one who names is the one who takes control" (Montejo, *Voices from Exile: Violence and Survival in Modern Maya History* 188–89).

4. The anthropologist Kay Warren makes note of the urgency of the movement's historical consciousness when she writes: "Another striking characteristic of the movement is its historical consciousness—its multiculturalist sense of the ways Mayas were written out of national history and its urgency to imagine new histories" (*Indigenous Movements and Their Critics: Pan-Maya Activism in Guatemala* 39).

5. The writings of many Maya intellectuals, who have gained prominence with their contributions to the field of Maya Studies, have become widely available. To name only a few: Demetrio Cojtí Cuxil

holds a PhD in communications from the University of Louvain, Belgium, has worked with UNICEF, and has published several articles and books, including *Configuración del pensamiento político del pueblo maya*, Part 1 (1990) and Part 2 (1995), and *Políticas para la reivindicación de los mayas de hoy (fundamento de los derechos específicos de los pueblos maya* (1994). Novelist Gaspar Pedro González, the author of *A Mayan Life* (1995) and *Return of the Maya* (1998), holds a degree in educational planning and is a university instructor, and has been a consultant in the Ministry of Culture. And anthropologist Victor Montejo, a professor in the Department of Native American Studies at the University of California, Davis, is the author of many texts, including *Maya Intellectual Renaissance: Identity, Representation and Leadership* (2005), *Voices from Exile: Violence and Survival in Modern Maya History* (1999), *Testimony: Death of a Guatemalan Village* (1987), *Las aventuras de Mister Puttison entre los mayas* (1998), and *Brevísima relación testimonial de la continua destrucción del Mayab' (Guatemala)* (1992).

6. Refer to Charles R. Hale's article "Travel Warning: Elite Appropriations of Hybridity, Mestizaje, Antiracism, Equality, and Other Progressive-Sounding Discourses in Highland Guatemala" for a useful account of the problematic application of theories with flawed assumptions of universal resonance, and the search, instead, for theories "in an active engagement with the politics of a particular place, time, and people" as it applies to the current pan-Maya movement in Guatemala (Hale 1999).

7. Morales has published a personal account of his twenty-five year militancy as a member of the guerrilla in his *folletimonio* (a testimonio delivered in installments to the newspaper), later revised and published as a book under the title *Los que se fueron por la libre (Historia personal de la lucha armada y la guerra popular)* (1998). *Los que se fueron por la libre* refers to his splinter group within the guerrilla forces that became extremely critical of the more orthodox umbrella organization, the Unidad Revolucionaria Nacional Guatemalteca (URNG), particularly after 1982, when the army's counterrevolutionary offensive had decimated the guerrilla forces' initiatives in the countryside. Morales's political writings, critical of the mainstream guerrilla coalition, resulted in his incarceration in Nicaragua when he was denounced by URNG supporters as a traitor to their cause. In his memoirs, Morales writes with much bitterness of the incarceration and subsequent posttraumatic stress disorder caused by the betrayal and hostility from his rivals within the guerrilla forces.

8. In *Voices from Exile*, published by the University of Oklahoma Press, Victor Montejo writes about the significance of a Maya "renaissance" and its role for the many displaced people who are now trying to reintegrate into national life: "The experience of the 'remembered community' that bound the refugees to their culture in exile will

support and build a transnational Maya culture. Our ability to be Mayas is not limited to any one place or time. It is not forever rooted in the past. It can be our identity and our strength wherever we are. And that identity and strength can also guide Guatemala to a better future" (243). For Montejo, the emphasis of revitalization is clearly on nurturing a strong sense of community as a source of strength, not as a process of authenticating a static notion of what it means to be Maya.

9. A few of the many texts on the subject of interethnic relations and cultural activism include Edward F. Fischer and R. McKenna Brown's *Maya Cultural Activism in Guatemala* (1996), Santiago Bastos and Manuela Camus' *Quebrando el silencio: Organizaciones del pueblo maya y sus demandas 1986–1992* (1996) and *Entre el mecapal y el cielo: desarrollo del movimiento maya en Guatemala* (2003), Marta Elena Casáus Arzú's *La metamorfosis del racismo en Guatemala* (1998) and *Desarrollo y diversidad cultural en Guatemala* that was edited with Juan Carlos Gimeneo (2000), *More Than an Indian: Racial Ambivalence and Neoliberal Multiculturalism in Guatemala* by Charles R. Hale (2006), and Victor Montejo's *Maya Intellectual Renaissance: Identity, Representation and Leadership* (2005). Notably, the newspapers provided an important forum for the exchange of ideas in the years leading up to the 1996 peace accords through the present for both Maya and Ladino perspectives. Many Maya scholars have theorized about the movement's goals and activities in the national press—perhaps the most notable is Dr. Demetrio Cojtí Cuxil, whose reflections and numerous articles have been reprinted in several books.

10. It is not only non-Maya observers who have critiqued the essential categories put forth in the movement's discourse. Estuardo Zapeta, a journalist, Maya intellectual, and anthropologist trained at State University of New York, Albany, in New York, has argued against such an essentialist stance in "El discurso indígena" ("Indigenous Discourse"), an article published in the newspaper *Siglo XXI* on July 4, 1994: "Nuestro discurso es el reciclaje de las ideas de la neoizquierda europea, con parches de ecologismo gringo, sazonado con derrotismo latinoamericano [...] Si tanto estamos en contra del colonialismo, ¿cómo es que nuestros líderes y lideresas se han dejado colonizar por el discurso populista? [...] Culturalmente, con nuestro énfasis en las diferencias, nos hemos transformado en victimarios raciales. De discriminados nos hemos convertido en racistas y etnocentristas. Con la falsedad de *lo puro* estamos creando comunidades cerradas en un tiempo en que en el mundo se habla de apertura. No hemos comprendido que *lo puro* no existe. La *pureza* es la transformación continua de nuestra cultura. Las culturas son dinámicas. Soñamos con un pasado grandioso pero no hemos aterrizado en el presente. Mucho menos sabemos a dónde queremos llegar. Con un discurso cargado

de portentos pasados nos hemos recreado como seres exóticos. Nos hemos olvidado de nuestra normalidad, de nuestra humanidad, de nuestra imperfección. No hemos comprendido que nuestra identidad la hemos reformulado en relación al *otro*. Con ese *otro* con quien precisamente tenemos que buscar las convergencias para el desarrollo común, pero parece que de entrada lo hemos rechazado" (Zapeta 26) ["Our discourse is a recycling of the ideas of Europe's neo-left, with patches of gringo ecological concerns, seasoned with Latin American defeatism ... If we are so opposed to colonialism, why is it that our leaders (men and women) have allowed themselves to be colonized by the populist discourse? ... Culturally, with our emphasis on differences, we have transformed ourselves into racial perpetrators. From being discriminated against we have become racist and ethnocentric. With the falsehood of *the pure* we are creating closed communities at a time in which there is talk of openness. We have not understood that *the pure* does not exist. *Purity* is the continuous transformation of our culture. Cultures are dynamic. We dream of a grandiose past but we have not landed in the present. Much less do we know where it is we want to go. With a discourse that is charged with marvels from the past we have recreated ourselves as exotic beings. We have forgotten our normalcy, our humanity, our imperfection. We have not understood that we have reformulated our identity in relation to the *Other*. Precisely with that *Other* with whom we need to search for converging commonalities for a common development, but it seems as though we have rejected him from the start"].

11. The global market can weigh heavily into the issue of identity formation in the sense that many important choices have to be made when deciding to enter the labor force under certain capacities, working in the *maquiladoras*, for instance, or adapting traditional *artesanías* by changing the standard colors used in indigenous textiles to suit the tastes of consumers, et cetera.

12. David Stoll is a North American anthropologist who sparked a heated controversy with the publication of his book *Rigoberta Menchú and the Story of All Poor Guatemalans* in 1999. Stoll points to inconsistencies between details in Rigoberta Menchú's account as they appear in her well-known *testimonio,* edited by Elizabeth Burgos in the early 1980s, and field research that Stoll has conducted. He criticizes in particular the way in which foreign scholars have privileged the perspective put forth in Menchú's *testimonio* and points to specific instances in which the way that Menchú tells her story is charged with ideological intent. His own agenda is to demonstrate that armed resistance was not the only option in the late 1970s and early 1980s, and he criticizes her account for making it seem as though it was.

13. "The argument between Menchú and Stoll is not so much about what really happened as it is about who has the authority to narrate.

What seems to bother Stoll above all is that Menchú *has* an agenda"
(Beverley 221, author's emphasis).

14. Nelson uses the notion of the "inappropriate(d) other," by citing
Trinh Minh-ha.

15. Even though the leadership of the *movimiento maya* does not
always represent the "Maya" coalition in its totality, as no collective
organization can, the fact that the cultural movement has attracted
adherents on many levels indicates that it does appeal to the anxieties
and desires of such activists and participants to a certain extent. It is
in this way that the voice and social agency of those who decide to
participate in different capacities becomes manifest.

16. Nelson comments about Morales: "In the past few years, his columns
have become increasingly mean-spirited and acerbic, projecting racism onto the Maya because they don't accept his version of *mestizo*
unity" (232).

17. One must keep in mind the particular national and local politics to
which the *movimiento maya* responds and the sociopolitical circumstances that make any notions of "Maya domination" or "Ladino
extermination" not only unfeasible but cynical, given the widespread
massacres of Guatemala's indigenous population during the violence of 1978–1985. One cannot bracket out the discourse of the
movimiento maya and deconstruct it in a vacuum. It emerges from
a particular set of circumstances that must be taken into account.
Moreover, Kay Warren reminds us of the importance of contextual
circumstances in the process of identity negotiations when she writes:
"Due to powerful economic, cultural, and political constraints on
individual and collective action, identity formation is not a free
market of personal options for self-definition" (Warren, *Indigenous
Movements and Their Critics: Pan-Maya Activism in Guatemala* 72).
The fact that speaking in terms of cultural concerns has emerged, in
part, as a strategic way to gain a voice for open sociopolitical critique
and activism within a state that has been so violent in its response to
previous attempts at advocating change *must* be considered within
this specific historical context.

18. Later on she does marry and have children, also as a matter of personal choice.

19. The neologism "fluidarity" plays with the idea of going from
notions of a *solid* identity implied in a relationship of *solidarity* to
the fluidity of boundaries that are aspired to in a new relation of
fluidarity.

20. Montejo has also served as a congressman in Guatemala and has held
the position of head of the Guatemalan Ministry of Peace.

21. Montejo writes of this unique perspective and what he terms his
"double identity" in his study of the exiled Guatemalan community
in Chiapas, Mexico, titled *Voices from Exile*: "I have the advantage of a
Western education *and* a Maya upbringing. I speak two Maya languages,

Popb'al Ti' and Q'anjob'al, in addition to Spanish and English. However, I have lived outside my culture for the past ten years and have acquired some Western and academic ethnocentrisms from that experience. Because of my double identity, this work is directed to two audiences: the Maya themselves, so that they have this document as a commemoration of their struggles; and the general Western community, academic and nonacademic, so that our work becomes relevant to and respectful of indigenous cultures" (Montejo 11–12).

22. The translation of the novel that I have used is the one by Susan Giersbach Rascón and Fernando Peñalosa, *The Adventures of Mr. Puttison Among the Maya* (2002).

23. All selections from the novel are cited with kind permission from the author, Victor D. Montejo.

24. The translation of the preface is mine. It is not taken from Susan Giersbach Rascón and Fernando Peñalosa's translation of the novel.

25. In his article "La población indígena en el Estado Liberal," Richard Adams describes in detail the legislation under the dictatorships of Manuel Estrada Cabrera and Jorge Ubico that required compulsory labor to carry out the state's projects of modernization. Some of the laws passed in the 1930s, the period in which Montejo's novel is set, include the *Ley de Vialidad* and the *Ley contra la Vagancia:* "En 1933 se emitió la Ley de Vialidad (Decreto 1474) por la cual el trabajo de construcción de carreteras ya no fue tarea de las compañías de zapadores. Se requería, en cambio, que todas las personas pagaran un impuesto de dos quetzales al año para la construcción de carreteras, y quienes no pudieran hacerlo quedaban obligadas a trabajar durante dos semanas [...] Puesto que se trataba del pago de un impuesto, el trabajo no era remunerado ni tampoco se daban las provisiones" [...] "Aunque la vagancia ya era ilegal, Ubico garantizó que satisfaría las necesidades de mano de obra en las fincas y decretó una nueva Ley contra la Vagancia [...] quienes poseían poca o ninguna tierra, tenían que demostrar entre 100 a 150 días de trabajo en una finca" (Adams 191) ["In 1933 the Roads and Highways Department Law (Decree 1474) was passed; under which the job of building roads ceased to be the responsibility of sapper (military engineer) companies. It was required instead, for all people to pay a tax of two *quetzales* a year for the construction of roads, and whoever could not afford it would be forced to work for two weeks ... Since it was considered to be the payment of a tax, the labor was not remunerated nor were any provisions given ... Even though vagrancy was already illegal, Ubico guaranteed that he would satisfy the labor force needs of the farms and he decreed a new Law Against Vagrancy ... whoever possessed little or no land had to demonstrate that they had carried out 100 to 150 days of work in a farm"].

26. Refer again to Richard Adam's article "La población indígena en el Estado Liberal" for an account of the increased foreign interest in

Guatemala's indigenous communites in the 1930s: "La riqueza del mundo industrial penetró lentamente en Guatemala con la presencia de turistas y de ciertos etnólogos que comenzaron a convivir con las comunidades mayas [...] Los efectos a largo plazo en la vida y economía indígenas provocados por el turismo no eran predecibles entonces, pero la nueva importancia económica que representaban los mayas para el ladino y el Estado sí eran una novedad. Anteriormente, el indígena había contribuido al proceso capitalista, a través de la represión política y la explotación económica; pero, en esta nueva etapa, parecía posible que la exaltación de lo maya tenía un valor económico" (Adams 182–83) ["The wealth of the industrialized world penetrated into Guatemala slowly with the presence of tourists and of certain ethnologists who began to live among the Maya communities ... The long term effects on the indigenous life and economy provoked by tourism were not then predictable, but the new economic importance that the Maya represented for the Ladino and the state were indeed something new. Previously, indigenous people had contributed to the capitalist process under political repression and economic exploitation; but in this new phase it seemed possible that the exaltation of all that was Maya had an economic value in itself"].

27. The translation of the dedication is mine. It is not taken from Susan Giersbach Rascón and Fernando Peñalosa's translation of the novel.

28. Kay Warren writes of her own experience in a conference in Guatemala in 1989 when a Maya linguist had asked her directly: "What are you doing here in Guatemala? What benefit does your research have for the Mayas of San Andrés?" (*Indigenous Movements and Their Critics: Pan-Maya Activism in Guatemala* 76). As questions such as these are posed in public and private dialogues between Maya communities and researchers, the opportunity arises for rethinking how best to remedy the power discrepancies and failures of academic projects that forget to include the collaborators that make their research possible in either the planning stages or inform them of the conclusions drawn from their work in the field. One of the strategies within the *movimiento maya* has been to ask these potentially uncomfortable questions in hopes of provoking a change in the methodologies of field research and the distribution of academic findings.

29. Refer also to Warren's text "Interpreting *la Violencia* in Guatemala: Shapes of Mayan Silence and Resistance" (1993) for an analysis of "the cultural construction of terror" in San Andrés Semetabaj. The author provides an account of a region that by 1975 appeared to have turned away from its traditionalist Maya spiritual practices, shaken by orthodox Catholic and Protestant conversions and the younger generation's refusal to participate in traditional institutions, such as the local brotherhoods (*cofradías*). Despite this turn away from ancestral *costumbre*, Warren encounters and documents many stories of transforming beings taken from oral tradition that she interprets

as a cultural expression of the effects of the unspeakable terror of *la violencia*. The author provides a synopsis of her argument in her own words: "My analysis argued that townspeople survived the silence imposed by the corrosion of trust in others in part by revitalizing traditionalist magical realist narratives of transforming selves to address the haunting issue of interpersonal betrayal [...] I found that Maya culture—both in what we would consider its realist and magical realist ways of representing the world—was used by particular individuals to address the existential dilemmas and human costs of a world spinning out of control" (Warren, *Indigenous Movements and Their Critics: Pan-Maya Activism in Guatemala* 129).

30. All poems cited with kind permission from the author, Calixta Gabriel Xiquín.
31. The English translation of Calixta Gabriel Xiquín's poems is by Susan G. Rascón and Suzanne M. Strugalla.
32. Poems are cited with kind permission from the author, Humberto Ak'abal.
33. This is the Spanish version of the poem.
34. This is the K'iché version of the poem.
35. The unsettling implication is that one can only perform one's identity according to the expectations of a hegemonic definition of what that identity should be, or according to a market demand for goods to be consumed. As everyone performs their identity, why would it be duplicitous for an indigenous poet to embrace his Maya "look," as he chooses to express it, with pride?
36. Cited from the back cover of *Guardián de la caída de agua* published in 1996.
37. This is the Spanish version of the poem.
38. This is the K'iché version of the same poem.
39. This is the Spanish version of the poem.
40. This is the K'iché version of the same poem.
41. Rigoberta Menchú provides a definition of the "nahual" to Elizabeth Burgos, also noted in the glossary of her *testimonio:* "Nahual: designa el doble, el *alter ego* animal o de otra naturaleza que, según la tradición indígena, posee todo ser humano. Está en correspondencia con la personalidad de las personas. La atribución del nahual conlleva el reconocimiento del recién nacido como parte integrante de la comunidad" (285) ["Nahual: designates the double, the animal or other sort of alter ego, which according to indigenous tradition, every human being possesses. It corresponds to the personality of people. The attribution of a nahual carries with it the recognition of the newborn as an integral part of the community."]
42. This is the Spanish version of the poem.
43. This is the K'iché version of the same poem.

BIBLIOGRAPHY

Acevedo, Ramón Luis. "La nueva novela histórica en Guatemala y Honduras." *Letras de Guatemala: Instituto de Estudios de la Literatura Nacional (INESLIN)* [Facultad de Humanidades, Universidad de San Carlos de Guatemala] 18–19 (1998): 1–19.

Adams, Richard N. "La población indígena en el Estado Liberal." *Historia General de Guatemala: Época Contemporánea 1898–1944.* Ed. J. Daniel Contreras R. (director del Tomo) and Jorge Luján Muñoz (director general). Tomo V. Guatemala: Asociación de Amigos del País, Fundación para la Cultura y el Desarrollo, 1996. 173–98.

Agüero, Raúl. *Guatemala, la Revolución Liberal de 1871 y las administraciones del Benemérito Licenciado don Manuel Estrada Cabrera.* Costa Rica: Imprenta Alsina, 1914.

_____. *Guatemala y el Licenciado Estrada Cabrera: Perfil biográfico.* Costa Rica: Imprenta Alsina, 1911.

Aínsa, Fernando. "La reescritura de la historia en la nueva narrativa latinoamericana." *Cuadernos Americanos* 28 (1991): 13–31.

Ak'abal, Humberto. *Ajkem Tzij Tejedor de palabras.* Guatemala: Fundación Carlos Novella, 1996.

_____. *Aqajtzij Palabramiel.* Guatemala: Cholsamaj, 2001.

_____. *Con los ojos después del mar.* México, D.F.: Editorial Praxis, 2000.

_____. *Guardián de la caída del agua.* 1993. Guatemala: Artemis-Edinter, 1996.

Anderson, Thomas P. *Politics in Central America: Guatemala, El Salvador, Honduras and Nicaragua.* Politics in Latin America: A Hoover Institution Series. Ed. Robert Wesson. New York: Praeger Publishers, 1982.

Anderson Imbert, Enrique, and Eugenio Florit. *Literatura Hispanoamericana: antología e introducción histórica.* 1960. Vol. 1. Chicago: Holt, Rinehart and Winston, 1988.

Arévalo Martínez, Rafael. *Ecce Pericles: la tiranía de Manuel Estrada Cabrera en Guatemala.* Colección Séptimo Día. Tercera edición. San José: EDUCA, 1982.

Argueta, Manlio. "Autovaloración Literaria." *Cambios estéticos y nuevos proyectos culturales en Centroamérica: testimonios, entrevistas y ensayos.* Ed. Amelia Mondragón. Washington D.C.: Literal Books, 1994. 27–33.

_____. *Caperucita en la zona roja.* 1977. San Salvador, El Salvador: UCA Editores, 1999.

_____. *Little Red Riding Hood in the Red Light District*. Trans. Edward Waters Hood. Willimantic, CT: Curbstone Press, 1998.

Arias, Arturo. *After the Bombs*. Trans. Asa Zatz. Willimantic, CT: Curbstone Press, 1990.

_____. *Después de las bombas*. 1979. Guatemala: Artemis-Edinter, 1997.

_____. *Gestos ceremoniales: narrativa centroamericana 1960–1990*. Guatemala: Artemis-Edinter, 1998.

_____. *La identidad de la palabra: narrativa guatemalteca a la luz del siglo XX*. Guatemala: Artemis-Edinter, 1998.

_____. *Taking Their Word: Literature and the Signs of Central America*. Minneapolis and London: University of Minnesota Press, 2007.

_____, ed. *The Rigoberta Menchú Controversy*. Minneapolis and London: University of Minnesota Press, 2001.

Armstrong, Robert, and Janet Shenk. *El Salvador: The Face of Revolution*. Boston: South End Press, 1982.

Arzú, Marta Elena Casáus, and Carlos Gimenez, eds. *Guatemala hoy: reflexiones y perspectivas interdisciplinares*. Madrid: Servicio de publicaciones de la Universidad Autónoma de Madrid, 2000.

Arzú, Marta Elena Casáus, and Juan Carlos Gimeno, eds. *Desarrollo y diversidad cultural en Guatemala*. Guatemala: Cholsamaj, 2000.

Asturias, Miguel Angel. *El Señor Presidente*. 1946. Madrid: Alianza/Losada, 1984.

_____. *El Señor Presidente*. Trans. Frances Partridge. New York: Atheneum, 1969.

_____. "*El Señor Presidente* como mito." *El Señor Presidente: Edición crítica*. Ed. Gerald Martin. Colección Archivos. Madrid y Barcelona: ALLCA XX 2000. 468–78.

_____. *El Señor Presidente: Edición crítica*. Ed. Editions Klincksieck. Madrid: Fondo de Cultura Económica, 1978.

_____. *Hombres de maíz (edición crítica)*. 1992. Ed. Gerald Martin. Colección Archivos. 2nda edición. Madrid, Paris, México, Buenos Aires, Sao Paulo, Río de Janeiro, Lima: ALLCA XX, 1996.

_____. *Week-End en Guatemala*. 1956. Buenos Aires: Editorial Losada, 2006.

Astvaldsson, Astvaldur. "Toward a New Humanism: Narrative Voice, Narrative Structure and Narrative Strategy in Manlio Argueta's *Cuzcatlán, donde bate la mar del sur*." *Bulletin of Hispanic Studies* LXXVII.4 (2000): 603–15.

Aydelotte, William O. "The Detective Story as a Historical Source." *Dimensions of Detective Fiction*. Ed. Pat Browne, Ray B. Browne, and Larry N. Landrum. Bowling Green, Ohio: Popular Press, 1976. 68–82.

Bakhtin, Mikhail. *The Dialogic Imagination*. Trans. Caryl Emerson and Michael Holquist. Austin: University of Texas Press, 1981.

Bastos, Santiago, and Manuela Camus. *Entre el mecapal y el cielo: desarrollo del movimiento maya en Guatemala*. Guatemala: Cholsamaj, 2003.

_____. *Quebrando el silencio: Organizaciones del pueblo maya y sus demandas 1986–1992*. 3era. edición. Guatemala: FLACSO, 1996.

Bauman, Kevin M. "Novelistic Discourse as History: Asturias's (Re) Vision of Estrada Cabrera's Guatemala, 1898–1920." *RLA: Romance Languages Annual* [West Lafayette, IN] 4 (1992): 387–90.

Belli, Gioconda. *El país bajo mi piel: memorias de amor y guerra.* 2000. Barcelona: Plaza y Janés Editores, 2002.

Benedetti, Mario. "Ernesto Cardenal: evangelio y revolución (entrevista)." *Casa de las Américas* 63 (1970): 174–83.

Benjamin, Walter. *Selected Writings.* Cambridge, Massachusetts and London, England: The Belknap Press of Harvard University Press, 2003.

Bethell, Leslie, ed. *Central America since Independence.* Cambridge and New York: Cambridge University Press, 1991.

Beverley, John. "What Happens When the Subaltern Speaks: Rigoberta Menchú, Multiculturalism, and the Presumption of Equal Worth." *The Rigoberta Menchú Controversy.* Ed. Arturo Arias. Minneapolis and London: University Press of Minnesota, 2001. 219–36.

Beverley, John, and Marc Zimmerman. *Literature and Politics in the Central American Revolutions.* Austin: University of Texas Press, 1990.

Bolívar, Simón. *Selected Writings of Bolívar.* Ed. Harold A. Bierck, Jr. Trans. Lewis Bertrand. Vol. 1. New York: The Colonial Press Inc., 1951.

Brown, James W. "A Topology of Dread: Spatial Oppositions in *El Señor Presidente*." *Romanische Forschungen* 98.3–4 (1986): 341–52.

Browning, John. "Corrientes filosóficas y políticas." *Historia General de Guatemala: desde la República Federal hasta 1898.* Ed. Jorge Luján Muñoz. Tomo IV. Guatemala: Asociación de Amigos del País, Fundación para la Cultura y el Desarrollo, 1995. 747–66.

Burgos, Elizabeth. *Me llamo Rigoberta Menchú y así me nació la conciencia.* 1985. Novena edición. México, Madrid, Buenos Aires, Bogotá: Siglo Veintiuno Editores, 1992.

Cardenal, Ernesto. *El estrecho dudoso.* 1966. Managua, Nicaragua: Ediciones Nicarao, 1991.

———. *El evangelio en Solentiname.* 1978. Managua, Nicaragua: Editorial Nueva Nicaragua / Ediciones Monimbó, 1983.

———. *The Doubtful Strait / El estrecho dudoso.* Trans. John Lyons. Bloomington and Indianapolis: Indiana University Press, 1995.

———. *Vida perdida.* Barcelona: Seix Barral, 1999.

———. *With Walker in Nicaragua and Other Early Poems, 1949–1954.* Trans. Jonathan Cohen. Middletown, CT: Wesleyan University Press, 1984.

Cardoso, Ciro F.S. "The Liberal Era, c. 1870–1930." *Central America since Independence.* Ed. Leslie Bethell. Cambridge and New York: Cambridge University Press, 1991. 37–67.

Cardoza y Aragón, Luis. *Guatemala: las líneas de su mano.* México: Fondo de Cultura Económica, 1955.

Casáus Arzú, Marta Elena. *La metamorfosis del racismo en Guatemala. Uk'exwachixiik ri Kaxlan Na'ooj pa Iximulew.* Guatemala: Cholsamaj, 1998.

Caso, Nicole. "Laberintos de apariencias y reiteraciones: reconstruyendo la integridad psíquica / nacional en *Laberintos de orgullo* de Rosa María Britton." *Rosa María Britton ante la crítica.* Ed. Humberto López Cruz. Madrid: Editorial Verbum, 2007.

Clary, William. "La máscara de la impostura: el retrato paródico de las Fiestas de Minerva en *El Señor Presidente.*" *El Señor Presidente: Edición Crítica.* Colección Archivos. Ed. Gerald Martin. Madrid y Barcelona: ALLCA XX, 2000. 668–78.

Cojtí Cuxil, Demetrio. *Configuración del pensamiento político del pueblo Maya.* Quetzaltenango, Guatemala: Asociación de escritores Mayances de Guatemala, 1991.

_____. *Configuración del pensamiento político del pueblo Maya (2da. Parte) Ub'aniik Ri Una'ooj Uchomab'aal Ri Maya' Tinamit.* Guatemala: Cholsamaj-Spem, 1995.

Contreras R., J. Daniel. "La Reforma Liberal." *Historia General de Guatemala: desde la República Federal hasta 1898.* Ed. Jorge Luján Muñoz. Tomo IV. Guatemala: Asociación de Amigos del País, Fundación para la Cultura y Desarrollo, 1995. 173–91.

Craft, Linda. "Ethnicity, Oral Tradition, and the Processed Word: Construction of a National Identity in Honduras." 1995. http://lanic.utexas.edu/project/lasa95/craft.html. Accessed on July 2, 2003.

_____. *Novels of Testimony and Resistance from Central America.* Gainesville, FL: University Press of Florida, 1997.

Dalton, Roque. *Poetry and Militancy in Latin America.* Trans. James Scully. Willimantic, CT: Curbstone Press, 1981.

Dawes, Greg. *Aesthetics and Revolution: Nicaraguan Poetry 1979–1990.* Minneapolis and London: University of Minnesota Press, 1993.

de Castañeda, Ester S. *Estudios sociales (primer curso).* 1962. 20th ed. Guatemala City: Editorial del ejército, 1984.

DeCerteau, Michel. *The Practice of Everyday Life.* 1984. Trans. Steven Rendall. Berkeley and Los Angeles: University of California Press, 1988.

_____. *The Writing of History.* 1975. Trans. Tom Conley. New York: Columbia University Press, 1988.

Derrida, Jacques. *Archive Fever: A Freudian Impression.* 1995. Trans. Eric Prenowitz. Religion and Postmodernism series. Ed. Mark C. Taylor. Chicago and London: University of Chicago Press, 1998.

Dunkerley, James. *Power in the Isthmus: A Political History of Modern Central America.* London and New York: Verso, 1988.

Elías, Eduardo F. "El estrecho dudoso: del discurso histórico a la épica contemporánea." *Revista Iberoamericana* 157 (1991): 923–31.

Escoto, Julio. *Rey del albor, Madrugada.* Honduras: Centro editorial S.R.L., 1993.

Estrada Paniagua, Felipe. *Administración Estrada Cabrera: Reseña de los progresos alcanzados en los ramos de adjudicación de terrenos, ferrocarriles, carreteras, puentes, comunicaciones por correo, telégrafo y teléfono, y producción agrícola.* Guatemala: Tipografía Nacional, 1904.

Euraque, Darío A. *Reinterpreting the Banana Republic: Region and State in Honduras. 1870-1972.* Chapel Hill and London: The University of North Carolina Press, 1996.

Fauriol, Georges A., and Eva Loser. *Guatemala's Political Puzzle.* New Brunswick and Oxford: Transaction Books, 1988.

Fayen, Tanya F. "Escritura y conciencia colectiva: una entrevista con Carmen Naranjo." *Cambios estéticos y nuevos proyectos culturales en Centroamérica: testimonios, entrevistas y ensayos.* Ed. Amelia Mondragón. Washington, D.C.: Literal Books, 1994.

Fischer, Edward F., and R. McKenna Brown, eds. *Maya Cultural Activism in Guatemala.* 1996. Critical Reflections on Latin America Series. Austin: University of Texas Press, 2001.

Gabriel Xiquín, Calixta. *Tejiendo los sucesos en el tiempo/ Weaving Events in Time.* Rancho Palos Verdes, CA: Yax Te' Foundation, 2002.

Gaitán, Héctor. *La calle donde tú vives.* Guatemala: Artemis/Edinter, 1981.

García Canclini, Néstor. *Consumidores y ciudadanos: conflictos multiculturales de la globalización.* México, D.F.: Grijalbo, 1995.

Gibian, Jill. "Carmen Naranjo: Mujer/Cultura." *Cambios estéticos y nuevos proyectos culturales en Centroamérica: testimonios, entrevistas y ensayos.* Ed. Amelia Mondragón. Washington D.C.: Literal Books, 1994.

Gleijeses, Piero. *Shattered Hope: The Guatemalan Revolution and the United States, 1944-1954.* 1991. Princeton, New Jersey: Princeton University Press, 1992.

Greene, Laurence. *The Filibuster: The Career of William Walker.* Indianapolis and New York: Bobbs-Merrill Company, 1937.

Guatemalan Commission for Historical Clarification (CEH). February 25, 1999. <http://hrdata.aaas.org/ceh/>. Accessed on August 16, 2001.

Guha, Ranajit. *History at the Limit of World-History.* New York: Columbia University Press, 2002.

Hale, Charles R. *More Than an Indian: Racial Ambivalence and Neoliberal Multiculturalism in Guatemala.* Santa Fe: School of American Research Press, 2006.

_____ "Travel Warning: Elite Appropriations of Hybridity, Mestizaje, Antiracism, Equality, and Other Progressive-Sounding Discourses in Highland Guatemala." *Journal of American Folklore* 112.445 (Summer 1999): 297-315.

Harvey, David. *Spaces of Capital: Towards a Critical Geography.* New York: Routledge, 2001.

Irigaray, Luce. *This Sex Which Is Not One.* 1977. Trans. Catherine Porter with Carolyn Burke. Ithaca, New York: Cornell University Press, 1985.

Jitrik, Noé. *Historia e imaginación literaria: Las posibilidades de un género.* Buenos Aires: Biblos, 1995.

Junta Libertadora. *Red Page Via Crucis of a Central American Republic: Victims of the President of Guatemala.* New York: Junta libertadora, 1914.

Krauel, Ricardo. "La república clausurada: análisis de los espacios opresivos en *El Señor Presidente.*" *Monographic Review/Revista Monográfica* 11. *Prison Literature* (1995): 220-34.

Kristeva, Julia. "Approaching Abjection." *Oxford Literary Review* 5.1–2 (1982): 125–49.

———. *Desire in Language: A Semiotic Approach to Literature and Art.* Trans. Alice Jardine, Thomas Gora, and Leon S. Roudiez. Ed. Leon S. Roudiez. New York: Columbia University Press, 1980.

Lacan, Jacques. *Ecrits: A Selection.* 1966. Trans. Bruce Fink. New York and London: W.W. Norton and Company, 2002.

LaFeber, Walter. *Inevitable Revolutions: The United States in Central America.* 1983. New York and London: W.W. Norton and Company, 1984.

Landrum, Larry N., Pat Browne, and Ray B. Browne. *Dimensions of Detective Fiction.* Bowling Green, Ohio: Popular Press, 1976.

Lara, Perfecto. *Divagaciones de un obrero: Homenaje al Excelentísimo Señor Presidente Constitucional de la República Licenciado don Manuel Estrada Cabrera.* Guatemala: Tipografía Nacional, 1917.

Liano, Dante. "La obsesión histórica en Arturo Arias." *Cambios estéticos y nuevos proyectos culturales en Centroamérica: testimonios, entrevistas y ensayos.* Ed. Amelia Mondragón. Washington, D.C.: Literal Books, 1994. 67–72.

———. *Visión crítica de la literatura guatemalteca.* Guatemala: Editorial universitaria Universidad San Carlos de Guatemala, 1997.

Lobo, Tatiana. "Abordar la historia desde la ficción literaria (o cómo destejer una bufanda)." *Literaturas centroamericanas hoy: Desde la dolorosa cintura de America.* Ed. Karl Kohut and Werner Mackenbach. Frankfurt/Madrid: Vervuert, 2005. 235–42.

Luján Muñoz, Jorge. "Hacia la emancipación." *Historia General de Guatemala: Siglo XVIII hasta la Independencia.* Ed. Cristina Zilbermann de Luján. Tomo III. Guatemala: Asociación de Amigos del País, Fundación para la Cultura y Desarrollo, 1994. 431–44.

Lukács, György. *The Theory of the Novel: A Historico-Philosophical Essay on the Forms of Great Epic Literature.* Trans. Anna Bostock. London: Merlin Press, 1971.

Mackenbach, Werner. "La historia como pretexto de literatura—la nueva novela histórica en Centroamérica." *Literaturas centroamericanas hoy: Desde la dolorosa cintura de America.* Ed. Karl Kohut and Werner Mackenbach. Frankfurt/Madrid: Vervuert, 2005. 179–200.

Markee, Patrick. "The Wolves Are at the Door." *New York Times Book Review* January 17, 1999: 7, 13.2.

Martin, Gail. "Manuel Estrada Cabrera 1898–1920: 'El Señor Presidente.'" *El Señor Presidente: Edición crítica.* Colección Archivos. Ed. Gerald Martin. Madrid y Barcelona: ALLCA XX, 2000. 534–65.

McCullough, David. *The Path between the Seas: The Creation of the Panama Canal 1870–1914.* A Touchstone Book. New York: Simon & Schuster, 1977.

Mellard, James M. *Using Lacan, Reading Fiction.* Urbana and Chicago: University of Illinois Press, 1991.

Menton, Seymour. *Caminata por la narrativa latinoamericana.* México: Universidad Veracruzana, Fondo de Cultura Económica, 2002.

_____. *Latin America's New Historical Novel.* Austin: University of Texas Press, 1993.

_____. *"Rey del Albor, Madrugada,* de Julio Escoto: La última novela nacional y la primera novela cibernética." *Caminata por la narrativa latinoamericana.* México: Universidad Veracruzana, Fondo de Cultura Económica, 2002. 273–94.

Miranda Hevia, Alicia. *Novela, discurso y sociedad.* Colección Convivio. Costa Rica: Mesén Editores, 1985.

Mondragón, Amelia, ed. *Cambios estéticos y nuevos proyectos culturales en Centroamérica: testimonios, entrevistas y ensayos.* Washington, D.C.: Literal Books, 1994.

Montejo, Víctor. *Las aventuras de Míster Puttison entre los Mayas.* Rancho Palos Verdes, CA: Fundación Yax Te', 1998.

_____. *Maya Intellectual Renaissance: Identity, Representation and Leadership.* Austin: University of Texas Press, 2005.

_____. *Voices from Exile: Violence and Survival in Modern Maya History.* Norman: University of Oklahoma Press, 1999.

Morales, Mario Roberto. *La articulación de las diferencias ó el síndrome de Maximón: los discursos literarios y políticos del debate interétnico en Guatemala.* Guatemala: FLACSO, 1998.

_____. *Los que se fueron por la libre (Historia personal de la lucha armada y la guerra popular).* México, D.F.: Editorial Praxis, 1998.

Muyolema C., Armando. "De la 'cuestión indígena' a lo 'indígena' como cuestionamiento. Hacia una crítica del latinoamericanismo, el indigenismo y el mestiz(o)aje." *Convergencia de tiempos: Estudios subalternos / contextos latinoamericanos. Estado, cultura, subalternidad.* Ed. Ileana Rodríguez. Amsterdam, Atlanta, GA: Rodopi, 2001. 327–63.

Nancy, Jean-Luc. *The Inoperative Community.* 1991. Theory and History of Literature Series. Ed. Peter Connor. Vol. 76. Fourth printing. Minneapolis and London: University of Minnesota Press, 2001.

Naranjo, Carmen. *Diario de una multitud.* 1974. Colección Séptimo Día. San José, Costa Rica: EDUCA, 1986.

Nelson, Ardis L. "Carmen Naranjo and Costa Rican Culture." *Reinterpreting the Spanish American Essay: Women Writers of the 19th and 20th Centuries.* Ed. Doris Meyer. Austin: University of Texas Press, 1995. 177–87.

Nelson, Diane M. *A Finger in the Wound: Body Politics in Quincentennial Guatemala.* Berkeley, Los Angeles and London: University Press of California, 1999.

Ortiz Guzmán, Rosaura. "'Torotumbo': Una Posible Interpretación." *Cupey: Revista del colegio universitario metropolitano* 1.2 (1984): 45–60.

Osses, Esther María. *La novela del imperialismo en Centroamérica.* Maracaibo: Universidad del Zulia, 1986.

Pérez, Alberto Julián. "La visión de la historia colonial en la poesía neo-épica post-vanguardista: Ernesto Cardenal." *Alba de América: Revista Literaria* 9. 16–17 (1991): 197–203.

Perkowska, Magdalena. *Historias híbridas: La nueva novela histórica latinoamericana (1985–2000) ante las teorías posmodernas de la historia.* Frankfurt
and Madrid: Iberoamericana Vervuert, 2008.

Phaf, Ineke. "Cómo narrar la historia viajando en microbús por El Salvador."
*Cambios estéticos y nuevos proyectos culturales en Centroamérica: testimo-
nios, entrevistas y ensayos.* Ed. Amelia Mondragón. Washington, D.C.:
Literal Books, 1994. 47–56.

Pinto Soria, Julio César. "La independencia y la federación (1810–1840)."
*Historia General de Centroamérica: de la ilustración al liberalismo
(1750–1870).* Ed. Héctor Pérez Brignoli. Tomo III. Edelberto Torres-
Rivas (coordinador general). Madrid: FLACSO y Sociedad Estatal Quinto
Centenario, 1993. 72–140.

Pons, María Cristina. *Memorias del olvido: La novela histórica de fines del siglo
XX.* México D.F.: Siglo veintiuno editores, 1996.

Prieto, René. *Miguel Angel Asturias's Archaeology of Return.* Cambridge:
Cambridge University Press, 1993.

Quint, David. *Epic and Empire: Politics and Generic Form from Virgil to Milton.* Princeton, New Jersey: Princeton University Press, 1993.

Rendon, Catherine. "El gobierno de Manuel Estrada Cabrera." *Historia
General de Guatemala: Epoca Contemporánea 1898–1944.* Ed. Jorge
Luján Muñoz. Tomo V. Guatemala: Asociación de Amigos del País, Fun-
dación para la Cultura y el Desarrollo, 1996. 15–36.

Rodríguez, Ana Patricia. *Dividing the Isthmus: Central American Transnational
Histories, Literatures and Cultures.* Austin: University of Texas Press, 2009.

Rodríguez, Ileana. "Dios/Pater-Patria/Libertad." *Cambios estéticos y nuevos
proyectos culturales en Centroamérica: testimonios, entrevistas y ensayos.* Ed.
Amelia Mondragón. Washington, D.C.: Literal Books, 1994. 95–104.

Rosengarten, Frederic. *William Walker y el ocaso del filibusterismo.* Trans.
Luciano Cuadra. Tegucigalpa, Honduras: Editorial Guaymuras, 1997.

Rotker, Susana. *Captive Women: Oblivion and Memory in Argentina.* Trans. Jennifer French. Minneapolis and London: University of Minnesota Press, 2002.

Rubio, Patricia. "Carmen Naranjo: From Poet to Minister." *A Dream of Light
and Shadow: Portraits of Latin American Women Writers.* Ed. Marjorie
Agosín. Albuquerque: University of New Mexico Press, 1995. 195–206.

Salgado, María A. "America and Guatemala in the Anti-Yankee Novels of
Miguel Ángel Asturias: A Love-Hate Relationship." *Hispanófila* 81.año
27, no. 3 (1984): 79–85.

Sauer, Carl Ortwin. *The Early Spanish Main.* 1966. A Centennial Book.
Berkeley and Los Angeles: University of California Press, 1992.

Schele, Linda, and David Freidel. *A Forest of Kings: The Untold Story of the
Ancient Maya.* New York: Quill William Morrow, 1990.

Schlesinger, Stephen, and Stephen Kinzer. *Bitter Fruit: The Untold Story
of the American Coup in Guatemala.* 1982. Anchor Books. New York:
Doubleday, 1990.

Soja, Edward W. *Postmodern Geographies: The Reassertion of Space in Critical
Social Theory.* 1989. Seventh impression. London and New York: Verso, 2001.

Sommer, Doris. *Foundational Fictions: The National Romances of Latin America.* 1991. Berkeley, Los Angeles, and London: University of California Press, 1993.

Sosa, Roberto. *Diálogo de sombras. Colección Lámpara (crítica y cultura).* Tegucigalpa: Editorial Guaymuras, 1993.

Squier, Ephraim George. *Nicaragua.* Oxford: Oxford University Press, 1852.

Stoll, David. *Rigoberta Menchú and the Story of All Poor Guatemalans.* Boulder, Colorado: Westview Press, 1999.

Szok, Peter. "Beyond the Canal: Recent Scholarship on Panama." *Latin American Research Review* 37.3 (2002): 247–59.

Taracena Arriola, Arturo. "Miguel Ángel Asturias y la búsqueda del 'alma nacional' guatemalteca. Itinerario político, 1920–1933." *Miguel Angel Asturias: Paris 1924–1933. Periodismo y creación literaria.* Ed. Amos Segala. Madrid: Colección Archivos, 1988. 679–708.

Umaña, Helen. *Estudios de literatura hondureña. Colección Lámpara (crítica y cultura).* Tegucigalpa: Editorial Guaymuras, 2000.

Varona-Lacey, Gladys M. *Introducción a la literatura Hispano-Americana de la conquista al siglo XX.* Ed. National Textbook Company. Lincolnwood, Illinois: Contemporary Publishing Company, 1997.

Walsh, Lawrence E. *Firewall: The Iran-Contra Conspiracy and Cover-Up.* 1997. New York and London: W.W. Norton and Company, 1998.

Warren, Kay B. *Indigenous Movements and Their Critics: Pan-Maya Activism in Guatemala.* Princeton, New Jersey: Princeton University Press, 1998.

———. "Interpreting *La Violencia* in Guatemala: Shapes of Mayan Silence & Resistance." *The Violence Within: Cultural and Political Opposition in Divided Nations.* Ed. Kay B. Warren. Boulder, San Francisco, and Oxford: Westview Press, 1993. 25–56.

White, Hayden. *Metahistory: The Historical Imagination in Nineteenth-Century Europe.* 1973. Baltimore and London: Johns Hopkins University Press, 1975.

White, Steven F. *Modern Nicaraguan Poetry: Dialogues with France and the United States.* London and Toronto: Associated University Presses, 1993.

Williams, Tamara. "Ernesto Cardenal and the New Latin American Epic." *RLA: Romance Languages Annual* 3 (1991): 638–41.

———. "Ernesto Cardenal's *El Estrecho Dudoso*: Reading/Re-Writing History." *Revista Canadiense de Estudios Hispánicos* XV.1 (1990): 111–21.

———. "Narrative Strategies and Counter-History in *El Estrecho Dudoso.*" *INTI: Revista de Literatura Hispánica*.39 (1994): 47–57.

Woodward, Jr., Ralph Lee. *Central America: A Nation Divided.* 1976. 2nd ed. New York and Oxford: Oxford University Press, 1985.

Zapeta, Estuardo. *Las Huellas de B'alam 1994–1996.* Guatemala: Cholsamaj, 1999.

Zeceña, Mariano. *La revolución de 1871 y sus caudillos.* Guatemala: Tipografía Sánchez y de Guise, 1898.

INDEX